Good Power

GINNI ROMETTY

Former Chairman and CEO, IBM

Good Power

Leading Positive Change
in Our Lives, Work,
and World

HARVARD BUSINESS REVIEW PRESS

BOSTON, MASSACHUSETTS

Copyright 2023 Harvard Business School Publishing Corporation

All rights reserved

Printed in the United States of America

10 9 8 7 6 5 4 3 2 1

No part of this publication may be reproduced, stored in or introduced into a retrieval system, or transmitted, in any form, or by any means (electronic, mechanical, photocopying, recording, or otherwise), without the prior permission of the publisher. Requests for permission should be directed to permissions@harvardbusiness.org, or mailed to Permissions, Harvard Business School Publishing, 60 Harvard Way, Boston, Massachusetts 02163.

The web addresses referenced in this book were live and correct at the time of the book's publication but may be subject to change.

Library of Congress Cataloging-in-Publication data is forthcoming.

ISBN: 978-1-64782-322-1
eISBN: 978-1-64782-323-8

The paper used in this publication meets the requirements of the American National Standard for Permanence of Paper for Publications and Documents in Libraries and Archives Z39.48-1992.

For the Love of My Life, Mark,
My Mother,
My Aunt Diane,
My Grandma Mary,
My Baba Ushka.

CONTENTS

What's Possible

My mother, brother, sisters, and I each have a different memory from when our father abandoned our family just before Thanksgiving.

My mother was packing moving boxes when my father told her that he wasn't coming with us to our new house on the outskirts of Chicago because he didn't love her anymore. My younger brother, Joe, cried when he found out his dad wasn't going to live with us. At fourteen, any hope Joe had that the man who never showed up to his baseball games would suddenly become a real father was shattered. Annette, the eldest of my two younger sisters, assumed that her father was giving up on her, that she wasn't important enough to come home to. She was only eight. Darlene was just five and remembers sitting on my lap, bawling when she heard the word *divorce* even though she had no idea what it meant.

My memory is specific. I was sixteen when I walked into the garage of our new house and overheard my mother telling my father how desperately she needed money.

"You're not paying for anything, Nick," she was saying, her voice echoing off the concrete walls. "We need to eat and pay the mortgage."

What my father said next upended everything for us, and for me.

"I'll never give you anything. For all I care, you can go work on the street."

Then he walked out and drove away, leaving my mother with no money, no education past high school, and no work experience outside our home. At thirty-four, she felt heartsick and terrified. She also had four kids who found themselves in an uncertain world and needed their mother to make things better.

My dad's leaving put our family at a crossroads. The path my mother chose—to take community college classes so she could get a job to support our family—showed me that no matter how desperate a situation gets, we each have within us the power to create opportunity for ourselves as well as others. It's a lesson I've tried to apply in my own life and work. While our mom went to school and worked two jobs, I helped care for my siblings until I graduated high school and became the second person in my extended family to go to a four-year college.

In 1981, I started as an entry-level systems engineer at International Business Machines (IBM), then as now one of America's longest-lasting and most iconic companies. After three decades learning and leading, in 2012 I became IBM's ninth chief executive officer, and the first woman CEO in its one-hundred-year history. I retired from IBM in 2020, after leading a period of necessary and tumultuous reinvention.

My journey has given me a front-row seat to five decades of technological and social change, and today I'm trying to do what my mother's example taught me—working to create better opportunities for more people, in part by writing this book.

If you're wondering if this book is mostly about leadership advice for women based on my experience as a woman in business, the answer is no. It's true that I grew my career in the male-dominated tech industry, and yes, I broke glass ceilings, but that's only one facet of a larger narrative and broader set of leadership lessons. Similarly, this is not a book about technology or IBM, a company I love and have been honored to work for—although, like my gender, IBM is intertwined with my stories and reflections.

Instead, I think the best way to describe what I've written is a memoir with purpose, because I write about my experiences through the lens of an idea much bigger than me and my life, one that relates to all of us: how we can drive meaningful change in positive ways for ourselves, our organizations, and for the many, not just the few. It's a concept I've come to call *good power*.

Discovering Good Power

I didn't set off to write about power, but that's what emerged.

As I connected the dots of my history, I realized that so much of my energy went into trying to make something better by solving a problem or working to achieve whatever mission was in front of me at a given time. This was first true for my family and myself, then later for clients and people I worked with, then for the company I worked for and larger communities.

In retrospect, I can see I grew up believing that I had it within me to change things for the better. With hard work and the support of people around me, I could influence outcomes. Even transform the status quo. Essentially, I believed that I had "power" even if I never used that word. Not power in a stereotypically negative sense—selfish, aggressive, hierarchical. I learned through experience that power didn't have to be bad to be potent. There's such a thing as good power.

Power, I observed, can be good when wielded with respect. When it unites people for a shared purpose and motivates them to be the best version of themselves. Power can be good when it seeks to maximize beneficial impacts and avert rather than ignore harmful consequences. Power can be good when it's inclusive, shared, and distributed.

There's another thing I noticed about power as I scoured my past. Problem-solving happens when people, in the spirit of bridging differences, embrace the tensions that arise from opposing forces. Answers to complex questions are rarely if ever "right *or* wrong," "yes *or* no," "this *or* that." Instead of insisting on "either X *or* Y," I've seen how much more is achieved when we consider "X *and* Y," accepting that the best resolution may be a third way. It's tempting to run from conflict, but it's more effective to face it. For years I've said that growth and comfort never coexist. This is true for people, for organizations, and for countries. If we want to fix what's broken, we have to feel uncomfortable, and that's okay.

One more truth I learned about power: for power to be of any real value, it must enable tangible progress. That means whatever results we're after are realized, in whole or in part. Something or someone must benefit. Intention without making headway is fruitless.

Essentially, writing this book helped me clarify that power is necessary to change things for the better, and that power can be good when it's wielded respectfully, when it navigates tensions, and when it strives for progress over one person's idea of perfection. Respect. Tension. Progress. You'll see these ideas threaded throughout the book, because they were threaded throughout my experiences. I hope they will emerge for you as they did for me, as keys to influencing meaningful change in positive ways.

Writing a Book in Three Parts: Me, We, Us

Our ability to induce positive change grows in scope and potency as our spheres of influence widen.

When we're young, we're more "me" centric. Our mission as we go to school and begin our working lives is to grow into adulthood as we adopt foundational values and character traits. As we take on more responsibilities, our mission becomes less "me" and more "we." Our decisions have consequences for others, like our partners, children, and the people and organizations we work with. At some point, we find ourselves in positions to effect positive change at real scale, and our mission expands to making all of "us" better—underserved groups, societies, countries, the environment, the world we share.

These spheres of influence—"me, we, us"—correspond with my own journey, and drove me to write this book in three distinct sections. Parts I, II, and III all share stories from my past, but each differs in structure and purpose.

In part I, "The Power of Me: Changing a Life," you'll experience formative milestones of my childhood and early career. Family struggles and triumphs. Financial woes and wins. College classes, the wisdom of mentors. These years taught me I had power to make a difference for myself and those I cared for. I share these years in detail because I believe that taking time to reflect on our past helps us know who we are and what matters to us, and why, as people and also as leaders.

In part II, "The Power of We: Changing Work," I reflect on ideas that, with the benefit of hindsight, emerged as what I call the five principles of good power. These are the "how" of good power, and the chapters include practical tools and insights, illustrated with stories.

Each chapter focuses on one principle:

Being in Service Of. This principle is good power's fundamental purpose, its intent, which is to help make someone or something better by meeting their needs, which in turn allows us to meet our own. I call this principle the soul of good power, and it fueled how I related to clients and coworkers and informed my advocacy efforts years later.

Building Belief. This principle is good power's heart, because we can choose to inspire, not force people to willingly embrace change, and take part in creating it. More than once, exercising my influence versus authority helped convince others to embrace a new reality.

Knowing What Must Change, What Must Endure. Change of any consequence requires critical thinking, bold creativity, and very tough choices. This is good power's brain. I called upon this principle and its practices to help reinvent the company.

Stewarding Good Tech. Even if we're not in tech, we all use technology. This principle is about driving trust and inclusion in our digital age so that technology augments humanity. Stewarding good tech is good power's muscle because it takes strength to do what's right for the long term, speak out, and advocate for others.

Being Resilient. Change takes time and perseverance. The right relationships and attitudes provide perspective and help us overcome obstacles, while maintaining conviction in ourselves and our mission. This is good power's unwavering spirit.

The five principles offer a conceptual way to think about good power. I've found them helpful to build mutually respectful relationships, bridge differences, and enable progress.

In part III, "The Power of Us: Changing Our World," I tell the story of my multiyear journey to drive societal change, which required rethinking broken systems. Do we reinvent pieces or dismantle everything? This is where scaling good power's principles can help navigate the tensions of opposition to bring people together to enact solutions. In these chapters, I share the work underway to increase access to good jobs for more people by getting employers to recruit and promote based on individuals' skills, not just their degrees and higher education credentials. This exciting, emerging approach to hiring and advancement is what I call SkillsFirst. My own experience championing SkillsFirst is just one example of how good power can be used to scale big ideas. Hopefully, it will encourage you to use your good power in ways that matter to you, and make a meaningful difference in our world.

Choosing Our Path Forward

Your own experiences, struggles, and beliefs will of course affect how you interpret these pages.

Maybe you'll see someone who rose from unfortunate circumstances to live the American Dream. Or perhaps you'll see a young woman who availed herself of privileges she was born into or was handed. Neither perspective is right or wrong. As you'll see, I had access to resources that others did not have, and my family lacked access to resources many others had.

I take nothing for granted, and I'm grateful for the opportunities I was given and the pathways I chose to take.

If you're an IBMer, please know that I tried to write with great respect and honesty about our company. While this is not IBM's story, or even my complete story, it is a book of stories and lessons, many from my years at IBM, because that's where I worked my entire life. What I share is my perspective as well as my gratitude for the 350,000 people who I worked side by side with as CEO, and many of whom continue to build on its 112-year-old legacy. I will always think of IBMers as family.

Two decades into the twenty-first century, it feels like our world is at another crossroads. We must choose how to proceed. We can either feel helpless, or we can discover good power within ourselves and exercise it in ways large and small to drive meaningful change. It's a choice available to all of us, because good power isn't reserved for people with big titles, money, or the loudest voice in the room. My mom had power even when she had little else, which is the point. After our father left and put our family at its crossroads, the choices my mother made helped us get off food stamps, save our home, and move closer to financial self-sufficiency, while regaining some dignity. Her actions influenced my own. Perhaps her good power will influence yours, too.

Thank you for reading,
Ginni

PART ONE

The Power of Me

Changing a Life

The people and events of our youth influence how we work and lead. That's why these first chapters tell the story of my childhood and early career. These are the faces and places I see when I close my eyes. My grandmother's lamp store. My sisters at our kitchen table. A first date by a lake. Being the only woman in many rooms. From family to friends to first bosses, the people you'll meet played outsize roles in shaping my character, values, and habits. I am me in part because of them.

These years also seeded three core beliefs, even if I couldn't articulate them until much later: One, access to opportunities like education and employment can unleash our potential. Two, a propensity to learn new skills at all stages of life is an invaluable asset. And three, we each have power within us to create positive change in our lives.

We all have the "power of me"—the choice to activate our talents, dreams, and will. We don't need to accept the status quo as fate. Instead, with this type of power, we can rise up against obstacles we face with grace and grit. That's what I hope you take away from part I.

I also hope the pages inspire you to consider how your past shaped how you work and lead. What moments moved you? What values stuck? Who do you see when you close your eyes?

1

Owning My Roots

My great-grandmother, Solemia Ushka, was the last member of her family left alive in Minsk, Belarus, during World War I. Before the war ended, she escaped to the United States with her husband, Dan, my great-grandfather, and they settled in Chicago.

Solemia later suffered two more tragedies in her life. Her two-year-old daughter was hit by a car at a picnic and killed, and her husband, a heavy drinker, died from diabetes, leaving her a widow with a son, Paul, but no money and no skills. Solemia also didn't speak English. A stout and sturdy woman, she took no shame in menial labor and got a job working the night shift as a cleaning woman in the two-towered Wrigley Building on Chicago's North Michigan Avenue. She spent most of her adult life mopping hallways and scrubbing bathrooms. When I was growing up, Baba, as we called her, would always gift me and Joe $10 at Christmas, plus a little tin box filled with sticks of Wrigley's gum.

When she stopped working, Baba moved to a one-story brick house in what was then farm country outside the city. My siblings and I visited her every few months and for two weeks during summers. We'd mow her lawn, pick tomatoes and strawberries from her garden, climb plum trees, and swim in nearby Griswold Lake. Baba's modest home felt like an oasis. She supported herself from a small pension, Social Security checks, and by cashing government savings bonds that she'd dutifully bought each week for thirty years. Baba was one resilient and resourceful lady with a survival instinct and a simple philosophy: work hard, save a lot.

She was also strong. In 1967, when Baba was diagnosed with breast cancer, doctors gave her six to eighteen months to live. She survived another ten years.

Baba's son, Paul, married a beautiful, hardy woman named Mary who gave birth to a baby girl, Arlene. Not long after, Paul died of rheumatic fever, leaving his wife, my Grandma Mary, in a tragic if familiar family situation: Mary, too, became a young widow with no money, no education, and a child to raise—my mom, Arlene.

Baba and Grandma Mary were a mother and wife grieving the same man, and they moved in together to save money and help raise Arlene. Baba spent nights at the Wrigley Building, and Mary worked various jobs during the day, including one on the shop floor of a clothing manufacturer, a dangerous place where she once got her hair caught in a cutting machine, luckily without serious injury.

Grandma Mary eventually remarried and moved in with her second husband, Theodore, and they had a daughter, Diane. Together, they opened a business making and selling lamps from their home, with Grandma designing and recovering ornate shades. Their black-and-white ads in the *Chicago Tribune* boasted "the largest selection of lamps and hand-sewn, washable shades at every price range and to match any décor." The business grew to include small pieces of furniture and gifts. By 1960, Mary and Ted had relocated the store to a two-story building on Belmont Avenue, with Mary's Lamp & Shade Shop on the first floor and their three-bedroom home above.

Ted died in 1966 from kidney failure, leaving my grandmother a two-time widow at forty-seven. She never remarried, but she continued to operate the lamp business on her own—sewing, selling, buying materials, paying bills, and opening the store from 9 a.m. to 9 p.m. seven days a week. She lived upstairs, quite happily, with her large German Shepherd, Cinders, for protection.

Like Baba's country house, my grandma's city home became a familiar, fun destination. Grandma would send Joe and me off with a few dollars and we'd walk to Woolworth's or the nearby hobby store and buy puzzles and model car kits that we painstakingly put together at her kitchen table. Sometimes we came back with workbooks full of math problems or word games to solve. Over the years she taught me and Annette how to sew, a skill that came in handy when I couldn't afford to buy a dress for my senior prom, and when my sister wanted a pink Gunne Sax dress for her eighth-grade graduation.

Also like Baba, Grandma was never too tired to cook or bake. Mashed potatoes, cupcakes, ribs, and steaming rice casseroles filled our visits. An impressive assortment of Christmas cookies (never without Imperial Margarine) emerged from her kitchen each December. For Baba and Grandma Mary, cooking and serving family was love. For me, food was comfort—particularly sweet, rich, and hearty meals and snacks. This continued throughout my life. I already was tall and big boned, and I vacillated from chubby to curvy in what became a lifelong struggle to maintain a steady weight.

My Grandma Mary was diagnosed with cancer in 1961, but like her mother-in-law, she outlived her doctors' predictions by almost fifty years. I come from hardy stock.

These two independent, industrious women were my earliest role models. They lived simply and with compassion, and yet were strong and epitomized the American work ethic: do what needs to be done for as long as it takes to get what you need. In retrospect, I can see that their choices embodied tenets of good power. Each saw herself as being in service of others, mainly family but also, in Baba's case, people who worked in the office buildings she cleaned, and for Mary, customers of the lamp shop. When tragedy disrupted each of their lives, they summoned resilience and reinvented themselves through fortitude and self-determination. I consider each woman the hero of her story, a role that my mother would emulate.

*　*　*

My mother and father waited weeks to tell anyone they had eloped.

My mom, Arlene, was just seventeen, a high school student living above her family's lamp store with her mom and stepfather. She had a wide, easy smile, inquiring eyes, and a spark that drew people to her. My father, Salvatore Nicosia, went by Nick, and was a charming if defiant nineteen-year-old. He left military high school early and got a job as a rate setter at General Electric before working with his father in commercial real estate.

When my parents first met, Nick was a night watchman guarding a construction site so that no one stole any of the equipment. The site was next to the lamp shop, so he must have noticed the pretty teenage girl coming and going from the building nearby. Eventually he asked her to go dancing. They dated, and in November 1956 they drove to Iowa to get married in secret. I was born less than a year later, on July 29, 1957. My father came from a big, boisterous Italian family that insisted on an official church wedding before I arrived.

When my brother was born less than two years later, our family of four moved to a one-bedroom apartment in the building my dad had been guarding when he met Mom. At nineteen, she had a one- and a two-year-old and a husband who wasn't around much. Grandma Mary came by the apartment a lot to make sure her grandchildren were doing okay; she taught my mother the basics of childcare. Not that my mom was irresponsible; she was just so young and had never lived on her own. She barely knew how to take care of herself, let alone two little ones. Various Nicosia cousins also popped by to make sure Nick's wife and kids had what they needed. My godfather, Sam, was my mother's age and came over after his classes at Wright Junior College to play cards with my mom while she rocked me in the cradle with one hand and held a cigarette with the other.

When I was in second grade we moved to a coach house above a four-car garage at my paternal grandparents' home in the upper-class suburb of River Forest. By that time my dad was spending even less time with us, his kids, and more time with his own father. My mother tolerated his absences because she loved him so much.

I was about eight when my sister, Annette, was born and our growing family moved again, into a larger but still small house in the lower-middle-class town of Bellwood, Illinois. The aluminum-sided, one-story bungalow was just six houses from the railroad tracks and had an attic my parents turned into two bedrooms, one for Joe and one for me, Annette, and Darlene, who was born in 1968.

We lived in Bellwood for eight years.

As the eldest, I helped my mom take care of my little sisters while she tried to keep up with housework and keep four children fed three times a day. She was not an especially interested cook, plus she was on a tight budget that meant a lot of canned tuna and soup. Sometimes she served us tripe, which is the stomach lining of farm animals like cows and pigs. Tripe was cheaper than meat, and she served it with spaghetti in place of meatballs. If cooked long enough in tomato sauce, the sliced tripe became tender and chewy, making a spaghetti dish heartier. Mom called the dish "stripe" to make it sound fancy. Not knowing any better, we were happy to eat it.

Our clothes were either handmade, hand-me-downs, gifted by relatives, or bought from the pages of the Sears, Roebuck & Co. catalog, the thick book that arrived by mail with a thud and sold everything from car tires to dresses. At the beginning of each school year I'd comb the thousand-plus pages of the catalog and pick two or three outfits that my mom sometimes had to put on layaway until she could afford to pay.

Our furniture was a random mix of French provincial–styled chairs and tables from my grandma's house, lamps from her shop, and odd pieces acquired through the S&H Green Stamps rewards program. Mom would collect the stamps for free from the grocery store, count all her red-and-green redeemable stamps, then peruse the S&H catalog to see what the stamps afforded her. One of her favorite acquisitions was a framed velvet picture of a river in Italy that was surrounded by tiny twinkling lights that lit up when the art piece was plugged in.

We rarely left Bellwood aside from visiting relatives. We couldn't afford vacations, although Joe and I do remember at least one camping trip, as well as our first time on an airplane when we all joined my dad on a business trip to Atlanta and packed into a hotel room. Darlene was so tiny she slept in the drawer of a hotel dresser.

Our family didn't have much, but we didn't want for what we lacked—at least not consciously—probably because the families around us also had just as little.

Our father came in and out of our lives. He was so routinely absent that the year he volunteered to lead Joe's Boy Scouts troop we were all shocked. When he was home, he usually sat solemnly in one of the S&H lounge chairs while we all watched *Bonanza* or ABC's *Wide World of Sports*.

My father wasn't abusive; he just wasn't around. And when he was, his presence felt more uncomfortable than special. On nights he joined us for dinner, meals were often interrupted by a phone call from a female business associate. I also have memories of him flirting with my mom's friends, yelling at me for something silly, and refusing to allow a boy from elementary school into the house because the boy was Black, much to my confusion and shame. I certainly did not see my dad as a protector, and I didn't much like being around him, especially alone, although I never put my finger on exactly why. I just know he did not make me feel loved or safe, like a child should feel with a parent.

My siblings and I were generally well-behaved and stayed out of trouble. Our neighborhood was idyllic for kids, especially active, athletic ones like Joe. Families lined our block and most kids had complete freedom beyond their front doors. We spent endless hours outside, drawing hopscotch squares on sidewalks, playing Wiffle ball, or running between houses for games of tag or hide-and-seek. During summers I'd ride my bike for blocks to meet friends at the community pool, where for a few dollars I could spend an entire summer. In the frigid winter, Joe and his friends packed the snow in the yard and then flooded it to make an uneven ice rink.

Our life in Bellwood gave me a sense of independence, as well as a sense of duty after being mother's helper for so many years. And thank goodness, because my mom would need me to be especially responsible once our family life imploded.

* * *

The house in Bellwood was feeling cramped for a family of six, which included two tall teenagers still occupying makeshift bedrooms in what was really an attic. The neighborhood was also changing. Its streets were no longer predictably safe for littler ones like my sisters to roam or walk to school. My mother wanted to live farther west, where Illinois's rural flatlands were budding with the suburban construction of new schools, new streets, new chances.

No bank would give my father a mortgage for a house because he and his dad were tied up in real estate disputes. Unbeknownst to my mom, my father had cosigned some loans, which made him an undesirable bank customer.

It was Baba, the Wrigley Building cleaning woman and irrepressible saver, who gave my parents the money for the down payment on a house. It was a brick-and-plywood split-level on Prince Edward Road in a new subdivision in the town of Glen Ellyn, Illinois, about fifteen miles west of Bellwood. Amazingly, Baba had enough money from government bonds to give my parents $12,500, knowing she would probably never get it back. My father's uncle—his dad's brother, Charlie—guaranteed the bank loan.

The moving truck was already on the way when my father told my mother that he was not coming with us. His declaration took her by utter surprise. She asked if he was in love with someone else. He lied and said no, there was not another woman—"I just don't love you."

She was devastated. Her pain compounded when she discovered that Dad was indeed having an affair with the woman whose calls had interrupted so many of our family dinners. Mom also found out that my father had tried to convince Uncle Charlie to sell the Glen Ellyn house for a profit after the mortgage was secured with Baba's money. Uncle Charlie, who had more sense and values than his selfish nephew, refused, asking my dad where else he expected his wife and four children to live.

Uncle Charlie never forgave my father for leaving us. In his eyes, abandoning your own children was an unforgivable sin.

The house in Glen Ellyn had four bedrooms, a living room, a den, and a harvest-gold and brown kitchen. It was not yet finished being built, however, and unless we paid more money the builders wouldn't install carpeting to cover the bare plywood floors, nor would they plant grass to cover the rocky dirt in the front and backyard. When we saw the house for the first time, the weedy rubble made it look more like an abandoned construction site, an eyesore among our new neighbors' well-tended gardens.

Days after we moved in, my father was at the house for some reason when I walked into the garage while he and my mother were arguing. Until that moment I assumed divorce would not change our life much from what it had been for years—we'd just see my dad even less. I still had no clue the damage his leaving would inflict. We were already scraping by on my father's inconsistent income and the allowance he gave my mom. Now we had no cash for food and no way to pay the mortgage or to finish the house.

My mother didn't see me enter the garage when I overheard her tell my father how desperately we needed money. Then I heard his horrible words: "I'll never give you anything. For all I care, you can go work on the street."

This coldhearted statement did not come as a shock. It stung, but it struck me as more wrong than painful. Unconscionable, an injustice.

Did I say something before he walked out and drove away, or did I just watch him go? I don't remember. But in that moment I decided to close my heart to my father after years of disappointment and indifference. Unlike my sisters, who were still so young and looked forward to days their dad took them for lunch at McDonald's or to Kmart to buy a toy, I had experienced his callousness for so long that I now expected nothing. As far as I was concerned, he ceased to matter.

*　*　*

For Darlene and Annette, our father's rare visits came to feel more like obligations. Darlene remembers sitting by the window for hours waiting for him to show up, then telling him about her first home run and how she wished he had been there to see it. But he never watched her play. Darlene didn't want to be mad at her dad, but he made it awfully hard to even like him.

My father's leaving thrust us from the lower-middle-class struggles we already knew into a kind of survival mode. We'd never thought of ourselves as poor, in part because other families in Bellwood were also barely staying financially afloat. In Glen Ellyn we seemed like the only family treading water.

My mother most feared losing the house. It was now in her name, thanks to Uncle Charlie who had guaranteed the loan and so was in a position to insist that my mom get the house in the divorce. (Uncle Charlie, furious at my dad, had also paid for my mom's divorce lawyer.) If we couldn't pay our mortgage, where would we live? My grandmother's city apartment was too small. Homes in other places were cheaper, sure, but the schools weren't as strong, and the streets weren't safe. Besides, who was going to rent to a single mother of four children with no job? We needed to keep that house!

In a gesture more contemptuous than kind, my dad bought us a used car so cheap and unsafe that his own cousin, a mechanic, refused to let my mom drive it. Instead, the cousin graciously gave us a beat-up vehicle that his six kids had used when they learned to drive. My brother and I called it the blue bomber. It had dents on every side, and even though the engine was in better condition than the heap my dad stuck us with, the blue bomber's body was in such atrocious shape that a jerry-rigged wire hanger was the only thing keeping the passenger door shut! Joe and I would drive to school and park the bomber in a far corner of the high school parking lot.

My mom was struggling with a profoundly broken heart. She had lost a love she once believed would last forever. Untimely deaths had stolen Baba and Grandma Mary's husbands. In contrast, Mom's husband departed willingly, leaving her with a different kind of grief to shoulder: loss mired by rejection. She tried to hide her tears, reserving them for visits with her sister, or at night behind her closed bedroom door.

She was also scared. Some days she had to will her body out of bed. "I have no money today," she would wake up and tell herself, "Hopefully tomorrow." That tomorrow never came. Her husband still wasn't giving her money even when he was legally obligated to pay $100 a week in child support. There was no way to force him to pay.

One of my mom's friends who was a social worker told her that our family was eligible for food stamps, the government-issued coupons to help people with no or low income afford staples. When my mom resisted, her friend insisted there was no shame in going on government assistance while she tried to get her life in order. She really had no choice—we needed to eat. When my mom began using food stamps, she insisted on shopping for groceries in another town where she was unlikely to run into someone we knew. The coupons came in booklets, and watching my mother tear the coupons from the booklet in front of cashiers while a line of customers waited behind us was one of the few times I felt self-conscious about our situation.

Mom didn't want to stay on government assistance, but she worried that no one would hire a single mother of four in her midthirties with no experience or college degree. She looked through the want ads and realized she had none of the skills higher-paying office jobs required. She did, however, have a warm personality and she was smart. Eventually she got a job as an operator on the night shift for a company that handled credit-card approvals by phone, mostly for hotels and gas stations. Several times a week she left the four of us home alone with me in charge and spent hours in a noisy room full of other operators. She actually enjoyed the work, especially being around other adults and talking to people all over the country.

She got a second part-time job working for the treasurer of the Chicago Teachers Union, a woman who had had relocated to Texas and needed someone trustworthy in Illinois to collect, document, and deposit checks from union members. It was a simple job, but it helped my mom to feel valued and trusted, and it helped her regain some confidence.

While she worked outside the house, I stepped into the roles of caretaker and cook. I already had what my siblings would one day call "mother hen" tendencies. Now I was "Mama Bear," making dinner most nights, mainly cheap, easy-to-fix meals like Hamburger Helper, tuna, or hot dogs. If my mom was too tired to go to my sisters' school to meet with teachers, I went in her place. When Annette asked for help studying for a spelling test—"Give me my words! Give me my words," an expression she picked up from me—I helped her practice. On the many nights my mom wasn't home until late, I got us all fed and off to bed.

My family still jokes that the reason I never had children of my own was because I had already raised my family. They are right.

* * *

For as hard as mom worked, the pay from her two jobs was still not enough. She needed a higher-salaried position, and the only way was to get more skills. That meant she had to go back to school.

The mere thought of being a college student was daunting. She had graduated high school more than a decade earlier and would be much older than other students. She worried there'd be so much she didn't know, and that she would feel stupid. Plus, she was already exhausted from her night job, which she had to keep so we had some money coming in. Just thinking about taking classes and doing homework overwhelmed her.

But she willed herself to overcome her angst and began taking courses at Wright Junior College, the same two-year college that my godfather Sam had also attended. She signed up for classes in basic accounting and even computing. Graduating was a hopeful but distant goal; more than a degree my mother needed skills that would make her employable.

One day the union treasurer told her about a full-time job answering phones and doing assorted office tasks for four union organizers. By this time Mom had some experience and skills to put on a résumé. She interviewed and got the job. The salary was higher than what she made as an operator, so she quit that job but stayed in school. She was the only woman in the office, and the men she worked for came to know her story and treated her well. Many days she joined them for lunch at a diner across the street. The camaraderie and respect she felt by being part of their crew was another confidence booster.

There's no doubt that work helped my mom recover some of the dignity she lost in the wake of my father's leaving. I look back on her choices, as well as my father's, and see two adults who wielded their inner power in vastly different ways. He was in service of himself, not others. My mother was in service of her children, even her coworkers, and transformed herself from an abandoned, penniless, jobless ex-wife to a hardworking income earner, and a trusted and well-liked employee. My mother, like Baba and Grandma Mary, showed resilience in the face of tragic circumstance.

Mom was doing her absolute best, modeling so many behaviors for me and my siblings. Still, our family needed different kinds of support. We could not reinvent ourselves alone.

* * *

My father's parents and sisters had all but disappeared from our lives, but we nonetheless had a diverse community of support.

Uncle Charlie still checked in on us from time to time, and at least once I saw him hand money to my mom. Sometimes he even paid our mortgage. Uncle Charlie still considered us family even though it caused a rift with his nephew and brother. His son Sam also insisted our cousins check in on us to make sure we had food in the refrigerator and gifts for Christmas and birthdays. They were doing what they thought was right.

Our next-door neighbors, Dale and Joan Fleming, owned an HVAC business. They had a beautifully landscaped yard and well-decorated home. By proximity alone they surely knew about my family's precarious circumstances—we couldn't afford drapes, so the Flemings saw straight into our house! They could have limited their involvement with our situation. Instead, they asked Annette to babysit when they didn't actually need a sitter, and they gave Joe a job cutting their grass so he could make money, too. Their son was Darlene's age, and over the years the Flemings took her with them on vacations. If Darlene got sick at school and no one in our family was home, Joan picked her up and brought Darlene back to her house.

When we needed a second car, Baba once again dipped into her savings, this time to put a down payment on a light brown Malibu Classic with a cream-colored vinyl roof. And then there was the day my Aunt Di and a bunch of folks I didn't recognize arrived with rolled planks of sod and, with the communal effort of an Amish barn raising, laid real grass in the front and back of our house. The lumpy, uneven result was not the most attractive yard, but it sure was a softer place for my sisters to play. Inside the house, my boyfriend, who was a professional house painter, helped me paint all the bare plywood floors dark brown so they would look like finished wood. Slowly, the house began to feel like a real home.

Joe had a serious girlfriend, Jeanna, whose large Italian family welcomed him for dinner many nights; their house became his second home. Annette recalls a girl she walked to school with, whose mother would poke her head out the front doorway to offer Annette something to eat, never letting on that she suspected the Nicosia girl may not have gotten breakfast. "Come on in, have some grapefruit." Annette would pull up a chair at the kitchen table and be invited to sprinkle sugar on top of a juicy half. We never had grapefruit at our house—it was too expensive.

The teachers in my life were part of my community of support. I recall the science teacher, Mrs. Corrigan, who told me I had a bright future and encouraged me to keep studying. The high school calculus teacher, Mr. Brown, who stayed after school and walked me through theorems until I understood them. The home economics teacher who helped me sew my prom dress. Their interest made me feel like I was worth time and attention.

So many people in my family's orbit refused to be bystanders, choosing to spend whatever resources they had—a grapefruit, an hour, a few dollars—to help us. Again, I see their choices as good power in action. The compassion-ate gestures added up, filling voids left by our dad so we could help ourselves move on.

*   *   *

Joe, Annette, Darlene, and I were our own little community. We developed a loyalty to each other, adhering to an unspoken expectation that we would not create more problems at home. Don't get into trouble at school, don't complain, say yes instead of no. Life was hard enough.

During the summer months, my sisters had no babysitter, but I had to lifeguard to make money, so they often came with me to the pool. "I'm working and need to be able to see you," I'd say as I set them up in a corner to play quietly for several hours. "You have to behave." And they always did.

Of course, there were times when my siblings and I argued. Aunt Di re-calls coming over and quelling the inevitable squabbles. And we were defi-nitely competitive when it came to sports and games. The four of us would huddle around Monopoly or Stratego, each one of us determined to win. To this day we still play games whenever we get together. Joe describes our competitiveness as being less about beating each other than not wanting to disappoint ourselves, and I think he's right.

Still, I don't remember much fighting. As the eldest, I was intensely pro-tective of my siblings, especially Annette and Darlene. I wanted to teach my young sisters a lesson that I'd internalized, which was the importance of being able to take care of yourself under any circumstance. Even before my dad left, I believed that self-reliance, self-sufficiency, and independence were traits women needed so we never had to rely on someone else. Remem-ber, this was still the era when a lot of wives did not work outside the home and were financially dependent on husbands. Yet like many women at the beginning of the 1970s, I was rejecting that model. Maybe my perspective originated from seeing Baba and Grandma Mary be such proficient provid-ers. I wanted my sisters to grow up with the ability to be independent.

My mother had to find her own independence, and in doing so she chose not to be a victim. She didn't want her children to see themselves as victims, either. Did she say this explicitly? No, at least not to me, but her choices demonstrated what it means to take control of your life and be accountable to yourself and others. Her example allowed my brother, sisters, and me to channel our energy into healthy outlets. Annette doubled down on her academics, emulating my homework habits, and playing teacher to younger kids. Joe became an all-star athlete in baseball and basketball, and when Darlene wanted to join the all-boys Little League, my mom didn't hesitate to sign her up. The two of them marched into the community center to do so, making Darlene the first girl in the league. By high school, she would be a star softball player.

I focused even more on studying because I was determined to go to college, maybe even medical school. By observing my mother, I learned to never let anyone else define who you are; only you define who you are.

2

Expanding My World

My Aunt Di is only twelve years older than me. When I was young, she would walk to my parents' apartment after school to play with Joe and me. After my family moved to Bellwood, she rode the train to see us. To me, she felt more like an older sister than an aunt. I looked up to Di, and I was just in elementary school when I visited her at Northern Illinois University, where she spent two years before transferring to DePaul University in Chicago. She was the first person in our family to get a higher education degree.

Di planned to become a teacher but switched to studying business. Her first job after graduating was at the Chicago Mercantile Exchange, a chaotic, loud, unruly environment with few women. Her job was to record trades, and because she was smart and hungry, Di quickly learned the securities business and made enough money to afford vacations and, eventually, to invest with her husband in a small business they built. Witnessing my beloved aunt become successful showed me that good grades could lead to a good education, which could lead to a good job and a secure, stable, even adventurous life.

I think I knew that my mother wanted us to go to college, but she never explicitly told my siblings and me that doing well in school was a priority, and she had no strict rules around homework. She just made sure we knew that we were capable. Most weekdays I came home, washed my hair, put on my pajamas, then sat at the kitchen table doing my homework. My favorite subject was math, even though algebra, trigonometry, and calculus didn't come easy. Unlike my brother Joe, I didn't have a photographic memory. I also didn't like just memorizing things. I considered it cheating. Memorizing isn't knowing, and I figured that only once I knew the roots of a problem or the logic of a theorem would I have enough confidence to solve, build, or rebuild something. If I could connect the knee bone to the thigh bone, I'd eventually find my way to the head. So I studied a lot.

I also did a bunch of extracurriculars but didn't excel at much. I played the piccolo and the flute, poorly. I wasn't good enough to make the swim team, so I participated in meets as a timer. I also played volleyball and basketball, but I was not an athlete like Joe and Darlene. Basically, my hobby was doing homework. I was determined to go to college, and I knew I needed high grades to get into one of the few top schools only a few hours away by car or train. We couldn't afford for me to go much farther.

Slowly, I began to see a path between school and the real world, and I believed that I had the power to choose and walk that path. One summer I got a job as a computer formatter, erasing and installing operating systems for a company called National Data Corp. Another summer I attended a "Women in Engineering" program at a nearby college. For a week in August, I was among one hundred young women invited to listen to lectures about all types of engineering jobs. It was hardly every teenager's ideal way to spend their last weeks of summer, but I loved it.

Twice I traveled to the Illinois State Capitol as part of youth-and-government programs. The first time our small group of students proposed a mock bill to congressional leaders, a law that would make it illegal for employers to ask job applicants if they had been convicted of a crime. The second mock bill we proposed would protect children of divorced parents who weren't paying legally mandated child support. Our proposed law required that parents sentenced to prison enroll in a work program; any money they made would go to their kids. Clearly my advocacy was sparked by an injustice I was all too familiar with.

During my senior year I ran for president of our high school's student union with the campaign slogan "Win with Gin." While I was not 100 percent confident that I, Gin, would win, I gave it a shot. In my speech, I promised that, as president, I would hold more meetings between the administration and students, and that we would have more dances after football games. I'm pretty sure the latter was the main reason I was elected.

When it came time to apply for college, Northwestern University in Evanston, Illinois, was my first choice. But even though I would graduate near the head of my class, the school was a stretch because my test scores on the ACT and SAT weren't as high as they needed to be. My application had to show who I was beyond my grades and test scores. I wrote my college essay about my father, and how his leaving us had made me more mature because of the responsibilities I took on at home, and less dependent on other people because I had learned to make decisions for myself, by myself. "As tragic as this situation may have been, I believe tragedy can either diminish a person, or make them stronger. Today, I am not afraid to make changes to help cope with any obstacle."

I was admitted to the University of Illinois College of Engineering one month before I walked to the mailbox at the end of our driveway and opened my acceptance letter from Northwestern. When Baba found out I was headed to college she said to me, "You're such a big strong girl! You really should work on a farm." I took it as a compliment.

Before I left, my mother was still taking community college classes and working full time. One day, as she sat in her school cafeteria eating dinner, she wrote me a letter:

> *As I sit here (I'm sure I'm the oldest person in this room), I look around at all the young people and think of you. How soon you will be leaving home and how we will all miss you. How you have brought so much pleasure and joy to our lives. What I have done to be part of you. How*

*much more grown up you are than I ever was at your age. How happy
I am that you are going away to school.*

*How sad I am because I will miss you. How I hope you will stick
with it and not be a dropout as most of us here, in this room, are
tonight. How proud I am to be your mother.*

I was as proud of her as she was of me.

* * *

Northwestern's tuition, room, and board cost about $6,500 a year in 1975.
Luckily for me, Northwestern's philosophy was that if a student had the aptitude to be admitted to the university, then the university had a responsibility
to help make it affordable for the student. My father had no intention of helping me pay. In fact, he wouldn't share information about his salary and taxes,
which made it more difficult for me to apply for financial aid. The aid I eventually got from the school covered about 70 percent of tuition, room, and board.

I cobbled together more money through student loans, my own savings,
and a smattering of scholarships, including $750 from my high school's
booster club, and some money from the National Society of Daughters of
the American Revolution, a scholarship I only knew about because a teacher
suggested I apply. Baba gifted me $100. Grandma Mary gave me another
$50. And I got about $500 from two dozen other relatives and family friends.
I needed every penny.

A lot of Northwestern's students came from families with financial
means. I wasn't preoccupied with not having money; I just didn't want to
stand out, and yet as winter approached and the wind started to whip off
Lake Michigan, there were women my age wearing fur coats! I couldn't
afford a fancy jacket, but I did use cash from my graduation gifts to buy two
Izod Lacoste button-downs, some corduroy pants, and a pair of Top-Siders.
The little alligator on my shirt and those boat shoes on my feet made me
feel like I fit in. I wore them a lot.

My first year I lived in the dorms and only went back to Glen Ellyn on holidays and during the summer to make money working the third shift at the post office, sorting mail from midnight to 8 a.m. My shift supervisor treated me terribly. He didn't like me and he could be quite mean. His bullying, combined with my trying to stay awake in the wee morning hours, made me so nauseous I would take Pepto-Bismol the minute I got home each morning. I didn't quit because the night shift paid 30 percent more than the daytime rate. I made my summer earnings stretch so I wouldn't have to work during the school year. That meant I had very little spending money, and I could only afford to eat what was served in the cafeteria Monday through Friday. By Sundays, I often had popcorn for dinner. I vividly remember the last two weeks of my freshman year, when I only had twenty-five cents left. I put the quarter in a clear plastic box on my desk and just stared at it. *This is it*, I thought, *no more money.*

For all my maternal tendencies, I was still learning to take care of myself and felt out of sorts for the first year or so as I tried to juggle a busy social life with classes and studying. I'd entered Northwestern intent on being a doctor because it seemed like a noble career path, but if I was really passionate about a career in medicine I would have stuck with it even after I didn't get As in physical chemistry and, of all things, human reproduction. By the end of my freshman year I decided that med school, no matter how noble, wasn't for me.

Engineering seemed an obvious major because I liked math, and it introduced me to computer science, a new field of study that was just getting popular. Technology was beginning its emergence into mainstream society. Coincidentally, the year I entered college was the same year that Bill Gates and Paul Allen began writing software programs for the first microcomputers; they cofounded Microsoft in 1975, one year before Steve Jobs and Steve Wozniak founded Apple. For the most part, though, the midseventies were still the era of typewriters, and computers were massive machines only experts knew how to operate. Students like me learned to write code using punch cards, a remnant from an era when those big machines could only do one task at a time. After my first coding class in the low-level computing language Assembler, I was hooked. Not because it was easy, but because the logic and creativity that programming demanded fit my brain.

Northwestern had one enormous computer on campus, a Control Data Corporation (CDC) computer housed in the tomb-like building called the Vogelback Computing Center. We'd write our code by hand, then make an appointment at Vogelback, where we painstakingly input our programs into a computer. A terminal read each line and punched holes in stiff rectangular cards; each punched card held one line of code and a thick deck of cards represented the ordered instructions for the CDC to generate whatever outcome we wanted. Next, we'd give our tray of cards to a computer operator, who fed the deck into a high-speed card reader. Sometimes we had to wait overnight to get a printout that either showed the results we hoped for or let us know there was an error with our code, in which case we had to go through each card to find the mistake or rewrite the code and repeat the entire process again. I have vivid memories of walking around campus, carrying my boxes of meticulously organized punch cards, being careful not to drop them.

There weren't a lot of women studying engineering, and in some classes I was the only female. For years in my adult life, I'd run into men who remembered me from this or that college engineering course. More often than not I had to apologize for not recognizing them. "But I have an excuse," I told them, "Back then there were thirty of you and only one of me!"

As one of the few women in the engineering school, I was aware that, like it or not, I stood out. That meant my wrong answers in class would be remembered, too, which was one reason I always came to class prepared. Like a lot of women of my era (and many women today), I expended extra energy to counter any stereotypes that existed.

None of that stopped me from asking questions, though. For me, being able to problem-solve was a path to success, and I intuitively understood that asking questions was part of problem-solving. That did not mean I wasn't smart; it meant I was smart enough to know what I didn't know, and confident enough to find out. Answers were breadcrumbs that led to knowledge, and knowledge was my path forward. If I wanted to move ahead, I had to ask questions.

I had a tutor at one point, and I have a vague memory of marching into his dorm room, ignoring the dirty clothes stacked near the doorway, shaking his hand, and then presenting him with my written list of questions about programming issues I was having trouble solving. I didn't want him to tell me the answers; I wanted him to explain the method of the solution. As he described it, I didn't want to be driven someplace but to be supplied with proper directions so I could find the destination myself.

In a way, we tutored each other. Once, he and I were in class and he raised his hand to challenge a professor who marked one of his answers on a test as wrong. "Put your hand down," I whispered to him, "You can win your argument in private later, or lose it in public now."

I liked using my right and left brain to get to the bottom of things or to invent a way to an outcome. Engineering also taught me how to seek solutions by dissecting problems into manageable pieces and thinking through each disparate part. As long as I could break something down, gather information, ask questions, validate points, and test hypotheses, I didn't get overwhelmed. Was my affinity to this way of thinking sparked by the strategic games I played with my siblings growing up? Did I develop it through the sewing projects I did with Grandma Mary, or by putting together model car kits? Maybe my penchant for problem-solving was a result of the uncertainty that our family had to navigate. All I know is that as a young woman I was eager to fix whatever was broken—a computer program, a law, a family— and willing to do what it took to create something new.

* * *

During my second year at Northwestern, a professor who knew I was on financial aid encouraged me to apply for a scholarship that General Motors was offering to women and minority engineering students at select top schools. I applied, crossed my fingers, and not long after I was named a GM Scholar along with another female student who was studying chemical engineering. The scholarship awarded full tuition for my last two years of school, plus covered all fees and a $200 book allowance. It also guaranteed me jobs for two summers at GM's headquarters in Detroit. All this, with no obligation to work for the company after graduation. I felt like I had won the lottery. Less than a year earlier I'd been staring at a quarter in a box! Now the rest of my college education was fully financed, and I had summer jobs that paid much more than working at the post office. If I did well at GM, I'd graduate with a job offer.

Each year I felt happier with the life I was building. I had joined a sorority, Kappa Kappa Gamma, whose dues my Aunt Di generously paid, and made great friends. Erin McInerney was a junior when she spotted me during sorority rush week. I knew nothing about the Greek system. I just saw it as a way to make friends and have a place to live. The other girls rushing seemed to know what to wear, what to say. Me? I was unsure which if any sorority would see me as a fit. I went through the process somewhat clueless, just smiling a lot and asking questions and hoping for the best.

Erin walked over to me during rush and we got to know each other. She also took computer classes and, like me, had a mother who worked a full-time job in an administrative role. She advocated for me during rush, which was a main reason I got in and chose Kappa. She introduced me to sorority life, making me feel like I belonged in an environment where I otherwise felt like an outsider. When Erin graduated with a degree in economics and went into banking, I watched her enter the professional world so fluidly that it influenced how I viewed my own postcollege prospects. Here was a woman I admired with a background like mine creating a very different life for herself.

Most students at Northwestern came equipped with all kinds of access and information that I didn't have, like family friends who could give them job referrals and references. They also knew stuff I was never taught, like which pieces of silverware to use at a dinner party. Just being around my friends gave me life tools and exposed me to more things, including stable, predictable home lives, even healthy marriages.

I took my first real vacation with Lauren Kohlenbrener, my friend and roommate who grew up in a well-to-do suburb of Chicago. The winter break she invited me to join her in Florida to stay at a condo was probably the third time I'd ever been on a plane. Lauren was also one of the first Jewish people I ever met. I recall being surprised when my Jewish friends told me they didn't have a Christmas tree, once again proving that college opened my worldview in different ways. Lauren and I didn't have similar backgrounds, but by exposing me to hers she provided a kind of access I didn't have.

I could be hard on myself at times, secretly vowing to be more organized, or a better friend, or less pessimistic. "The only thing that worries me," I wrote in an annual letter to myself as part of my sorority tradition, "is how long do good things last—for some reason I feel not forever." It was as if I was waiting for the other shoe to drop, doing what I could to prevent it from happening. And yet when bad things did happen, I didn't dwell on them.

There was an incident I only remember because of press clipping from a student newspaper that I saved. Senior year I was president of the sorority when several members were accused of violating our bylaws by drinking alcohol and smoking pot during a pledge activity. We risked losing our charter, and as punishment our alumnae banned alcohol and boys from the members' rooms, which had been allowed on special occasions. As president, I was the public face of the debacle, and while I don't remember much about what happened aside from what was reported, I imagine it was very stressful for me. The fact that I have no memory of it is telling. I did this prior to college, too. I look back on my family's early struggles not with grief but with gratitude, believing that if I could get through them, I could get through anything. My early family life came to symbolize survival, not loss.

* * *

In 1979, I graduated Northwestern University's Technological Institute (now called the Robert R. McCormick School of Engineering and Applied Science) with a Bachelor of Science in Computer Sciences, with distinction. It was an incredibly proud moment for me, but more so for my mom. My mother attended my graduation. So did my Grandma Mary, who had closed the lamp store and was now living with my Aunt Di.

I left college in 1979 with $4,000 in student debt (about $16,000 in today's dollars) and was eager to start earning money to pay it off. I was extremely thankful to General Motors, Northwestern, and others for all the scholarships and financial aid I received. Without their assistance my debt would have been over $130,000 in today's dollars. I interviewed with many large corporations and received many job offers, including from Ford, Honeywell, and Hewlett-Packard.

General Motors offered me a position as a junior programmer in its Chevrolet Information Systems division, with a starting salary of $20,000, including a cost-of-living allowance. I was most interested in HP and GM. HP had a compelling computer science division and wanted me to move to the West Coast, which was very exciting. The HP recruiter flew me out to their headquarters in Cupertino, California, and kept calling even after I turned down the job; he even sent a Western Union Mailgram asking me to call him collect to discuss the role. I think he couldn't believe I was choosing snow over sun, and a car company over computing. I finally had to tell him the two reasons why I decided to work for GM: I felt a great sense of loyalty to the company and wanted to give it the same chance it had given me. Also, I'd met a man in Detroit and fallen in love.

3

Listening to My Heart

My blind date picked me up in a dark-red Mercury Cougar. He was tall, light-haired, with brown eyes, and a quick smile. All I knew about Mark Rometty was that he was four years older than me— I had just turned nineteen—and that he worked for an automotive industry supplier in Detroit.

It was the first summer of my GM internship and I was renting a sparse room with a friend in a house that overlooked a cement plant. The woman who owned the house had set my friend and me up on separate blind dates— an attempt to get us to leave while she threw a party—and even though I had a boyfriend back at Northwestern I saw no harm in one night out.

Mark took me for dinner at a yacht club on the lake, where he proudly admitted he could only afford the membership because the club was having financial troubles at that time and gave him a discount. What he didn't tell me was that he didn't have a dollar on him that night because he hadn't planned on taking me to dinner but changed his mind once he picked me up. The club was the only place he could sign for a meal and not have to pay right away. I surprised myself by ordering a cocktail—a rarity because I've never been much of a drinker—and when I spilled my screwdriver all over my dinner plate, Mark didn't make me feel more embarrassed than I already was. He just reached across the table and used his napkin to mop it up.

Conversation was easy. Mark struck me as a kind man and definitely a jokester. I began to wonder if this might turn into more than one date. It did, and at the end of the summer I returned to Northwestern and broke up with my boyfriend.

The two of us had a lot in common. His dad had passed away when Mark was only ten, after his much older brothers had already moved out of the house. His mother had little education and no money, so at a young age Mark was mowing lawns, shoveling snow, and handling a paper route to earn cash to afford groceries. His mother remarried a man with six children, but being the sole Rometty child in the crowded household made for a stressful relationship with his stepdad, and from sixteen on Mark mostly stayed in his brother's basement, as well as with his Auntie Leona, who treated him like her son.

In school Mark played football and baseball, and he was on the all-city swim team. He, too, lifeguarded during the summer and was president of his class his senior year.

Mark's college years began when he walked into the registrar's office at Eastern Michigan University, filled out some forms, and was immediately admitted to the state school for about $300 a semester. He majored in marketing. To pay tuition and living expenses he used some money from his father's Social Security and he worked part-time at a stamping plant that made car parts, a dangerous job that paid $2.25 an hour. He could easily have lost a finger if he wasn't careful. He quit to work for a man who built swimming pools, which doubled Mark's pay but meant spending hours lifting heavy marble and bags of concrete.

After he graduated in 1975, he landed a job in the institutional division of General Foods selling huge bags of coffee, oversize jars of barbecue sauce, and other staples to commercial cafeterias. Eventually, one of Mark's lawn-cutting customers referred him to the job that became his true calling and lifelong career: a manufacturer's representative for the auto industry. He was such a joyful salesperson who breezily turned a cold call into a long lunch, a handshake into a relationship, and a stranger into a friend. He could talk to anyone, and adored banter and building rapport. When we met he was a few years into his career.

Behind his repartee was, and still is, a highly principled man. As well as a survivor. One of my favorite Mark stories, and there are countless, reveals his character. At his all-boys Catholic high school, it was common for priests to swat students with a paddle. One day Mark and the priest in charge of his homeroom disagreed about something. Mark held his ground because he knew he was right. The priest beat him severely. Mark went to the disciplinarian's office to report the beating, but instead of justice he got an ultimatum: go back to homeroom or sit in the hallway after school for everyone to see. For the rest of the year, Mark sat in detention despite being ridiculed.

Mark was also at my graduation, and we married seven months later, after I moved to Detroit. The ceremony was in a quaint chapel attached to the church where Mark had finished high school. My mother walked me down the aisle and gave me away.

It was important to Mark and me to celebrate the relatives and friends whose support had helped both of us navigate some tough times. Treating our loved ones to a special affair was a way to honor them. For me, that included providing a formal seated meal, not a buffet—I wanted every guest to feel served. We kept costs low because Mark and I were paying for the event. The family of one of Mark's high school friends owned a meatpacking plant, and they generously upgraded the steaks we selected for dinner. At the caterer's suggestion we saved money with a semifake wedding cake; only the top tier was real, the rest was frosting-covered cardboard. After we cut the ceremonial piece, the waitstaff rolled the tall cake into the kitchen and served everyone slices from sheet cakes, just as tasty but far less pricey. The day after the wedding Mark and I opened the envelopes we'd received and used the gifted checks and cash to pay the caterer and the banquet hall.

When we were ready to buy a house, the ones we could afford needed fixing up. Mark and I were employed by good companies but lived frugally to save as much as we could. Mark sold his red Mercury and was driving a company car. I drove the brown Chevy Malibu that Baba had helped pay for when I was in high school. The ranch house we found in Birmingham, just outside Detroit, required a new roof and fresh paint. The kitchen was also outdated, and for weeks Mark's brother, Steve, came by at night so he and Mark could put in new cabinets and floors. Almost every piece of furniture was a family hand-me-down, including our bedroom set, which was from Mark's childhood room.

To spruce up the yard, Mark bought a riding lawn mower, and I decided to learn how to plant flowers. One Saturday, I was digging in the dirt while Mark gleefully drove his new mower. After a few hours, I complained to Mark about the rotten vegetables I'd found in the ground. He walked over to inspect my work.

"Those are tulip bulbs," he said, deadpan.

It was too late, I'd already pulled them all out. Mark just laughed. I was grateful that my husband never took small things too seriously. I was also grateful to have a partner who was so supportive of my career. If it wasn't for Mark, I never would have found my way to IBM.

* * *

I liked my job at GM, and was grateful for it, but something was missing. I worked in the Chevrolet division, and because GM gave me two years seniority over other college hires due to my summer internships, I got the chance to work with people who were very experienced.

Our workday officially started at 7 a.m. and ended at 3 p.m., but we could also flex our hours as needed. More often than not I chose to stay later if a project wasn't done, or if there was something else I could do—and I always found something else to do! I liked staying and logging on to the computers to see how the programs we wrote could be improved or, better yet, to find new bugs in them. Like studying math and programming in school, I wanted to understand the "how" and "why" of things. I also hoped the knowledge would provide a foundation for whatever came next.

I remember looking at my coworkers and taking note of how much they loved the automobile industry. As much as I wanted to excel at my work and get paid well, at twenty-three, I knew I wasn't truly excited about trucks, buses, and cars. I was hungry for a type of work that used my engineering skills to solve problems but also engaged my heart. I couldn't articulate it then, but I was looking for a career I was passionate about, not just a job that paid well.

Mark saw my struggle and encouraged me to capitalize on my engineering and computer science degree and consider the burgeoning tech industry. He checked in with a friend who worked at IBM, and the friend passed on the name of someone I could call to ask about job openings. I called and set up an interview.

That year, 1981, IBM had introduced its first PC. The three-piece set had a bulky screen that sat atop a processing box, plus a six-pound keyboard. It was marketed as easy for anyone to use, even at home. I'd seen its ads on TV that showed silent film star Charlie Chaplin tottering into a computer store, quickly learning how to use the new technology. The PC was a departure from IBM's signature products, which were huge computers called mainframes that processed large volumes of information.

IBM's buttoned-up culture was widely known, so I purchased the second suit I'd ever owned, this one in a navy blue pinstripe. The office was located in downtown Detroit's Renaissance Center, seven round glass towers housing offices and retailers in a complex so massive it was dubbed a city within a city. The corporate campus was a hive of activity, a buzzing parade of professionals that exuded an ambitious energy I'd never experienced. I was eager to be part of it as I joined the flow of workers and rode an elevator up to one of the several floors that IBM occupied. Walking in with my résumé in hand, I felt excited, just a bit nervous, and grateful for my new blue suit.

I met with several people, including a woman who would be my boss if I was hired. I also interviewed with people who would be my peers, as well as an office administrator, before sitting down with the branch manager.

John Kennedy was a long, lean man in a plain dark suit, white shirt, and striped tie, with a presence I found more gracious than intimidating. He'd recently joined the branch to turn it around. I'd been referred to John just as he was staffing up with people whom IBM would train for entry-level positions in marketing or systems engineering. He explained that the branch mostly served financial services customers like banks and insurance companies, with a smattering of utilities, universities, and government operations. There was much to learn, and many chances to grow. I was intrigued that IBM's technologies were used to help so many different kinds of large businesses operate. That was a purpose I felt good about; my work would be a means to an end that engaged me. In addition, even as an entry-level engineer, I would be meeting directly with customers to install, run, even sell products, including the new PCs. I thought here I could have a career.

John was especially interested in a unique skill I had. At the time, banks were retiring older computers from a company called Burroughs, and I'd taught myself how to program and use Burroughs systems while at GM. In me, John had someone who could jump in and convert customers' Burroughs systems to IBM. My after-hours education had paid off!

I left the interview hoping I'd made a good impression. Not until I was home taking off my new suit jacket did I notice the large white tag loosely sewn into the blazer's outer sleeve, just above the cuff. It was supposed to be clipped off before wearing the suit. I was mortified.

Apparently, it didn't matter because I was offered a job as an assistant systems engineer in the Detroit commercial office of IBM's Data Processing Division. My starting salary was $2,000 a month, with opportunities for cash bonuses. Still, the salary was less than I was making if I factored in all of GM's benefits. I put that aside. John was taking a chance on me. In turn, I was taking a chance on IBM by embarking on a career doing something that mattered to me: applying my engineering and technology skills to a broad range of problems.

On Monday, November 2, 1981, at 8:30 a.m., I arrived for my first day at IBM. Before I left the house, I may have asked Mark to check my suit.

4

Learning to Learn

My first boss John Kennedy had a trait I'd never really experienced in the workplace: gravitas, that combination of confidence, integrity, expertise, and what today we call emotional intelligence. He was respected because he was respectful. While kind, he could also be quite frank if you weren't performing up to his standards. His ability to combine soft and hard leadership styles is an essence of good power.

Branch manager was a coveted role in IBM's corporate hierarchy, a sure step to promotions that usually required relocating. IBM moved employees to other states and countries so often that people joked its acronym stood for "I've Been Moved." John, however, didn't want to leave Detroit. With no intention of uprooting his wife and nine children, he took a long-term view of his position, and intentionally staffed his office with friendly people who would create a collegial atmosphere and also the drive "to do whatever needs to be done in the timeframe we need to get it done," as he put it. John hired for character as well as talent.

"Good people attract good people," he liked to say. And John was good people.

He was especially interested in helping those who worked for him learn and grow. A systems engineer's role was part technical, part sales. SEs like me were paired with traditional marketing specialists and together we sold and supported IBM products; the SEs told customers how our hardware and software functioned and would be installed, while the marketers touted its features and told them what it cost.

Most young hires went through a yearlong training program, but because I had work experience I did an abbreviated version. Still, half my job description was dedicated to education, which included shadowing veteran engineers. This would be my first time as an apprentice, working side by side with seasoned technicians so I could watch, do, and question in a safe environment because I was expected to be a student, not an expert.

In addition to hands-on learning, I traveled to IBM's education campus in Dallas to take a variety of courses, including one titled Effective Presentations. I was stiff when I was called upon to demonstrate my speaking skills in front of my peers, and it showed. In her evaluation, the instructor lauded my verbal delivery and effective flips of the flip chart, but also noted that I failed to communicate the topic's main ideas and needed to work on basic elements like eye contact and body movement.

"Don't read the charts or turn your back to us," she wrote in my evaluation, "and please use humor and interaction to relax the audience and keep them involved. If you don't love your topic, we won't!" All in all, I was pretty horrible.

Another class introduced me to IBM's methodical approach to sales calls. First, establish rapport with open-ended questions. Next, identify the prospect's business needs using a five-step "funneling" technique. Then, summarize what you heard and transition to a possible solution using the "F-A-R" approach to describe the product's Features, relate its Advantages, and seek a Reaction. Always close with a plan of action, detailing what you'll do next, what they will do, and the basis for the next meeting. I got kudos for my preparation and rapport building, but I was counseled to "work on those FARs," speak more precisely, and show more enthusiasm.

Clearly my communication skills needed an upgrade, but these foundational concepts—clarity, caring, listening with an intent to learn, and speaking with an intent to provide value—would stick with me. I would come to see communications as a science I could learn, versus an art that re-quired innate talent I didn't possess. With practice and guidance I believed I would improve. I approached public speaking with the same curiosity that I brought to math, engineering, and IBM's technology. I wanted to under-stand how it worked.

Our branch focused on selling and maintaining computer hardware like mainframes, printers, terminals, and data storage systems, as well as software. Knowing how to read and write different coding languages would allow me to communicate with the IT experts and buyers at our customers.

One of our industrial customers was Grand Trunk Western Railroad, a subsidiary of a Canadian company that still runs one of the oldest railway lines in North America. I was assigned to help sell our PC software to one of Grand Trunk's regional office managers, a gruff railroad man who'd spent years working in and around trains. He was a journeyman who knew his trade, and I imagined he'd be skeptical about someone half his age telling him how to do his job. I wasn't nervous about being young or the only female in the room. These realities didn't distract me. I was focused on sharing how the new software could track the contents of boxcars.

I wanted to practice using the software on Grand Trunk's own PCs, using their data, so I got permission to go into Grand Trunk on a Sunday before the presentation. The railroad's office was located in the financial district of downtown Detroit, which was deserted on weekends. Mark insisted on coming with me so I wouldn't be alone.

"It'll be a long day," I warned him. He didn't mind.

We drove the half hour from Birmingham to 171 West Lafayette Boule-vard. Grand Trunk's building was old, with an ancient elevator and narrow hallways that seemed even darker after hours. Its offices were sparse and gritty. Gray metal desks. Typewriters. Reams of papers stacked in small of-fices. I found a PC and for the next eight hours I dug in.

To entertain himself, Mark brought a hot new gadget with us, a Sony Watchman. The miniature TV was about the size of a brick and had a tiny, one-inch black-and-white screen. He got comfortable and turned on the football game.

The only nearby restaurant that was open was American Coney Island, which served frankfurters slathered with chili, diced white onions, and mustard. Mark loved his Coney dogs, and that Sunday he must have eaten at least six. I can still see him, sitting there eating those Coney dogs and watching the Detroit Lions on his tiny TV.

It's funny that I remember that day at Grand Trunk's offices more than the meeting with the supervisor, which went quite well. Our team showed him how to use the program to collect and track shipments, discover if quantities were increasing or shrinking, and what percentage of trains arrived on time. This kind of information could take weeks to get from other departments; with our program, he'd have it at his fingertips. Grand Trunk bought the software, and I was assigned to help implement it. I would work with Grand Trunk for a while, and because I was becoming an expert on the product, I was asked to assist with other sales and install efforts.

I was learning that the more I knew how things worked, the more confident I was talking to customers. I was also learning more about the man I'd married. Mark genuinely wanted to be there for me and would continue to show up for me without making it seem like a burden on him. Sitting in the lifeless railroad offices for eight hours was nothing compared to the lengths he would go, and the miles he would travel, to support me.

* * *

I was being assigned to more accounts. One week I was at a courthouse, the next at a medical facility. One of my first big projects was to help sell a new line of IBM mainframes to a large insurance company. The marketing effort was being run by a demanding but good-hearted senior marketing representative named John Nern. John was an IBM veteran and the consummate sales professional. He had a friendly, personable rapport with his customers. He knew their families and whether they spent weekends fishing or watching their kids' football games. He understood their business and was dead serious about never letting them down.

"Always keep your promise to a customer," he told me over and over. He was brash and would deviate from protocol if it meant getting something done. He just never went too far. John's dedication earned his customers' trust, and thus their allegiance, which they exercised by buying more IBM products. He just had to keep delivering on his promises.

After I helped his marketing team sell two large systems to the insurance company, replacing a competitor's machines, John took me under his wing and became a mentor, teaching me what he knew and giving me access to opportunities, like asking me to coordinate the installation of the two mainframes we sold.

Mainframes were housed in spacious rooms where they could be kept cool enough to operate. Air conditioning wasn't sufficient, so a liquid cooling system circulated water through its insides, absorbing heat. Massive cables had to be laid under the room's raised floor to link the mainframes to power and water. The complex task was executed by field engineers who were highly skilled technicians. I'd never met the engineers assigned to the insurance install, yet it was my duty to organize them.

I also had never led an installation, although I had two weeks of formal training and one hands-on experience, when I joined a crew of field engineers installing a mainframe at a government customer's office. Mainframes were installed late at night on weekends when no one was in the office, and I remember arriving on a Friday evening, before the engineers, so I could study one of the mainframe's thick manuals, which IBM called a Red Book. Once the engineers showed up, I did my best to assist as they snaked thick, heavy cables and bundles of electrical wires through the floor. I also vividly recall all the engineers deciding to break for the night and go off to a local bar. I can still hear their voices trailing off as they wandered out, leaving me there alone.

"You're still training, Ginni. We'll come back and get you . . ."

Being the only woman among a bunch of male coworkers, drinking was not an option I was interested in—not to mention that I wasn't even invited!

So I stayed at the site, alone for hours, pulling those cables and wires across the room.

At the insurance company installation with John's team, I was more than a trainee. I was in charge. I'd written a detailed plan and worked side by side with the engineers late into the night. They certainly didn't need my technical help, but I think they appreciated that I understood what had to be done and was willing to do the heavy lifting. After, I received an extra $1,500 in recognition for coordinating a successful install, and John asked me to be the systems engineer assigned to the insurance account. I may have also earned the respect of the field engineers, considering they didn't leave me to finish the job on my own.

*   *   *

"When you aren't sure how to handle a tough situation," John Nern once told me, "hunt down someone, anyone, who can." This was his way of teaching me to build a network. At his urging, I started to introduce myself to product specialists around the country and coalesced a collection of experts I could reach in a pinch. Because they knew me, they took my calls.

I cultivated my network by checking in with people for no particular reason, or to see if they needed anything, and by taking time to answer their questions. If a marketing rep from another office asked me to lend a hand closing a deal, I got on a train or plane. I never said no to a request regardless of how busy I was. That also helped me be a better communicator. John instructed me never to use canned presentations, but not to shoot from the hip, either. "Prepare what you want to say and personalize it so people feel you are talking to them." Asking account reps in my network to share information about customers allowed me to better understand a company and its operations before I stepped in front of them. I was learning that networks were really just supportive communities nurtured through genuine interest in people and by sharing what I knew.

In 1985 I was promoted to a large systems specialist, which relocated me into a regional office to handle sales and support of IBM's new product, the 3820, a high-end laser printer. These machines were the length of cars and taller than most humans. One of my first projects was helping the local telephone company laser print millions of customer phone bills. For weeks the bills kept coming out wrong. I had to diagnose each error, then run the job again. I spent many nights and weekends reading the "dumps," which were pages of code and data, to identify why the printer was screwing up. Eventually we got it running right.

Soon I was overseeing marketing and support for the 3820 across a five-state region, which required networking with marketers and systems engineers in other offices. If they had confidence in my willingness and ability to assist them, they wouldn't hesitate to contact me and together we could capitalize on sales opportunities or fend off a brewing crisis. I visited branches in person and reached out to share creative sales strategies. Potential buyers were skeptical and wanted to see the 3820 in action, but it was too immense to bring to customers so I had to bring them to us. In Columbus, Ohio, we hosted "Executive Printer Briefings," and in Detroit, "Spotlight on Printing!" Not the sexiest of events, but they paid off. Our printers were being installed at Chrysler, Progressive Insurance, and Dow Chemical. Inside IBM, our region became known as having one of the best laser printer programs in the country. I came to enjoy the troubleshooting, and all the problem-solving made me a bit of a laser printing expert. IBM even flew me to Gaithersburg, Maryland, for several weeks to help write the technical guide for the 3820.

In 1987 I was promoted to my first management position. Other systems engineers would now report directly to me. This was a vote of confidence at IBM, where people rose through the ranks by increasingly larger management roles, from overseeing a team, then a branch, then a region, to eventually leading IBM's business in a country. My new role put me on that path. I even received a congratulatory letter from IBM's CEO, John Akers. I'd never met John and doubted he knew who I was. Still, it felt like a big deal to hear from the head of the company.

The person who appointed me as a manager was Pat O'Brien, who managed all the systems engineering talent in the branch where I now worked.

He'd been a math teacher before joining IBM as a systems engineer in the late 1960s, and during my three years working for Pat I would oversee about twelve people and twenty-four client accounts.

Pat taught me how to manage people by how he managed me. He was honest, whether what he had to say was positive or negative. He could be firm without exerting heavy emotion. In meetings, Pat listened and let others talk first, even when he was the most senior one in the room. When he did speak, he got to the point. Pat told me it was a manager's duty to help people develop their careers. The learning and education that was so vital to me was now something I needed to help others access. I tried to pick up on people's strengths and weaknesses, ask about their aspirations, then come up with plans to build their skills. I encouraged those who reported to me to learn as much as they could, and in turn I shared as much as I could. During my second full year working for Pat, my team averaged twenty-five days of formal education, which was 60 percent more class time than IBM required. Our revenues from software, services, and maintenance exceeded our quotas, reinforcing the positive correlation between learning and earning.

Pat also taught me to make decisions based on values. One of my most talented engineers had an ugly habit of telling off-color, misogynistic jokes, and several women complained to me. I asked Pat how I should handle the situation. His response was unequivocal: "You have to address it," he said. "Get rid of him if you have to; it doesn't matter how good he is." Pat was giving me permission to prioritize people and recognize that a healthy workplace is a humane workplace. In a letter to the technician, I made it clear that his offensive behavior was unacceptable, and that he would be fired if there was one more infraction.

I was learning that business is rife with situations that require us to choose between ethical and fiscal responsibilities; between doing what is right and doing what is simple, or most profitable, or more popular. The right choice is not always obvious, but Pat taught me that it should be. His values-driven approach would influence my priorities as a manager and a leader for decades to come.

Given Pat's steadfast moral code, it was ironic, then, that he broached an inappropriate topic with me, one that today would be completely unacceptable.

"Listen Ginni," he said one day, "this is scary for me to say but the only reason I am bringing this up is to help you." I leaned in, all ears. "You are smart and a hard worker and can go far here, but if you look at the high-level executives, most seem to be in good physical shape."

Pat was talking about my weight.

I'd struggled with it all my life. As a little girl I was chubby. During high school I went through chunky periods before thinning out in college and when I got married. Now, well into my twenties, my weight was creeping up again. Gaining and losing weight was a cycle I was all too familiar with, but this was the first time my appearance had ever been presented as an obstacle to my aspirations, or a factor that could overshadow my mind or my work ethic. My first instinct was to react with humor to defuse the awkwardness. "Pat, you think I eat too much?"

"I have no idea," he said, flustered. He was trying to coach, not offend.

I have no memory of being upset with Pat, although I was probably a little embarrassed. I'm sure I understood that he was looking out for my best career interests; Pat had twice nominated me for manager of the year, and I was confident that he saw my potential and didn't personally judge my appearance. He was speaking on behalf of others who might, which he knew from his own experience. When Pat first joined the company, he was once sent home for wearing a light-yellow shirt instead of a white one!

I also don't think I thought Pat was wrong in his concern. But I didn't interpret his observation as a critique of my appearance as much as a concern that some might think I had a weakness of self-discipline. Whether or not that was how Pat or others perceived my weight I can't say, but that's how it landed for me.

"I'm just saying that if you want to move up, and I think you can, consider how senior executives *look* . . . and how they dress. They wear suits," he added. With that, he was also suggesting that I replace the bright dresses

I wore with the monochromatic skirts, blazers, and tie-like scarves many women donned. IBMers weren't flashy. The corporate uniform back then was cookie-cutter conservative. Meanwhile, I had an affinity for dresses with a touch of flair. Dresses were also far more comfortable than tight-waisted skirts, especially if I was heavier. Was it fair? No. Was it the reality of the era we lived in? Unfortunately, yes.

Obviously what was appropriate to say to an employee back then was very different in everyone's eyes, Pat's as well as mine. His intention was pure: he just wanted me to fit in so I could get ahead, so he was urging me to look professional and back then looking professional meant not standing out. (Granted, I was also five feet, nine inches tall, so there was only so much I could blend in.)

Remember, this was the eighties. Women's participation in management and professional roles had been rising for years, but we were trying to fit ourselves into male-dominant cultures. We just wanted to be noticed for the right reasons: our talents. I didn't see myself as a feminist, per se, perhaps because I just didn't see being female as a disadvantage or worry that my future was capped by a so-called glass ceiling. In my mind, the best way for anyone to get ahead was to do great work. Maybe I was naive in wanting to believe that being a woman wouldn't hinder my career. Or maybe I was just being optimistic.

Also, I had yet to find myself in a situation where I felt compromised or harassed. Maybe I wasn't looking for it. Maybe I was okay ignoring inappropriate comments. When one man referred to me and another woman colleague as "skirts," we laughed it off. When he also remarked that we were going to play with "the big boys" when we both got promoted, we just shot back, "you mean the big *girls*," and rolled our eyes. I wasn't insulted because I truly believed people took me seriously.

Did I begin dressing a bit more conservatively after Pat and I spoke? Did I go out and buy a slew of suits, or go on a diet after the conversation? Honestly, I can't remember. But I did gain more weight throughout the nineties. Did it hinder my career as Pat feared? I have no proof either way. But Pat was right about one thing: women in the workplace are judged more harshly than men on appearance—and in many ways that hasn't changed.

* * *

During this period in my career, I was also trying to work on my own weaknesses very deliberately. I had perfectionist tendencies that customers appreciated, but that could drive my colleagues crazy. Specifically, I was a nitpicky editor, often returning reports and other documents with so many handwritten notes and crossed-out words that my direct reports nicknamed me Ginni "Red Pen" Rometty.

"Take the red pen away from her!" they'd chide. This was not whispered behind my back; I was in on the joke. More than once I received a red pen as a gift. There was a lesson in the humor. My drive for perfection often meant I only focused on what needed to change without acknowledging the positive. This could keep people from trusting themselves. It would take me a while to learn that just because I could point something out didn't mean I should. I still spotted errors, but I became more deliberate about what I mentioned and sent back to get fixed. I also tried to curtail my tendency to micromanage and let people execute; I had to stop assuming my way was the best or only way. I was learning that giving others control builds their confidence, and that constantly trying to control people destroys it. In general, I became more selective on where I put my energy, and where I asked others to put theirs.

I was also learning how to better manage my own time. My efforts knew no boundaries. Staying at my desk until 9 p.m. was not unusual; nor was working Saturdays, Sundays, and holidays. This was in stark contrast to my dear husband, who often said that if someone couldn't get a job done by 3:30 p.m., they were inefficient. Luckily, Mark accepted, supported, and at times just tolerated my very different philosophy. Once, after a string of late nights, a coworker called out my tending to "overoptimize" and put it this way, "Ginni, how do you expect to do more in this company if you can't get a first-line manager job done in eight hours?" Was I not being efficient, or was I going the extra mile? Probably a bit of both.

At some point I was introduced to the ABC rule. As are your most important tasks, and usually the most difficult, the activities that require the most brain power. Bs have medium importance, and Cs are the least vital and usually the easiest. Most people spend their days doing C work and confuse being busy with being productive. I began to start my days with A activities, like writing proposals, because I was sharpest in the morning. And yet . . . I could always find something else to do after finishing the C work.

My intense focus could also be myopic. At times I was so committed to getting something done that I'd abruptly cut short friendly chitchat before a meeting began or cut off a colleague if his ideas weren't absolutely relevant to the topic at hand. Some people appreciated what one person labeled my "aggressive impatience," because it kept meetings on track to meet deadlines. Others probably found it a bit cold. I never wanted to offend anyone; I just wanted to get stuff done. I would learn ways to be productive and more personable because both mattered to me.

Some people assumed I expected the same long, intense hours from them, which was not the case; I just enjoyed working. My tendency to work so much was partly rooted in my youth: I never wanted to be in a position where I couldn't take care of myself financially, and hard work was a means to that end.

* * *

Reflecting back on these years, I can see I was establishing foundational behaviors.

First, I was developing a propensity for continuous learning, approaching every situation with the attitude that I could glean something new if I observed, listened, and asked questions with that intent. Everyone had something to teach, and I didn't always wait for a mentor to find me. When I made it known to someone that I wanted to learn from them, they tended to adopt me and become invested in my success. Over the years, I established a mosaic of mentors and tried to become a composite of their best behaviors. I also was becoming a "T-shaped" professional, developing a breadth but also a depth of knowledge in a particular area. In my case, I was digging deep into computing technology while learning how to communicate and sell. When I didn't comprehend something, I asked questions.

In essence, I was learning the value of learning.

Knowledge, however, is not enough. In researching this book, I read over performance reviews from my first years at IBM. In them, my managers often cited my professionalism as a strength. No one taught me how to be "professional," although my early family life certainly hoisted on me a heavy, if premature, sense of responsibility and accountability. Rereading the appraisals reminded me just how much people value seemingly simple acts like being prepared, being on time, being responsive, keeping others informed so they're never surprised, or just having a positive attitude, especially under stress. Reliability. Dependability. Initiative. Anticipating problems and addressing them before they fester. These are all things people appreciate. And when all else was equal, I think professionalism helped me stand out.

During my first ten years at IBM, I felt then as I'd felt during school: if I learned as much as I could and met or exceeded expectations with a level of professionalism—maybe even gravitas if I was lucky—I would have access to more opportunities.

5

Being Uncomfortable

I couldn't sleep. It was Labor Day weekend, 1991, and Mark and I were spending the holiday at my brother Joe's house in Memphis with my mom, Annette, and Darlene. I had until the end of the weekend to decide whether or not to take a new job, which meant a risky career move.

That year, IBM had entered the consulting business. The company already provided IT services, which focused on running and maintaining its hardware and software. This new unit would sell business strategy and management advice by analyzing organizations and recommending ways to be more competitive and profitable, in part by using technology. It's one thing to go into a company to hook up and run computers. It's another thing to provide a five-year plan about how to change processes and approach. The latter talent IBM lacked.

IBM invested quite a bit to build its new business, and recruited a senior partner from a high-end management consulting firm to convince other career consultants to quit their boutique firms to build the IBM Consulting Group. These outsiders, with their MBAs and experience with C-suite executives, came into IBM with acumen and methodologies IBM needed, as well as a bit of swagger.

A handful of veteran IBMers from across the company were being asked to join the new group, which wasn't meant to stand alone but be an integrated arm that leveraged IBM's existing resources. IBM was a complex place to navigate, and the new employees needed the current ones to lead them around, sort of like seeing-eye dogs.

In turn, IBMers would learn how to be consultants.

When I was approached to join, I hesitated for a few reasons. First, I worried it would derail my current career trajectory. Opportunities to lead branches didn't come along often, and moving into consulting meant giving up my spot in line, stepping off IBM's well-paved management track. I'd also go back to being a practitioner, even an apprentice, as I shadowed the veteran consultants. That kind of felt like a demotion even though it was considered an honor to be asked to join the new business.

I also questioned whether I could succeed. Instead of selling systems, I'd be selling solutions to business problems. And I would be selling myself. My performance would be judged on whether a customer was willing to pay for my advice, not whether they bought a computer. I'd only be as good as the quality of the recommendations my teams and I came up with and executed, and that felt like a very vulnerable place to be. What if no one was willing to pay for my advice?

The mere thought of switching was terribly nerve-racking. I fretted over it, and of course I talked to Mark, who harbored none of my hesitancy.

"This sounds like something you'd be really good at, that uses skills you've already built," he said. "What do you have to lose?" If it went awry, his salary would cover us until I found a new job. I was grateful for the financial cushion but still concerned I'd halt my momentum. If I failed at it or disliked the work, or if the new business flopped, would I be considered for future management roles, or be forgotten? Even if I enjoyed consulting, what did the future look like? So many unknowns.

I also wondered how the inevitable travel could affect my marriage. Consultants can spend long periods away from home. "We'll make it work," was Mark's grinning response. "We'll have a new rule, and never go more than two weeks without seeing each other."

I tossed and turned all weekend and discussed my dilemma with my family while we ate burgers and hot dogs at our Labor Day barbecue. A weekend of thinking and talking revealed a tough truth: I'd become really good at being a really good IBM employee. I knew our products cold, and I was frequently asked to help others sell them. I also taught our systems internally. I knew who to call for support, and how to plow through our thickets of notorious bureaucracy. I was an expert at IBM's processes, but that wasn't necessarily a marketable skill in the external world. I needed to cultivate new transferable skills valued by the external market just in case things didn't work out at IBM.

That revelation, along with my family's support and Mark's optimism, inspired me to build belief in myself and my future and led me to closure. I decided to leave the known for the unknown and become a practice leader for the consulting unit's Information Technology Strategy and Planning Group. I was thirty-four, embarking on the biggest risk I'd taken in my young career, and feeling very uncomfortable.

* * *

Ineedajob.

This was the password I used to access my voicemail months into my consulting adventure because, well, I needed a job. I'd yet to sell my own client project. Bringing in new business was part of my job description, as was getting myself and our practice certified to meet industry standards so we would be taken more seriously in the marketplace. Companies didn't think of IBM for strategic business advice, so to be in a position to prove ourselves, we were instructed to offer our time and advice for free. "Give us a chance," we'd say, "If you don't like us, don't pay us." I had made lots of presentations but hadn't closed a thing.

Finally, in 1992, I helped land a project developing an IT strategy for a large grocery store chain. The company was a longtime client of a competing management consulting firm and was initially reluctant to accept our offer to assess their operations. They acquiesced when we presented a proposal that gave them our time for pennies on the dollar.

The days were long, but I was growing, using my brain in new ways every day. Consulting was honing my deductive reasoning skills and exercising my logical approach to problem-solving. It was teaching me how to translate the value of technology into business results and introducing me to more sophisticated business discourse. I was conversing with senior executives about all aspects of their companies, and these face-to-face encounters with bright, impassioned leaders energized me. I was establishing a service mindset. The consultants I apprenticed under were showing me the difference between customers and clients: customers are transactions; clients are relationships. Maintaining relationships requires a high level of commitment, genuine caring, curiosity, and attention to details. I came to see my role, no matter my title, as being in service of clients.

My original fear that no one would be willing to pay for my advice hadn't materialized. Feedback from clients was positive enough that I began to think I could do the job. Even though I didn't have an MBA like many of the professional consultants IBM hired, I seemed to have an aptitude for the work. In short, I realized that I didn't need a business degree to succeed. By 1993, I was exceeding my revenue targets and was the first new consultant to certify myself and my regional practice. I was being asked to speak at IBM career days to recruit more consultants.

I had no regrets about going into consulting. I had escaped a process job and was acquiring new skills and knowledge that I could apply to any number of roles inside and beyond IBM. But it was still unclear where my career was headed.

* * *

Fred Amoroso flashed his wide, infectious grin and pitched the job as one with a purpose beyond just consulting for insurance companies.

"You'll have great opportunities no matter where you go," he said, hoping to inspire me to work for him, "but if you come with me, we'd have the chance to transform IBM, too. And if that's what you're interested in, then I would love to have you as part of the insurance team. Together we'll not just do consulting work but figure out ways to help change the IBM company." I was impressed by Fred's outsize passion for the staid insurance business.

Fred was an engineer-turned-entrepreneur who had cofounded a business that he sold to the accounting firm Pricewaterhouse. He was at the firm when IBM recruited him in 1993 to oversee all its insurance business around the world. I met Fred not long after, and now I was being given a choice between two opportunities: work for Fred and oversee all consulting for the insurance industry, or work for someone else and do the same for banking. Insurance did not inherently entice me (IBM's own CEO would one day tell me he found insurance about as exciting as watching grass grow), but Fred painted such a compelling picture that I decided to take him up on his offer.

As an IBM outsider, Fred was outspoken about what he saw as IBM's frustrating flaws, including its bureaucracy and a lack of hands-on work by some people who'd risen into executive ranks. Fred insisted that everyone "get dirt under their nails" by being informed and engaged in the departments and clients we oversaw, versus leaving the details to people who reported to us. Managers had to be knowers, and doers.

I observed Fred's charismatic leadership with fascination. His enthusiasm could mount an army. Just expressing a strong point of view brought people into Fred's orbit, and built belief in his vision, even among those who didn't work for him or know much about insurance. People followed his energy and trusted his knowledge. Behind his style was a simple secret.

"I wasn't born with it," he told me when I commented on his effusive passion. "You can learn to be passionate about what you do." Then he added, "But being passionate is also exhausting." Fred explained that he turned his passion on and off. All that outward charisma attracts followers. "But the energy can drain you," he said.

The notion that passion can be acquired when it doesn't come naturally, even summoned, conserved, and applied selectively, were revelatory insights for me, perhaps because it expanded my own possibilities. If I could acquire a passion for anything, I could do anything—including insurance.

* * *

Fred proved to be an incredible mentor and sponsor, and his advocacy helped fuel my growth in many ways.

He gave me a lot of responsibility and made sure I got credit for things I did well. He respected my drive and genuinely wanted to see me excel. But Fred also knew that I needed more than strong results and excellent performance reviews to get ahead. He understood the value of exposure and what it could mean for someone's future, and he encouraged me to establish a more public presence inside and outside the company. I began authoring articles, getting quoted in trade publications, and speaking at external events. With Fred's support, I was one of just four US employees invited to attend a global education seminar for newly named executives. And it was Fred who first introduced me to Louis V. Gerstner Jr., IBM's legendary CEO from 1993 to 2002, by asking me to host Lou at a conference and introduce him to clients.

Lou was orchestrating his own transformation of IBM, bringing it back from the brink of a potential bankruptcy, and taking the company into the internet age. Fred believed that if Lou could see me in action, as he put it, he and IBM would value me more. Unbeknownst to me, Fred approached another colleague, Phil Guido, to coordinate a way to increase my visibility with Lou. I didn't know Phil yet, but he was and remains one of the very best executive leaders in IBM, and the two brainstormed how to include me in an upcoming meeting that Lou had with the chairman and top executives at a big life insurance client. They asked me to speak about technology trends I'd been researching, which turned into a spirited, substantive discussion about how the client could deal with disruption. Looking back, I appreciate that Fred and Phil created an environment where I could excel just by being myself.

When Fred thought my raises from HR didn't adequately reflect my work or were lower than what I could earn at other companies, he fought HR to get me more cash and equity. IBM had strict rules about who received what and when, and Fred continuously warned HR that a client or a competitor was likely to poach me if my overall compensation didn't reflect my value. It helped that I was an educated advocate on my own behalf, and I made a point of showing Fred lists of projects that I had sold, and the monetary value of each engagement and its follow-on business.

The result of our joint advocacy was that, under Fred, I received my most substantive jumps in pay since joining IBM. I also learned a lesson as a manager: pay people competitively before they ask. Not having to fight Fred for a raise I had earned engendered my appreciation and loyalty.

Fred also cared about my well-being as much as my results, and he didn't hide his concern that my unrelenting pace was impossible to sustain. I would easily travel to six different locations in a five-day period to visit clients. In a note he sent me in September 1994, his last sentence read, "I enjoy working with you—don't burn yourself out." He once recommended that I only work four days a week given how much I packed in a day. I never took that advice.

Three years later, I still hadn't slowed down, and in my performance review Fred wrote, "I have never seen someone with that capacity of work, but I see the toll it takes." He was right. I was not exercising, and I probably needed more sleep, less travel, and more fun. "Be more selfish," was his advice, "take time to smell the roses." Fred's concern would eventually be an impetus for me to finally start paying attention to my health, as well as to more productively manage my time, identify priorities, set boundaries, get comfortable delegating, and even let the occasional detail fall through the cracks. But I wasn't there quite yet.

During my years working for Fred, I was promoted faster than most people typically moved up, and by 1997, I was running all of IBM's insurance-industry consulting and software business on a global basis. Fred's faith in me boosted my faith in myself.

"You could run an entire vertical one day," he said, meaning an entire industry. I assumed he meant well into the future.

* * *

In the late spring of 1997, Fred called me into his office. We were at an IBM campus in Westchester County, not far from IBM's Armonk, New York, headquarters. I was still living in Detroit, but I was commuting to Armonk regularly.

"I have great news for you," he said. I knew Fred was moving to Tokyo to oversee all of IBM's services business in the Asia-Pacific region, and that someone had to replace him to lead the global insurance unit for IBM. "I believe you should be my successor."

My first reaction was *Wow, that sounds wonderful*, which was quickly followed by a less enthusiastic thought, *I'm not ready*. The unit I currently ran was doing well. I did not, however, have responsibility for all functions. Taking Fred's job meant overseeing profit and loss across every geography and every product and service that IBM sold to insurance clients, including responsibilities for the staff functions. With another year or so I would be more prepared, and that's what I told Fred. He looked at me quizzically, as if to ask, *Isn't this the promotion you've been working toward?* He then suggested I go ahead and interview with a senior vice president who led all of IBM's sales and global industries.

The next day I drove twenty minutes to the SVP's office in another sprawling IBM campus, this one with sleek white buildings, including a glass pyramid structure, all designed by the architect I. M. Pei. We spoke about the role, and to my surprise I was offered the job at the end of our conversation. "I'd like to go home and talk to my husband about this," I said. "I'll get back to you on Monday." I hesitated for several reasons. For one, Fred was an admired, well-liked leader. Stepping into his beloved shoes was daunting. More worrisome was that there was so much I didn't know. I flew back to Detroit and talked to Mark about all the reasons I wasn't quite ready for the role, and my response when I was offered the job. Mark listened patiently before asking me only one question.

"Do you think a man would've answered it that way?"

Mark knew a lot of the people at IBM who I thought were talented. "I'm sure they would have accepted the job and focused on all the reasons they deserved it and why they were ready," he said. "Ginni, you're ready. Plus, I know you, and in six months you'll be telling me that you want more challenges."

His observation made me pause. Mark's point wasn't just about differences between men and women, but about choosing to have confidence even in the face of risk. Going into consulting a few years back seemed like a small change compared to what Fred wanted me to do, which was to run an entire business. And yet, hadn't I learned so much as a consultant, and grown exponentially as a result of taking that risk? I knew I had.

My biggest obstacle was not a lack of ability, but self-imposed self-doubt. I could have been celebrating! Instead, I was obsessing over an inner voice that said, "If only I had more knowledge, or a little more time, then I could do this." The voice then listed ten reasons why I couldn't do it, versus ten reasons why I could. Luckily, I also had Mark's and Fred's voices.

I flew back to New York and told Fred I would accept the job. He smiled, then looked me in the eyes, "Don't do that again," he said, confirming Mark's point that feeling a lack of confidence and risk is no reason not to proceed. In fact, risk is a reason to forge ahead. If I wanted to grow my skills, advance my career, and widen my impact, I had to embrace risk and the discomfort that came with it. Taking risks meant that I was bound to learn and grow.

That episode began to crystallize an idea that would prove true time and again: growth and comfort never coexist.

PART TWO

The Power of We

Changing Work

At some point in our lives and careers, our attention turns from ourselves to others. We still have our own goals, but we recognize that our actions affect many, and that it's impossible to achieve anything truly meaningful alone. As we help others and ask for their help, our perspective transitions from me to we. My journey learning to apply "the power of we" forms the arc of part II.

These chapters define and illustrate five principles that emerged over decades as my responsibilities grew: Being in service of. Building belief. Knowing what must change, what must endure. Stewarding good tech and inclusion. And being resilient. Only in retrospect could I see that each principle was a galvanizing lens through which I tried to work and lead.

What follows is not my full history but selected memories that occasionally go back and forth in time between the years I was a consultant through my years as IBM's CEO and Chairman. In sum, these stories and reflections show how the five principles came to life for me and my teams, and the ways we tried to address difficulties and make progress by navigating the tensions inherent to each, like trying to meet the needs of multiple stakeholders, bridge emotion and execution, and muster optimism despite setbacks. Some lessons are practical and you can apply them tomorrow. Others are more ambitious, so embrace them today and let them evolve.

It's my hope that these ideas translate to your own work and leadership. Although it's my journey, I share it in service of you and the positive changes you seek for others.

6

Being in Service Of

It's a blistering-hot midwestern summer day, but the air-conditioned office is chilly. I sit down next to the CEO of a large grocery retailer and hand him a multipage report that my team and I put together after months of studying his company. This is the first major consulting engagement I'd personally sold on my own. We've interviewed dozens of the company's executives, studied store aisles, toured warehouses, and researched the industry to know how the retailer compares to competitors. We found problems ranging from inventory shrinkage, as shoppers ate strawberries from the display, to low cashier productivity, and a slow supply chain.

I've been traveling Sundays to Fridays, and I am so busy that I've forfeited vacation days and celebrated my birthday behind the deli counter in a store, where the manager presented me with a personalized cake from the bakery. Now the team is tired after a long night preparing for the meeting, and we're gathered around the table anxious to present months of work.

I begin walking the CEO through the report, starting at the top of the first page and going through each of the paragraphs. He turns the page, then looks me straight in the eyes. I stop talking.

"Ginni, give me your copy of the report that's highlighted," he says.

"Well, this is my version," I reply, drawing my packet a little closer, hesitant to show him my notes. He then holds up the voluminous mass of densely printed pages I'd given him.

"Why do you make me read all this other stuff?" he says. "Ginni, please give me your copy that's highlighted." He has a full day ahead of him (years into the future, I'll know firsthand just how full a CEO's days can get), and he only has time to hear the most salient points. He doesn't need to know how my team and I arrived at those points, but I'm trying to impress him with our process. He is not impressed yet.

That exchange very early in my career revealed to me a basic truth about what it means to be in service of others: time is the most valuable thing someone can give, and you must give them value in return.

The Soul of Good Power

When I started thinking about what makes power "good," one of the first things that came to my mind was this notion of being in service of others. Not in a lofty sense, but in a practical, tactical sense.

To be in service of, as I see it, is to consider and fulfill someone or something's needs to the best of our abilities, before or in parallel with fulfilling our own. When we are in service of, our intention is to make someone or something better by helping them realize their potential. I consider this the soul of good power—its fundamental intention. The worthwhile "why" for all that we do.

Conceptually, I see "being in service of others" as different from "serving others." Waiters can serve you a meal but not care if you enjoy yourself. In contrast, waitstaff in service of their guests do more than just take an order and bring food. They really want to create an enjoyable experience, and as a result of trying to deliver, will hopefully get a bigger tip. But the experience, not the tip, was their first intent.

Being in service of others is not a means to an end, but a means in and of itself. It manifests in how we act and the behaviors we choose in moments of preparation, interaction, and follow-up. And while it starts with those closest to us, what we do one-on-one can extrapolate to organizations, and even ideas. Being in service of a purpose can manifest in how we spend resources like time, energy, intellectual capital, and money.

In many cases, balancing the needs of others with our own is the tension we must navigate. Being in service of should be a win-win.

When we're in service of people, we also speak to and treat them with respect, dignity, and civility. We emotionally connect, collaborate, ask, and listen. We have empathy, and we step into their shoes.

Who or what we're in service of changes throughout our lifetimes. It begins with our families, the people that care for us, and that we care for. As we grow up, we're in positions to be in service of our friends and neighbors, which means looking beyond ourselves and refusing to be bystanders when others need help. In our work, we are most directly in service of customers and clients. We can also be in service of our coworkers by creating healthy workplaces and helping them reach their potential. Leaders are in service of their organizations, and all those invested in it, by how they manage, and in the programs, policies, and cultures they craft and champion. Companies also have a responsibility to be in service of communities and society, as corporate citizens, in addition to shareholders. I follow in the footsteps of leaders who for decades have believed that businesses have a role in maintaining the health and prosperity of the societies in which they operate.

Working at IBM was, for me, about being in service of changing the way the world works. I know that's a lofty purpose, but it started on a less lofty plane—learning how to be in service of clients. It evolved from there.

Delivering Value

I learned the most about how to be in service of clients during my years in consulting, before I replaced Fred and became the head of the Global Insurance Unit. Our clients could be tough. They had high standards because our work was complex and often critical to their operations. They wanted returns on their investments in us, and it was during this time that I developed habits I stuck with for years and scaled as projects got larger and more intense. They were all about how to bring a client value.

For one, analyzing a client's business was just a first step—but analysis was not the goal.

We had to extract the "ah-ha."

Extracting the "ah-ha" meant coming up with new conclusions and recommendations that would benefit a client's business. To get me to the "ah-ha," my consulting managers would rip holes in my reports, pushing me to think strategically, not just operationally. They tested my assumptions and made sure I was validating my hypotheses to boost the quality of my ideas. They constantly reminded me that I was not just supposed to provide facts, but to solve problems.

I came to see that when a client shared a problem, my colleagues and I could respond in one of three ways: We could reiterate the problem, which demonstrated to the client that we heard them, but it didn't enhance their business. We could reiterate what they said and segue into describing our products and services. That approach set us up for a transaction: look what you can buy from us. This wasn't the truest way to be in service of them. A third way to respond was to engage in conversation, and augment what they told us with our own knowledge, asking questions to probe deeper into their business. This was a more collaborative approach, a two-way dialogue informed by what the client told us that then went further by integrating information we brought to the table about industry trends, for example, and connecting dots. The back-and-forth could lead to an original, strategic solution that established trust, and a relationship that led to mutual opportunities.

To even begin to arrive at an "ah-ha" in concert with a client, I had to do my homework.

Shortly after I began managing other consultants, I told one of my bosses that I was worried about my team's readiness for a presentation.

"Ginni, you must be prepared to dance when your team cannot," he said. His message? Managers must also be doers, and never just preside. I adopted a mantra to ensure my teams and I delivered value in the moment: think, prepare, rehearse.

I did a lot of research before meetings, which I'll remind you was much more time-consuming in the days before search engines like Google. I didn't want to walk in cold; I wanted to know where a company had been, what it was doing now, and where it wanted to go. How could I deliver value if we didn't know the client really well?

Looking back, I can see another impetus for my ruthless preparation: I was a woman in a man's world. There were, of course, other women at the company, many of whom I worked for and worked with. Some were my managers, others were assigned to me as mentors. Each had unique abilities, and as a cohort I found my female colleagues intelligent, professional, ambitious, and dedicated. And they were always prepared. Every woman I knew worked incredibly hard. They showed me through example that the way to distinguish yourself is to know your stuff.

IBM was ahead of its time in advancing women, especially in the tech industry. Still, there were usually more men than women in the meetings, especially at our clients' offices. When I went to see a client, I suspected that I had a higher bar to hurdle than if I was male. In some cases I had to overcome so-called wife, daughter, or granddaughter syndrome because some men I met subconsciously cast me in one of those roles; I reminded them of the most significant females in their life. In those cases, I needed to recast myself as a businessperson in their eyes.

Preparation helped protect me, at least in my own mind, from gender bias, conscious or otherwise. Was it fair? No. But I was and remain a product of the times in which women have to work extra hard to prove themselves— thirty years later this is still true in so many places, including the tech industry as a whole and the ranks of senior management across the board. For me, being prepared staved off any self-doubt. Knowledge led to more confidence, and when I felt confident I felt like I belonged in the room or on a stage. So, in those moments when some impostor syndrome crept in, I countered it by bolstering my knowledge.

The irony, of course, is that being uber prepared made me more capable and better equipped to be in service of clients. Doing my homework allowed me to be fully present. I could ask probing questions instead of basic ones. I could truly hear what a client meant, not just what they said, because I had context. Before walking into any meeting, I always checked the day's headlines just in case something had happened that affected our client. The more I knew going in, the more equipped I was to "dance," as well as to connect dots on the fly, synthesize themes, and have a conversation that moved everyone forward. More than preparation, I'd also built the companion skill of anticipation.

Being curious helped. For years I filled two or three pages with thoughts and observations and collected tidbits of information about a client without knowing how they might come in handy. When I later sat down with a client, I might pluck a point from my penciled notes depending on where the conversation went. Having a menu of ideas at the ready made me feel more confident. Clients appreciated this habit, I think, and came to expect it. "What else is on your list, Ginni?" they'd ask, peering into my notes. Even though I never kept my notes, the process of writing was one of the ways I learned.

It was Lou Gerstner who showed me that no one is above homework. Lou's accomplishments as a leader and in both saving and transforming IBM are well chronicled. Lou was a brilliant and principled leader. He became the person who taught me the most about leadership and stewardship, and he remained a treasured mentor and friend for decades. Lou was extremely focused, able to ask the most important and penetrating questions and lead via intellect versus fear. He was also maniacally centered on clients. In fact, to this day, there is an annual IBM award in his honor given for excellence in client service.

Not long after we met, Lou and I were scheduled to visit the CEO of a big insurance client together.

Before the meeting, Lou told me that he'd been reading Tom Brokaw's book *The Greatest Generation,* and it included an entire chapter on the CEO we were about to see. What I couldn't believe was that the person running the company was researching so diligently. I realized then that if my CEO takes time to prepare, so should I.

I still consider preparation the ultimate compliment to anyone and essential to being in service of others. That said, no matter how much I prepared, I never assumed I knew it all.

I also discovered how to bring value by *not* talking, but by listening with the intent to learn.

I'm genuinely curious about people and never particularly liked talking about myself. I'd much rather hear about others. With clients, I became strategically curious, listening for insights and information that I could use to help them. I also listened for points of connection; having something or someone in common helped us relate and establish an authentic bond.

Listening with the intent to learn allowed me to make better decisions on behalf of others.

Ed Liddy, the former CEO of Allstate, was a client I worked closely with in the 1990s. He had a saying that paraphrased a Greek philosopher, "The good Lord gave us two ears and one mouth for a reason; you should conduct yourself in roughly that proportion." Ed was a values-based leader, well respected in the company and outside, and a voracious learner. Under his leadership, the seventy-year-old insurance company was grappling with issues of reinvention as internet startups began selling policies online, impacting Allstate's revenue. Ed was trying to figure out how Allstate could integrate online sales without alienating its retail agents. I traveled regularly to Allstate's headquarters just outside Chicago. Ed and I sat in his office and talked. Our dialogues were a safe space for him to ponder out loud, away from scrutiny, in his efforts to move his company forward.

"I feel like a tortoise at the starting line," he told me during one of my visits, as we overlooked an expansive corporate campus and talked about his industry's shifting landscape.

To help Ed and other insurance industry clients, I started a research group to study industry trends. Not many if any tech companies created original content back then, and I wanted us to be smart about the big business picture, not just the technology. Without context we couldn't problem-solve. We partnered with outside organizations, including the University of North Carolina, to examine how people were starting to use the internet to access, distribute, and analyze information. Realize, only about around fifty million people used the internet back then; today it's about five billion. We published reports with our own "ah-ha" conclusions. Being relevant in the future meant incumbent insurance businesses like Allstate had to develop "high-tech touch" with customers as consumers got more electronically connected. No more paper- and face-to-face-only interactions.

One of our reports, "Landscaping the Future," identified four scenarios that might unfold over the next decade, including one predicting that by 2005 every consumer would be using the internet to patch together insurance products from multiple vendors, without ever interacting with humans. That's standard practice today, but twenty years ago it was a disruptive, even scary notion for an established company.

I could see how proactive research made me and my team smarter about our clients' businesses and elevated our conversations from sales to business strategy so we could provide more value. For clients like Ed, this kind of insight made us more than salespeople in his eyes, but people that truly wanted to help them solve problems.

I discovered that listening breeds knowledge, knowledge breeds credibility, and credibility earns trust that allows relationships to flourish. It's in candid collaboration with those I was in service of that I often discovered the most valuable "ah-has."

There were also times I had to deliver bad news. One year I conveyed an unfavorable assessment of a financial firm's operations to its leadership team, which was seated around a huge round table. It was a bit intimidating, and I wasn't sure how everyone would respond to what I had to say. Afterward, the CEO came up to me, and I have never forgotten his comment.

"Ginni, you have such a velvet hammer."

"Is that a good thing?" I asked, worried that I'd overstepped. He said it was good because I'd told him things that were hard to hear, but in a way he could accept. He became a client I worked with for many years.

What made the hammer land more softly? Speaking about tough truths in affirmative tones let critiques land constructively. So did beginning a difficult conversation by emphasizing something positive, as well as citing facts instead of opinion to support a controversial conclusion, and ending on a note of optimism and with potential solutions. Using a velvet hammer helped clients become part of a solution, versus having a solution foisted upon them.

I also tried not to confuse being in service of with being a pushover. Sometimes the best way to be in service of is to say no. In those situations, honesty was my ally because it made it possible for everyone to get to a better place.

Communicating Value

Around the height of the dot-com era, I was sitting in a large auditorium among dozens of clients listening to Lou Gerstner deliver a talk about the rise of e-business. I was using a little black notebook to diagram speeches, but instead of focusing on content I was dissecting Lou's logic, nesting key points into an outline so I could map his delivery. I wanted to figure out what made Lou and others such memorable communicators. That black notebook was filled with my observations and diagramming exercises as I looked for patterns. I wanted to observe from the best but build my own style.

Being in service of clients and leading ever-larger groups put a premium on my ability to communicate well. You may recall that I did not start my career as a naturally skilled speaker or presenter. My performance assessments can attest to that! "If you don't love your topic, we won't" and "Work on those FARs" hung in my head for years.

I became a student of compelling communications.

The best talks were structured in just a few parts—often three. Key messages were infused with stories, and the very best speeches felt authentic because they had vulnerability and wit.

I made the time to logically structure my own communications, not just presentations but also what I planned to say to someone in private meetings. I preferred to chunk ideas into groupings of three, embracing the widely accepted and scientifically proven rule of three. A trio is more approachable and memorable than other configurations. In the context of being in service of clients, the rule of three forced me to critically assess what I wanted to say and edit my ideas to the most essential. Value! The intent was to make it easy to be clearly understood.

Simplicity is a silver thread of stellar communicators, and clear communication is a silver thread of delivering value.

Being clear isn't always easy when you're in the business of selling complex technologies. Many of my IBM colleagues were incredibly intelligent. It wasn't unusual to find myself in a meeting with engineers, scientists, PhDs, and experts whose body of knowledge on a topic was unimaginably deep. I was constantly impressed by, and in awe of, the breadth of intellect around me. But even as an engineer myself, I couldn't afford to be intimidated or pretend I understood what they were saying if I didn't. My job was to translate complexity to clients. So when I was introduced to a new scientific concept, I asked question after question until I grasped it. I'd then paraphrase a concept in simpler language, sometimes with an analogy, so I could explain it to a client with less technical background than me. I never wanted them to feel stupid or stop listening to me because they got lost. If they remembered what I said, and really understood it, our odds for progress were much greater.

If I worked hard to communicate simply, others didn't have to work hard to understand me. It's also why I eventually stopped using visuals or slides: they can be a distraction or a crutch. I would either have the key points in my head, or maybe I would hold a small piece of paper. I wanted the audience to know I cared enough about them to think through in advance what I was going to say. So in that moment, it was me and them.

On stage I wasn't easily distracted. Once, I gave a speech wearing two unmatched shoes because I'd dressed in such a hurry. Another time, I was giving a keynote to a large group of clients. My boss, Fred Amoroso, introduced me, then sat down on stage behind me while I launched into my prelunch talk about the future of the insurance industry. I was wearing a black suit with a long scarf draped around my neck, and midway through my presentation, the scarf started slipping. One end began to inch closer and closer to the floor at a pace I didn't detect but everyone else noticed. People in the audience apparently became fixated on the drooping scarf; some even took bets on how long before the thing hit the ground. I felt a tap on my shoulder and Fred whispered to me that I may want to adjust my scarf. I looked down and one end was at my knee. I pulled it back into place and made a joke that got a nice laugh before I jumped back into my talk.

Now, with all my preparation and focus, I never forgot something else I was taught when it came to public speaking, a famous quote often attributed to Maya Angelou that stuck in my head: "I've learned that people will forget what you said, people will forget what you did, but people will never forget how you made them feel."

Teaching

It's natural for a professional in their career to look for ways to build their own skills, but at some point we transition and our focus becomes how to build others' skills and enable them to be the best version of themselves. My early managers were the first to point this out, and ever since developing people is one way I try to be in service of people on my teams.

Developing others, versus just ourselves, is a signal we're transitioning to the power of we. Sometimes it took the form of coaching, and I tried to use a velvet hammer. Other times it took the form of teaching.

In the late 1990s, when I ran IBM's worldwide insurance business, I organized its first-ever global conference. The evolution of the internet was transforming our industry so fast that I wanted all one thousand of us—sales, engineering, project managers—under one roof to talk about it. The main purpose was education. To ensure the largest possible turnout we picked a hotel in California by analyzing the city that would reduce the travel time for the most people from around the globe.

I could've kicked off the conference with a spirited welcome before turning it over to the professional speakers. But I had it in my head I should teach something, too. Not because I wanted the spotlight, but teaching, like I did with my little sisters, was my way of caring. For almost ninety minutes I presented the "Landscaping the Future" research I'd shared with Ed at Allstate, describing four potential future scenarios, including two we called "wired wired world" and "big brother." My hope was that people would be more likely to share the insights with their clients, too. Now, sitting and listening for that long would kill most audiences, especially one with so many nonnative English speakers. To be fair, I probably went on about thirty minutes too long (I still needed to be more ruthless about my communications). But instead of the audience being annoyed, I remember sensing appreciation for such a personal level of development.

When I arrived back at my office in New York after the conference, a package was waiting for me. Someone had already shipped me a book about Mount Everest inscribed with a personal note: "In appreciation of great days . . . your highly motivated and energized sherpas." *Had I worked everyone that hard?* I thought after looking up the definition of *sherpa.* I'm pretty sure he meant that he and others were as dedicated to our shared journey as the renowned mountain guides of the Himalayas. I was grateful for the loyalty.

Stretching

By 2000, I'd developed very deep technical, consulting, and industry-specific skills, and was being challenged to develop even broader skills by leading strategy for all of IBM's Global Services business. In other words, the horizontal part of being a T-shaped professional. One day in 2001, I was in the office of my boss, Doug Elix. Doug was IBM's senior vice president running all of Global Services, and in addition to being a keen business leader, he took great joy in the achievements of those around him, never focusing on himself. People loved working for Doug. That day in his office, he told me I was being asked to step out of my job leading strategy to take on an assignment that I don't think many people wanted: reorganizing the entire company's go-to-market strategy. Basically, my new job was to help us become more client-focused by changing how we segmented our clients and incented and organized our sales resources for those clients. The cross-company task was, at that time in my career, the quintessential stretch assignment. Revamping any sales force is high risk. It was also going to be a stretch for a lot of other people whose jobs would materially change.

One part of the strategy shift involved changing how we marketed to the company's largest clients. About half of IBM's revenue came from a subset of big corporations with endless possibilities for us to be in service of them. Lou, our CEO, and Sam Palmisano, our new president, wanted IBM to better serve these clients, increase our business with them, stop a few frustrated ones from leaving, and launch some new relationships. Their plan was to also put some of our most talented internal leaders in these client-facing roles, which we later named managing directors (MDs).

Developing people often sits at the intersection of growing a company and growing its people. For IBM to strengthen its client relationships and boost revenues, we needed about fifty high-level execs to stretch themselves into a new professional role. A common thing that happens at many companies is when people get promoted, they move further away from direct client-facing roles. Instead of managing clients, they manage businesses. IBM went to market by product and geography, so as IBMers' careers progressed in the field, they usually led larger and larger internal business units.

My assignment was to create a new career track, one that culminated with the new position of managing director, that could have as much prestige, compensation, and value as the usual business leadership roles. In essence, I had to convince people—many in much higher-ranking roles than mine—to give up their senior posts running an entire product line or region to oversee one client. I had no operational authority to do this; it was an assignment of influence.

Taking on the MD role was daunting for some; their reputation would be on the line every day. Yes, the proposition was risky, much like my own decision to go into consulting years prior. They, too, could stretch themselves and develop a wider suite of skills that the company and the market valued.

I wanted people to see the new MD role as an opportunity for them to grow, not a sacrifice they had to make so the company could grow. A small team and I traveled the world to meet with potential MDs so we could match them with the right clients. We listened to their career histories, their aspirations, and their reservations. Many worried the new structure would derail their careers. Egos were also involved. Would they be forgotten? Would they be respected? Would they make more money? We explained how a new incentive structure could boost their compensation exponentially. We also said they'd have tools to succeed, including the authority to make decisions that cut across the company—no waiting for permission— and being in charge of their own P&L. Sam also met with candidates. He understood their concerns, and reassured them of the importance of the role, its potential for their careers, and the support they'd get from senior leadership.

Getting two dozen executives to say yes for the first round was just half the battle. Integrating the MD roles into our corporate structure was a longer-term challenge.

To bolster MD enthusiasm at the outset, I organized an inaugural meeting of our first thirty MDs at IBM's Armonk headquarters. I wanted people to feel as special as they were—they'd been picked for a reason, because they had what it took to stretch.

I seated everyone at the large round table in IBM's boardroom and congratulated the group on being pioneers. Lou also joined the meeting. One by one I went around the table and looked at each person and told them exactly why they'd been handpicked. I called out their strengths and their

track record, and why their skills and expertise were the right fit for their chosen client. I'd spent so much time getting to know each new MD that I didn't
need notes to remind me of their attributes. I could have told you their shoe
sizes! Tybra Arthur's banking skills, technology depth, and problem-solving
capabilities made her the right candidate to fix and rebuild our relationship
with a major European bank. Martin Jetter's deep engineering skills and
global experience made him the perfect match for a global manufacturing
client that was also a bit of a competitor with IBM, and whose business we
could only grow through expertise and trust. Dino Trevisani's ability to navigate complex organizations, build trusted relationships, and create win-win
solutions made him the right fit for a global financial services firm. Will
Ulaszek's ability to unite people around a goal and his understanding of ar-
chitectures made him the ideal fit for a mega telecommunications company
formed by the merger of two very different companies and cultures.

It was a rocky year or two as some MDs got familiar with new industries
and others tried to get many clients to fall in love with IBM again. But MDs
who dug in and stretched themselves excelled.

Anita Sabatino, a wicked-smart, hard-charging, fast-talking executive
with a thick New York accent, became MD of a troubled financial services
account. I spent some time with Anita, and she embodied being in service
of with energy and rigor. In the process of doing her job and developing herself, Anita was also developing her team. She insisted they rehearse before
client meetings. "Have a plan and work your plan," she told them. "Know
what you're going to say, and how you'll react to whatever they say." She
began meetings by stating her values before launching into a pitch. She
spent more time at clients' offices than at IBM's. She had clients speak to
IBMers about their business, and she got herself and colleagues in front of
decision-makers to earn their trust. After, she'd huddle with the team to assess, asking, "How's our trust level with the client on a scale of one to ten?"
Then they workshopped how to raise the number.

Anita rarely took no for an answer, but she didn't push when IBM wasn't
the best alternative. And she didn't hesitate to ask me to join a meeting or

settle an issue. I always took her calls. She eventually took over a financial services client overseas, even though she didn't speak their language and had to move her family across the world. She beautifully turned around a troubled situation by being in service of the client as her primary goal, and actively developing her colleagues. Later, Anita spearheaded the MD mentoring program so others could follow.

It was a delight to watch Anita and others excel.

Tybra Arthur was another superstar MD. After her first assignment, I gave her the opportunity to work in France to salvage a teetering client relationship. Tybra didn't speak French, and she was the only Black woman among many white men. She had the skills the client needed and the capacity and will to learn their language, as well as the presence to assert herself. Tybra belonged in any room, and I was proud to sponsor her. Years later, after she retired, Tybra and I reflected on her career progression in an email exchange. First, she wrote about her mom, her biggest cheerleader and a woman who made education a priority for Tybra and her three sisters. I could relate to that! What she wrote next made me feel like a teacher hearing from a former student.

"Ginni, you were a role model for me. Observing how you engaged with others, giving us stretch assignments and coaching us. If I didn't get it quite right, your feedback was always about what I might have done differently, an enabler for what to try next, not a reprimand of what went wrong. You made me feel that I was capable, even when I didn't believe it myself, and opened doors with leadership roles that allowed others to recognize my capabilities."

The best part is that Tybra paid forward what she received by building a pipeline of Black and underrepresented minority MD candidates. That was among her greatest accomplishments, and I have no doubt she has received sentiments like the ones she shared with me from people she stretched and coached.

We get to a place in our careers when we look back and wonder, *Did we make a difference?* Sometimes it can be hard to remember. Those words from Tybra not only moved me but they crystallize what makes power good versus bad: other people experiencing our influence in positive ways.

Accepting Impact

I'd just finished giving a speech at a conference in Melbourne, Australia, when a man in the audience came up to me and introduced himself. I assumed he had a question or comment on the material I'd presented. Instead, he said, "I wish my daughter could have been here."

His comment came out of left field for me. I didn't go through my days thinking I was a role model for other women, and I admit that I resisted the idea of seeing myself as a female role model because I just wanted to be seen for my work, not my gender. Why couldn't I be a role model for everyone? But the father's reaction to me in Australia was a moment of recognition: I *was* a role model for women, whether I wanted to be or not.

As my profile grew inside and outside IBM, I recognized that just by doing my job I was in a position to be in service of other women. I became cognizant that I was being viewed through that lens. How I acted, and reacted, had dual contexts. I may give a speech as Ginni Rometty, business professional, but I was also Ginni Rometty, female professional. I came to see that my actions had implications for me and for women in business. In that sense, I was in service of other women who wanted to build their own careers, or go into fields and jobs dominated by men, and gain the confidence to believe they could because, perhaps, someone else had done it.

Women were one of many overlapping but different groups that my working life touched. Each had its own interests and needs, and as my career grew I discovered that my opportunity and responsibility to be in service of these groups grew, too.

The more power I had at work, the more my influence rippled out— inevitably, and by choice.

Over time my thinking would mature and evolve, and I came to firmly believe that leaders and businesses have a responsibility to be in service of society broadly, contributing to the health and prosperity of the communities and countries in which they operate.

None of us are *in* society, but *of* society. The same is true for our places of work, and our families. As such, we're always in a position, regardless of age or title, to ask how we might use the resources at our disposal—our time, our talents, our money, our influence, our power—to deliver value to others. When we do, we get value in return.

Reflecting

In this chapter, I hope I've shown how being in service of others became the lens through which I did my work. I tried to deliver value to clients and colleagues through habits, rituals, and beliefs that I formed, and that were instilled in me by so many wise people. I learned that by focusing on the needs of others first, we can fulfill our own needs as a result. Being in service of others also can be an incredibly fulfilling way to spend our days, and hopefully I've also conveyed why it's the soul of good power: a purpose that inspires actions and shapes outcomes.

In tandem with these learnings, I discovered something else about good power: trying to affect positive change is rarely if ever a solo endeavor. It's hard to achieve anything of real meaning on our own, so we need others to help bring about whatever positive outcomes we're after, whether it's closing a sale, building a business, or something as systemic as reducing homelessness. Whatever the mission, we're more likely to achieve it if we can bring people along with us. My career would soon take another unexpected twist, and I would learn just how tough this can be to do, especially at scale.

7

Building Belief

It's July 2002, and two secret meetings are taking place in two conference rooms at a Marriott Hotel in New York City. In one room, partners from the accounting firm PricewaterhouseCoopers (PwC) are preparing to spin off the firm's thirty-thousand-person consulting unit with an IPO. Most people involved in the planning have no clue that on another floor, my colleagues from IBM are negotiating to buy PwC's consulting unit, which will cancel the public offering.

I am running one of the company's largest units, IBM Global Services Americas, which includes all IT consulting and outsourcing. I think the potential acquisition has exciting implications for IBM's future. Our own IT consulting business has grown, but we're missing opportunities to do larger, more substantial and impactful projects for clients. Companies are eager to benefit from those who understand the intersection of business and technology, and they are hungry for new, more strategic ways to run their operations. IBM doesn't yet have the business strategy acumen or enough relationships with C-level executives to take advantage of this opportunity. Fusing PwC's business and industry consulting with our IT consulting, outsourcing, and technology expertise will give us capabilities no other company offers.

I'm asked to help with the negotiations, so I go to the Marriott, where I find my coworkers diligently poring over numbers behind closed doors.

There's a sense of urgency in the conference room because IBM must decide what to do before PwC goes forward with an IPO.

In theory, IBM and PwC Consulting (PwCC) make a compelling match. Of course, just because something looks good on paper doesn't mean it's doable in the real world. A spate of mergers in the professional services industry have already failed, and there's no successful precedent for merging a private, people-based partnership like PwCC with a public technology corporation, especially one as big and complex as IBM. As I dig in, the scope of the challenges becomes clear.

Wooing PwCC consultants to join IBM is going to be a tough sell. A majority of its twelve hundred partner-owners have to vote in favor of becoming IBM employees, and most are intensely loyal to their firm, the people who worked with them, and their clients, especially after working years to build their business and achieve coveted partner status, which comes with independence, authority, prestige, and hefty compensation packages that include salaries much higher than IBM pays, and perks like club memberships and first-class travel. In contrast, IBM is a more hierarchical, corporate, and cost-conscious place to work. We will have to remix the consultants' compensation to get it more in line with our own. Harder to account for will be the loss of the consultants' beloved culture. It's part of their professional identity. We'll need the consultants to stay at IBM and perform to their potential. A swift, mass exodus is a real danger; if too many flee, taking their talent and client relationships with them, IBM will have invested billions of dollars for nothing.

Integrating the two very different businesses poses another hurdle. PwCC can't operate as an appendage; we have to meld the two disparate organizations into one collaborative entity to realize genuine value for everyone. This won't be like our usual acquisitions, which are mostly products that we wrap into existing offerings and/or scale through our distribution channels. This time we'd be gaining thousands of hearts and minds.

In short, IBM needs to buy PwCC to grow, but PwCC's people must want to give their all for years to come. I'm wondering if enough people from both organizations can come to believe that, together, they could create a great new business, better than either one of them alone. This is the daunting and intriguing problem we have to solve.

The Heart of Good Power

Building belief is about moving people to embrace an alternate reality for themselves and others, and then to willingly participate in creating it. It's the first major step if you want people to change, because they have to understand and believe in the change.

If "being in service of" is the "soul" of good power—its fundamental "why"—then "building belief" is good power's "heart"—the vital "how" of exercising influence to bring people on a change journey.

To build belief is to win voluntary, enthusiastic buy-in. That's what unleashes discretionary effort. The opposite of building belief is ordering people to do something they don't buy into and expecting them to perform as if they did. That's not good power, at least not in my book. We want people to follow us because they choose to. Change constantly fueled by authority or fear is simply not sustainable; it's also not in service of anyone except those who demand it. I just don't think that long-lasting productive shifts in behavior and perspective can be dictated.

Building followership doesn't just happen through rah-rah words and inspiring speeches. Emotional connection is essential to spark belief, but belief is sealed with information, honesty, and clarity about a situation and the path forward. Facts *and* feelings. Bridging emotion and execution is the tension of building belief.

Who we want to bring along ranges and changes. It might be an individual, a team we manage, a community, or an entire society. Similarly, *what* we try to build belief in might be our own leadership, an institution, or a new idea that disrupts the status quo. Throughout my life, I've had to build belief among different people in different things. I've also had to build belief in myself; titles alone don't magically confer self-confidence.

The need to build belief is ongoing. For me, it was especially crucial at two times in my career: the PwCC merger, and almost a decade later, during my first one hundred days as CEO. Both offer many lessons.

Merging

I remember the first time I entered the bustling conference room at the Marriott back in the summer of 2002, where my colleagues from IBM and a few people from PwCC were trying to figure out if an acquisition was even feasible. I took a seat and looked across the conference table at a smiling but unfamiliar face.

"Ginni, I'm Mike Collins." I'd never met Mike, but I knew his name and was instantly delighted to discover that the person leading negotiations for PwCC was the former business partner of my former boss, Fred Amoroso. Mike and Fred had cofounded a business together, which they sold to Pricewaterhouse before Fred joined IBM. Fred had raved to me about Mike's integrity, operational discipline, and courage to stand up for what he believed in. Apparently, Fred told Mike about me, too. We'd each been influenced by Fred's leadership and values, and we came to the table with similar priorities: an acquisition was only worthwhile if it benefited our two companies' financials, our clients, and our people.

Mike led PwCC in the Americas and was among the few people at his firm who knew selling to IBM was an alternative to an IPO. For days, Mike had been walking back and forth between the two conference rooms, weighing the options with his PwCC colleagues David Dockray, Peggy Vaughan, Ric Andersen, and Jim Bramante. Originally, Mike had been in favor of going public. Now, he worried PwCC wasn't prepared for the drastic change. Private businesses don't have to report their revenues or earnings or abide by strict SEC regulations. The more Mike got to know IBM, the more he recognized that PwCC didn't yet have the mindset or the infrastructure to operate as a publicly owned entity. At one point, Mike had asked one of my colleagues how long he'd been with IBM.

"One-hundred-and-three quarters," was the reply, a phrase that signaled to Mike just how central financial reporting was to public-company life.

PwC had no choice but to spin off its consulting business in some form, for a variety of reasons, and Mike was beginning to believe that IBM not only seemed like a safer place for his colleagues to land, but more meaningfully a destination with potential to grow their business and impact. Still, an acquisition would be complicated. We were making progress at the Marriott, hashing through a variety of issues while grazing on handfuls of hotel snacks. One afternoon I found myself in a taxicab with my IBM colleague who was in charge of the negotiations. He was also the most likely candidate to put be in charge of the acquisition if it went ahead.

"You know, Ginni, they have confidence in you," he said, referring to Mike and the PwCC team. I was flattered, then surprised by his next comment. "You're the right person to lead this, not me. I believe you will be the only one they'll accept as a leader." He said this graciously, and with humility and respect to everyone involved. "I'm really happy to support you, if you take the job."

By "job" he meant negotiating final terms of an agreement, helping secure votes, then building the new business over several years. One of my first reactions was admiration. He was stepping aside, voluntarily giving up power, and not for my benefit but for the good of the business. It was selfless.

I was at a point in my career where many professionals plateau, excel, or switch careers. I seemed to be on an upward trajectory, and leaving my current role to oversee a massive, high-profile acquisition was a bear of an assignment, and very risky. I didn't see myself as more or less qualified than anyone else; however, two things did make the job especially attractive to me.

First, I championed the merger because it was in service of clients and of IBM. Our union would establish one of the world's largest consulting services organizations, and a new category in the consulting field. Second, the leadership role would require a balance of skills. The engineer in me was intrigued by the prospect of analyzing two businesses and concluding which pieces should endure and which should be replaced or reworked. More than an intellectual exercise, it also required a human touch. We'd be acquiring people, not products, and unlike buying a software company, these "assets" had mouths and legs that could refuse to perform and choose to leave. The consultants also had hearts, not parts. They'd only stay and do their best if they believed that IBM valued them and that they could bring value to clients. The same was true for IBMers. The dual tasks of building a new business and building more belief in that business were compelling. So was the prospect of merging systems as well as people—because that's really what had to happen.

I knew if I didn't have genuine confidence in the mission and faith in myself, doubt would seep through everything I did and said, dampening enthusiasm and drowning out followership. The question I had to ask myself was if I authentically believed in what we wanted to achieve. I did.

By late July we had a tentative agreement to buy PwCC for $3.5 billion in cash and stock. As a result, IBM would establish a new, sixty-thousand-person unit, IBM Business Consulting Services, which I would lead—if the merger was approved by all PwCC partners around the world. Winning their approval, and building the potential new business inside IBM, had to happen in tandem.

At that moment, the reality of what was ahead became very clear to me. There would be unpredictable, uncomfortable moments. Success wasn't guaranteed. And, unlike past career decisions, this one would have a binary outcome: this will either kill me, or catapult me, I remember saying to myself as the adventure began.

Cocreating

I wanted people at both companies to feel part of the new reality being created. If others felt that their ideas, individuality, and needs were valued, they'd be more inspired to take part.

Even though IBM was technically acquiring the consultants, I treated it as a merger, and made a point of using that language because it connoted a coming together instead of just folding PwCC's people into IBM's ways. For words to mean something, though, they had to be backed up with actions.

I immediately assembled a transition team of three hundred people from each business, and for six weeks everyone hunkered down in offices and hotel ballrooms to get acquainted and figure out what a combined organization would look like. These collaborative work sessions included people that played a wide array of roles, from IBM's finance and contract specialists to PwCC's consultants themselves. Everyone had a chance to contribute ideas and see how they fit in, and, I hoped, to feel a sense of belonging.

I took an "adopt and go" mentality. Once we made decisions we went with them. No more debate. That was about speed, and it countered the expectation that IBM was slow to move.

But there were other decisions where the two options proposed were on opposite extremes, and we had heated debates. The answer did not lie in a compromise—in some cases that was worse. We called these dilemmas and spent endless hours working together to find a third way forward. It was painful as we had to get to the real outcomes needed, and it took time to re-imagine how to achieve those. But people came to see how we were unique as a business, and we focused on changing the things that supported that differentiation.

I considered myself in service of PwCC consultants. I spent a lot of time listening to them, and I had empathy for the loss many felt, as well as their concern that colleagues who had been on track to become partner before the merger would still have opportunities that had been presented to them. I was also genuinely curious about what it was like to work in a partnership. I'd grown up in a hierarchical corporate culture and had no clue, and I couldn't make them feel more at home at IBM unless I understood what home looked and felt like to them. I tried to listen without judgment to what they valued and disliked about their new reality, which was my only reality.

Coming up with the leadership structure and policies required an inclusive approach. PwCCers would know I was dead serious about merging versus engulfing them if they saw some familiar faces in senior spots. I asked PwCC's own leaders, including Mike, to fill our top three positions, reporting directly to me. I insisted that our CFO come from IBM, not uncommon for an acquiring company, especially a public one buying a private one. I was especially conscious about getting women into more consulting roles; at the time of the merger, IBM's consulting business employed more senior women than PwCC.

Operationally, we used PwCC's partner matriculation process and performance evaluation method, which emphasized and rewarded skills acquisition, not just how much revenue someone generated. Structurally, we decided to go to market by industry, PwCC's approach, instead of IBM's product orientation.

Restructuring the partners' compensation was tricky. We were trying to serve multiple purposes: honor the consultants' value, motivate them to stay, lay a framework consistent with public company compensation, and keep the arrangement cost-effective. We remixed components of their compensation by replacing some cash with equity, a new equation since they were used to only getting cash. The IBM stock vested immediately as well as over a period of several years. In the long run, the equity would more than compensate for the cash reductions. Still, the consultants were used to higher paychecks, and the remix took some getting used to.

To take some sting out of the compensation change and the transition to a corporate hierarchy, we agreed that consultants who had achieved partner and managing partner status should keep those titles. We also extended the title to IBMers. For all up-and-comers, the partner title, and financial incentives that came with it, became something to aspire to.

While we couldn't keep everything that made PwCC unique, nor replicate the unique culture of a private partnership, our intent was to preserve enough of the consultants' way of life to make them feel that sense of belonging, while at the same making choices that made sense for the new business. I accepted that not everyone would be happy.

Making It Personal

As the new organization took shape, I traveled around the world to meet with PwCC's partners in North and South America, Asia, and Europe. Under partnership rules, regional offices could vote against joining us and instead go off on their own. My intent was to convince them to want to come and stay by explaining, in person, why it was good for everyone at the firm as well as their clients, and what the new organization would look like. I tried to express that acquiring their firm was not a knee-jerk decision. IBM had been preparing to expand into strategic consulting for years. We were ready to welcome them and take our business to a level that only they could help us achieve.

"We need you," I said. "And you need us."

Access to IBM's technology, engineers, scientists, and research meant the consultants could finally implement their advice and be even more influential. The conversations really got going when we talked about specific clients.

One weekend, I invited PwCC partners to my home in Detroit for a working session. The relaxed setting, being surrounded by photos of my family, and Mark and his humor joining us for dinner, allowed them to get to know me as a person, not just a boss. I remember being very candid with people, letting them know that I believed in the merger so much that I was staking my own career on it. I, too, had a lot to win, or lose.

Sometimes Mike and I met with consultants, clients, and staff together. Mike's respect for me reassured PwCC partners and clients. We made a good team.

By October, the acquisition was overwhelmingly approved by PwCC member firms. The day we announced that IBM had bought PwC Consulting, we ran full-page ads in several newspapers: "This changes everything," read one of our headlines. "So many good players, we're buying the team," read another.

I also left a voicemail for the over one thousand PwCC partners, introducing myself. Remember, this was 2002, before you could connect with thousands of others at once via social media or videoconferencing. A PwCC employee described it as "the voicemail that rang around the world" in the Huffington Post: "Many of us were highly skeptical of how tech-driven IBM would manage a services business like ours. In roughly two minutes, [Ginni] would welcome us to the IBM family, tell us we were very special, and that we would retain the best of our culture, and—make no mistake—we'd very soon be part of IBM. No question about who was in charge."

Those gestures were further attempts to be authentic, inclusive, and personal, especially to those for whom the news was just breaking. That first day, within hours, I also called CEOs at PwCC's clients to introduce myself and talk about our vision and the work we were already doing for them.

Analysts applauded the move, and the news made the front page of the *New York Times*. One *Wall Street Journal* article began, "Contrary to expectations of a culture clash, IBM's efforts to integrate the 30,000-person PwC Consulting unit appear to have gone off with a minimum of divisiveness." Of course, there were skeptics whispering we'd never succeed, and many who hoped we'd fail.

Building belief didn't stop then, or in January 2003 when the acquisition became binding. To say that every consultant was excited and happy from day one would be a lie. Keeping people's hearts and minds engaged was a herculean mission without end, especially while we got our bearings during the first few years.

In the early 2000s, Ken Chenault, then Chairman and CEO of American Express, spoke at one of IBM's leadership meetings. I always remembered what Ken said: "The role of a leader is to define reality and give hope." Ken was paraphrasing a quote attributed to Napoleon Bonaparte, and I interpreted it as meaning we should be brutally honest about difficult situations, then positively focus on the actions that move us forward. I adopted the sentiment and made it my own, always trying to "paint reality and give hope." I did a lot of painting those initial years of the merger, and it felt never-ending.

Painting Reality, Giving Hope

In the early days, we weren't meeting our initial profit targets. PwCC's attractive profit margins began to shrink as their existing clients realized that the consultants were now under pressure to meet quarterly revenue targets. Enough clients began negotiating lower fees in return for booking projects by our desired dates, and our profits were impacted. I expected this, but it happened much sooner than anticipated. We were a big enough business unit that our performance had an impact on IBM's overall results.

Months and quarters went by and we weren't making progress fast enough on profit. Every day that I walked into our headquarters I felt the intense pressure growing on me exponentially. We had to change the trajectory.

One weekend I went home to Detroit and went to dinner at a small restaurant with Mark and four of our best friends. Since we hadn't seen our friends in quite some time there was much bantering and a lot of laughter. For a brief few moments I forgot about the pressure cooker that was my life. Suddenly one of my friends asked, "How's the big job going?" In that instance, without warning, I burst into tears. My friends and my husband were stunned. Everyone became silent. They had never seen me cry.

"Ginni, what's wrong? Are you okay?" Their cacophony of concern was genuine. I collected myself, took a few bites of my fish, and recounted a recent moment where I'd been told, "If you can't get this turned around, you're no longer a welcome member of the family."

Being spoken to that way was demoralizing and definitely not motivating. But I didn't want to let it paralyze me because there was work to do. Getting my emotions out among friends was actually a huge relief, versus just letting it fester. The comment was obnoxious, definitely uncalled for, even though I knew it came from a very real truth: the merger was not yet yielding the profit results the company needed, and it was my responsibility to change that.

My way of dealing with the issue was not to bully my teams, but to be honest that something was clearly not working, and we needed to be more precise with our efforts and do something different. I brought my team in and told them that there must be things we were missing. The time had come to accept some extra help. It was a proud group of people that didn't necessarily want outside assistance. After a few false starts, we found the right mix of talent to integrate with our own. This was the moment I came to realize that asking for help as a leader is a sign of strength, not weakness.

As we set out to make some step changes, I was upfront and transparent with my disappointment. It wasn't a time for charm; I was matter-of-fact about what we needed to do next, like instill more discipline into how we estimated and tracked consulting hours, for instance. The added operational rigor was not enjoyable for anyone, but it was necessary to maximize profits and be successful. We were in service of multiple stakeholders.

As much as I wanted the PwCC consultants to feel at home, they'd also moved into a very different house.

Over time I noticed that not all PwCC consultants challenged their clients as rigorously as was sometimes needed. Their culture tended to be conflict averse. I tried to steer them away from this habit, urging them not to fear conflict because conflict can lead to a closer relationship.

A colleague who excelled at doing this was Bridget van Kralingen. I recruited Bridget from another consulting firm to help us grow our business. I'd heard about her from a client who thought she was terrific, and I quickly saw why. Bridget was exceptionally adept at confronting clients in ways that resolved conflict but also strengthened the relationship. In other words, she wielded her own velvet hammer. I remember a client calling irate about a pricing issue. Bridget offered to jump in and deal with it, without blinking. I watched her in action. Seasoned and polished, Bridget knew that pricing issues were rarely ever just about pricing; they were often a question of timing, implementation, or value. She also called the client and listened to learn and to get to the underlying issue. She wanted to know the personal impact the problem was having on the individual. Was his job at risk? Was his boss angry? Throughout the back-and-forth discussions Bridget never got defensive. I was impressed with how she arrived at a win-win solution with such empathy and gravitas. Others noticed her style, too, and she became a role model.

I gleaned much from Bridget about the benefits of running toward conflict. It has the potential to foster a sense of intimacy among people because we get to know each other. What upsets them. What they really want. What's at stake. Embracing conflict also reduced my own anxiety, because my energy went into solving versus stewing.

One day, a colleague came into my office and shut the door. The person wanted me to be aware that there were a few vocal leaders who didn't believe we'd ever perform at the operating levels we'd been asked to. In my heart this wasn't new news; I'd been hoping they would come around. But the fact is, if people don't genuinely believe they can do something, they will never achieve that outcome. Their intractable mindset left me no choice. I confronted the individuals and made changes I should have made earlier—some left, some retired, and some went to jobs that suited them better.

Throughout it all, I tried not to lose sight of what was going well, and I shared widely the things that clients uniquely appreciated about our work.

"Look at what we're capable of," I'd tell people, including myself. "We just have to get it right more often than not and keep improving. Don't give up!" There were a lot of days when it was tempting.

The bureaucracy inherent to some parts of IBM drove everyone nuts and confirmed some PwCCers' fears. For example, some admin processes weren't set up to accommodate the size and pace of expenses from so many consultants traveling so much for such long stints. Sometimes it took far too long to approve expenses and reimburse people. There was one episode where a traveling consulting team was in Switzerland for months working with Nestlé. The team was paying for hotels and meals out of their own pockets, as the unpaid amounts were maxing out some of their credit cards. I learned about the unpaid expenses just as I was flying to Switzerland.

I called my CFO. "Honest, I'm going to sit here and write personal checks to each person if we don't get our people paid!" I was angry and had my pen poised and checkbook open. The needle moved and I never had to write any checks, but I would have! Hopefully, my response let the consultants know that I was serious about fixing what was broken.

I also tried to paint reality and give hope to my fellow IBMers. I didn't want them to feel overrun. We held town halls to explain that the marketplace was shifting. Some parts of the hardware business were continuing to commoditize; to stay relevant, IBM had to refocus on delivering consulting services that transformed how companies operated by mixing business knowledge and technology. I acknowledged their discomfort, and pointed out longer-term opportunities, like broadening their skills, building new products, and growing IBM's overall business, thanks to access to PwCC's expertise and relationships.

Among my own challenges was not getting so distracted by integration issues that I lost focus on our clients. I had to remember to be in service of them, not just IBM, because their success would be the ultimate arbiter of ours. In 2003, a journalist writing about the acquisition asked me how I would know when we had "arrived."

"That's something that your clients vote on," I said. "When they turn to you—and then continue to turn to you over time." I tried to keep the consultants' minds off internal operations and focus on the problems facing their clients.

By 2008, our consulting services business had revenues of more than $19.5 billion and was earning $2.7 billion in profit. The vast majority of the PwCC partners were still with IBM. The consulting group had grown to over one hundred thousand people.

Success isn't measured by perfection at every turn. What the team did was extremely hard. It took a while, and not everyone was pleased all the time. Some very talented PwCC folks chose to join other consulting partnerships. But we succeeded, and we did not allow internal struggles to disrupt our client work or tarnish our reputation in the marketplace. We built a healthy, highly profitable business during years when the economy was trying to bounce back from recession. The business we built also proved quite consequential for all of IBM, fundamentally changing the company. Today, IBM Consulting represents 30 percent of IBM's 2022 revenues.

Merging consulting with technology was a strategy that many companies copied. Today there are so many integrated services companies that it's hard to recall a time they were novel.

In one respect, the PwCC-IBM merger is a story about getting the strategy of a new business to take hold by building belief in people's hearts as well as their minds. At any time, enough consultants could have walked out and left IBM with little to show for its investment. I look back and can see how so many of us rode the tension between nurturing change and pushing it, between balancing people's needs and the business's needs. Personally, I was learning to be more sensitive as well as systemic.

Again, paraphrasing that famous Maya Angelou quote: people don't remember the specifics of history, but they remember how they felt. Former colleagues still send me notes reflecting on our time together during that period, and their sentiments reinforce that how we went about creating the business, the sense of belief and belonging, was as memorable as what we achieved.

In January 2009, I hosted one last meeting before going to head another unit. It was bittersweet, leaving the people and the journey, which would continue on without me. I handwrote a personal note to each of my top one hundred leaders, thanking each of them. I placed the notes on everyone's assigned chairs. Someone later told me they overheard a partner who found his seat, saw the envelope, recognized my handwriting, and said out loud, "That's so Ginni."

Writing those notes was not about me. It was my way of genuinely expressing that something many felt couldn't be done was achieved because of "the power of we."

The experience did not kill me or my career. The PwCC merger allowed me to build more belief in myself, giving me confidence in my own leadership style. I saw that I could persevere through tough assignments by doing things in a humane way. Positive change in a positive way. I also was learning to balance my own opposing forces: to be nurturing, caring, and supportive while also being analytical, rigorous, and demanding.

And, I no longer felt the same urgency to prove myself in the eyes of others. I still wanted to be the best professional I could be, but those years empowered and inspired me to further focus on developing the people around me to be the best version of themselves. Helping people grow and build belief in themselves continued to bring me immense pleasure and satisfaction.

The merger also elevated me inside and outside the company. In December 2002, *Time* named me to its Global Business Influentials list. In 2005, I made my initial debut as number fifteen on *Fortune* magazine's list of the 50 Most Powerful Women in Business, and I was also invited to join corporate and nonprofit boards. I served as the senior vice president of IBM's consulting services business for over seven years, until 2009, when I became senior vice president of global sales, with my scope later broadening to include all marketing, communications, and strategy. That was another risky assignment because the world was in the midst of the global financial crisis, and I was charged with trying to grow sales when our corporate clients' own revenues and budgets were shrinking. On the other hand, this was another opportunity for the company and my colleagues to build belief in me, and for me to build belief in my capabilities to one day lead a supertanker the size and scope of IBM.

I've often said that I've been lucky to have at least ten different jobs, all at one company. So many of my positions gave me deep vertical experience in a number of professions, from systems engineering, to sales, to consulting, to solutions and software development, to outsourcing.

Between 2009 and 2011, it was very clear that I was being challenged to grow horizontally and take an enterprise view in the biggest and broadest of senses. I was further becoming a T-shaped leader. This was, in fact, a signal to some people outside and inside the company that I could be a candidate to lead IBM when our current CEO Sam Palmisano stepped down. IBM had several very qualified leaders who could be chief, and they too were given stretch assignments.

Did I want to be CEO? It was absolutely not a singular goal I set for myself, but after decades of focusing on doing whatever job I had to the best of my abilities, I certainly hoped I was developing the skills and capabilities necessary to be considered to one day run the company I loved.

I'll never forget when Randy MacDonald, IBM's senior vice president of human resources since Lou's days as CEO, called me into his office. Randy was a firm, tough, bold leader, who was also quite creative and warm-hearted. He did not mince words. "Ginni, if you want the opportunity to be CEO of IBM, don't try to run for office." I translated his sage advice to mean put your focus on followership, not politics.

Deepening Followership

In March 2011, a magnitude 9.1 earthquake caused a tsunami along Japan's northeast coast. I remember watching devastating videos of massive waves crashing over sea walls, crushing boats and cars like toys. Entire towns were washed away in the sea's surge. In Tokyo, the quake and aftershocks had caused tall buildings to sway and chunks of scaffolding to fall onto streets. Trains had stopped running. Power had been lost. The tsunami also destabilized the Fukushima Nuclear Power Plant, about 137 miles outside the city, where engineers were trying to contain radioactive leaks.

A lot of foreign companies with offices in Japan insisted on flying their expat employees out of the country. For Japanese citizens, the exodus of expats in the wake of the earthquake was akin to abandonment. It was considered such a sign of disrespect that a derogatory term was coined for those who fled after the tsunami: *flyjin*, which combined the English word for *fly* and the Japanese word for foreigner, *gaijin*.

IBM had about twenty thousand employees in Tokyo and surrounding areas. Our Japanese clients included large banks, airlines, hospitals, utilities, and government offices—essential institutions that needed to keep operating. We chose to make our employees' evacuation voluntary after scientists reassured us that Tokyo was not at risk of radiation. Almost all IBMers chose to stay.

At the time, I volunteered to go to Tokyo to represent our most senior leadership. Even if there was nothing I could personally do, I wanted to be present. I remember arriving at the usually bustling Haneda Airport. I'd never seen the international terminal desolate. It was so empty I could hear the click-clack of my shoes as I walked alone toward Customs. Even the Customs agent asked if I was certain I wanted to enter the country because so few foreigners were coming into Japan.

I headed straight to IBM's largest office in Tokyo, where I was shown a makeshift control room that had been set up to track all the activities urgently unfolding at various IBM locations and client sites. I walked around the office, stopping at people's desks to shake hands and listen to their stories. Someone had swum through floodwaters to deliver computer parts to a bank. Other people had delivered food and water to clients and coworkers. I also visited several clients to ask what they needed and to thank them for working with IBM, and for trusting us.

What I remember most is the appreciation our clients expressed, not just for the work of our people, but for our presence. They also were especially grateful that a senior executive had flown into the country, given that so many leaders from other companies had flown out. Honor and respect are highly valued in the Japanese culture, and they remember people's actions for a long time, as well as the intent behind those actions.

I tell this story because going to Tokyo spoke louder than any words of condolence or gratitude I could have expressed via email or in a call.

More than a decade after the tsunami, in July 2022, the former Japanese prime minister Shinzo Abe was tragically assassinated. We'd worked together many times, and I had tremendous respect for his efforts both to build relations between countries and to support women. Like so many people around the world, especially the Japanese people, I was stunned and saddened by his death. I posted a few memories on LinkedIn to honor his legacy. After I posted, I was perusing the comments people left. "Thank you for the warm message," one person wrote. "We also remember you as the first senior executive to visit us in Japan after the earthquake in 2011 to share the pain and loss with us."

There are many faces of followership. The success of the PwCC merger and my time expanding IBM's global presence would be some of the reasons cited by others as to how I made my name inside IBM, most notably when I became CEO.

Honoring the Moment

For months there was discussion in the press about who would succeed Sam Palmisano as IBM's next CEO. I wanted the job, but no matter the outcome, I knew I had done all I could do to be in service of IBM and its clients—more than I ever thought I could. That's as far as I let my mind go.

On Monday, October 24, 2011, I was at my office in Armonk, New York, when Sam called to tell me that the board had selected me to be the ninth chief executive officer of IBM.

It's odd—I don't really remember the specifics of our call, except that it was emotional for each of us. We both had great respect and love for IBM. I do recall thanking Sam and telling him I was honored, then just sitting quietly. I had about two months to prepare for my first day as chief in January 2012, but less than twenty-four hours until my appointment was publicly announced. Until then it was confidential. The only person I could tell was Mark, who was back at our home in Detroit. After we spoke he boarded a flight for New York.

I had to be in Manhattan by late afternoon to meet with our board at IBM's New York City offices at 590 Madison Avenue, in the heart of bustling midtown. I walked into the seventeenth-floor boardroom and was greeted by a supportive round of applause. That evening, I joined the board for a small, intimate dinner. IBM's board was and is composed of distinguished and diverse leaders. Little did I realize then how much I would learn from each one of them over the decade to come.

The evening ended relatively early and I made my way back to my condo in White Plains. The gravity of the moment began to sink in as my mind wandered back in time to the many people whose guidance, teaching, and sponsorship made it possible for me to be in this position. I made a list before trying to get a good night's sleep. The next day would be eventful when the announcement was made public at 4 p.m., just after the US stock market closed.

The next day I woke up and went to work as usual. I had to carry on with my planned schedule while the clock ticked toward four o'clock. The office felt oddly quiet. Only a handful of people inside the company knew, although plenty had speculated. Throughout the day IBM's head of communications called me to review drafts of the press release.

Just prior to 4 p.m., I went into a conference room with a few people. We turned on CNBC and together listened to the closing bell of Wall Street, then watched the network's anchors inform viewers that IBM would soon have a new chief executive. A headshot of me stared back at us from the large screen while the TV personalities debated what my appointment meant for the company—and how to pronounce my last name. I listened to them postulate for about five minutes, then pushed my chair away from the conference table and stood up.

"Okay, time to make my calls," I said. Then I walked back to my office and closed the door.

I spent the next two hours calling the twenty or so names on my list, the people whose influence had been instrumental to this moment. Those I called included Pat O'Brien, who had promoted me to my first management position and taught me so much about leading with values; Fred Amoroso, who taught me about leading with passion; and Mike Collins, who had been in the trenches with me throughout the PwCC merger. Each picked up their phone when they saw my number, some a bit shocked to hear from me just minutes after learning the news for themselves.

I also called IBM's former CEOs, including John Akers (I still had the congratulatory letter his office sent me when I became a first-line manager in the 1980s), and Lou Gerstner, who more than anyone else taught me what it meant for a leader to be in service of clients and multiple stakeholders. Half a dozen clients were also on my call list. So were my mom, Annette, Joe, Darlene, dear friends, as well as several former colleagues and current direct reports.

Making these calls was the first thing I wanted to do after the news went public. The announcement was not just mine; it belonged to them, too. Hearing so many voices from my past is one of two memories I most cherish about that day.

The other memory I cherish began when I returned to my condo at around 7 p.m. to discover that Mark had arranged dinner for just the two of us on the forty-second floor of my building, in a large event space usually used for parties. The night sky was so clear we could see New York City's glimmering skyline in the distance. It reminded me how far I'd come from Glen Ellyn. I don't remember what Mark and I ate for dinner, but I do remember how I felt—first, grateful, and so very lucky to have Mark with me for decades, and thank goodness, for this next phase of my career, which would surely be the most difficult and eventful yet.

I also felt honored and humbled to be leading one of America's oldest and largest companies, which had survived decades of disruption by reinventing itself time and again, outlasting many competitors whose brands were once as ubiquitous as Apple or Microsoft but that few people remember now.

IBM was officially formed in 1911, when several smaller businesses merged to form the Computer Tabulating Recording Company. Back then the company manufactured automatic meat slicers, punch card equipment, and cash registers—business technologies of the day! In 1924, its president, Thomas Watson Sr., changed the name to International Business Machines, and the company's track record for history-changing technologies began with building the nation's first Social Security system in the 1930s. In the late 1960s, IBM's engineers helped put the first person on the moon. The company's massive, complex mainframes launched the business computing industry, and in the nineties and early aughts the push into services, consulting, and e-business reestablished the company yet again. In 2011, IBM celebrated one hundred years, a rare accomplishment for any business. Then, as now, IBM remains one of a handful of American companies to have survived and thrived through economic upheaval, two world wars, and the demise and invention of entire industries. Throughout its existence, IBM also had its own ups and downs, including a potential bankruptcy in the eighties.

Now here we were, at another crossroads. Our storied history and the strengths we had in the present were not going to be enough to keep us viable well into the future. Technology and our clients were changing so fast, and we had a lot of changing to do, too, much more than most people inside or outside the company realized.

I also was intensely aware that I was assuming responsibility for a vast, diverse population of stakeholders that depended on the company to make money—from retirees who counted on pensions, to employees and their families, to companies and governments that relied on IBM to operate their most critical systems every day, to shareholders that deserved returns on their investments.

So much was at stake.

That moment—with my husband across the table, the twinkling city in view, and the dawning of an awesome task before me—is when I really came to understand the concept of stewardship. Being CEO was not about some title I had achieved; it was about all the people for whom I was now in service of.

Seeing the Future

Underneath that immense sense of duty was both some fear and the anticipation of a new journey. IBM was one of the largest single suppliers of IT to many corporations worldwide. We ran big, vital, complex systems behind the scenes for thousands of businesses and governments. Our clients depended on us to keep them operating. Without IBM, banks couldn't operate. Railroads couldn't move. Airlines couldn't fly. Thousands of organizations—including 95 percent of companies in the *Fortune* 500—relied on IBM to handle enormous amounts of sensitive, private data.

And yet, we were also the oldest kid on the technology-sector block, and we were losing ground to new competitors that were less than a quarter of our age. Amazon and Google had started as consumer brands and expanded into business computing with new offerings like cloud and software as a service (SaaS). Meanwhile, we'd been successful under my predecessor by becoming a globally integrated enterprise, by acquiring companies that could benefit from our global distribution model, delivering efficiency and productivity gains, as well as executing share buybacks. For the last six years our earnings growth routinely surpassed expectations, making investors very happy. Despite those efforts, our sales were basically flat. There were no new products or services, in the market or in our pipeline, that were significant enough to offset the decline of some of our products that were commoditizing.

Media coverage about my appointment as CEO reinforced the problems: "Rometty will have to find ways to reenergize the top line, something that will likely push IBM outside its comfort zone," wrote *Bloomberg News*. An analyst from Morningstar put it this way: "The company will have to reinvent itself for the future, stay with the times, and maintain the revenue base when they do that."

We'd have to do all this while maintaining the margins shareholders wanted and maintaining the current products and services our long-term clients relied on. We couldn't abandon banks, airlines, and governments— even though they wanted us to lower our prices every year. In one sense, our challenge was to find that balance between being in service of our existing clients and surviving as a business. Deciding our future was nothing less than a question of identity: Who is IBM now? What should we become?

The fact that I was a woman was also a big part of the news coverage, especially in an industry still dominated by men. "IBM Names Virginia Rometty as Its First Female CEO" and "Rometty Breaks Ground" were indicative of many headlines. At the time there were just eighteen women running *Fortune* 500 companies, and IBM was nineteenth on that list. For some, my gender was a reason to celebrate. For others it was reason to speculate, and IBM had to push back, even insisting that "progressive social politics" was not the reason for my ascent.

For me it was an interesting position to be in, full of contradictions. On one hand, I was proud to be among breakers of the so-called glass ceilings that still kept women from advancing into positions of power. I could imagine parents like the father I'd met in Australia showing their daughters headlines and saying things like, "See, you can be whatever you want to be." On the other hand, I wanted to be acknowledged for accomplishments, or leadership style, regardless of my gender. There were articles about that, too.

The *Financial Times* framed the situation bluntly: "As a woman rising to the top of one of the bastions of the male dominated IT industry—and an icon of corporate America to boot—she will inevitably become a symbol for other aspiring female executives. For some, her success or failure will come to shape opinions about the progress in the business world of her entire sex." This unofficial responsibility was not one my eight male predecessors got handed, or any male CEO for that matter. It was a blessing and a burden. Such were the tensions of my new job.

As I planned how I would spend my first one hundred days, I sought guidance for incoming and first-time CEOs. An article someone sent me had this nugget of advice: a new CEO must begin to build "an embedded degree of belief," which I interpreted to mean others had to believe in me, in themselves, and in our future. My job now was to envision the broad contours of change that would prepare the team for the difficult journey ahead. It was again time to paint reality and give hope.

Being Essential from Day One

On Tuesday, January 3, 2012, IBMers returned to work after the holiday. It was also my first official day as CEO. I arrived at IBM's primary research labs in Yorktown Heights, New York, at 7 a.m. to broadcast live to IBMers around the world. I chose the location because research had long been our company's differentiator, something I'd been saying all the way back to my days in insurance and with the PwCC merger. Now, the company's almost thirty-five hundred researchers would be critical to reinventing our innovation engine. I wanted my presence among them to reinforce just how much I—and all of IBM—valued them, and would need them for the journey ahead. I arrived early to mingle with as many people as I could before doing a live video that would be broadcast companywide.

My goal was to come out of the gate with a balance of optimism and realism, to paint reality and give hope. I'd prepared extensively for the moment so I could clearly communicate positivity about our future but also be truthful about the present.

I suggested that IBM aspire to "Be Essential" in the eyes of our clients, as well as to societies and the world at large. As an aspiration and purpose, "Be Essential" was an identity people could be proud of, in part because no one can call themselves essential—only others could confer that status. Being essential was also authentic to me because it reflected a mindset of being in service of, and it was true to IBM because so much of our work was mission critical for clients, like safeguarding millions of transactions for financial institutions and securing global supply chains.

We could only be essential if we gave clients what they wanted and needed, but unfortunately, some of what they believed they wanted and needed for their future we weren't yet able to deliver. So, I came up with something I called our Three Strategic Beliefs (of course there were three) to outline those broad contours of change ahead.

The first Strategic Belief was that a new era of computing had already begun, and we had to be a bigger part of it. It was an era driven by data and the cloud, and it included artificial intelligence–based systems. These trends were facts. We had no choice but to bring new products to the marketplace and reimagine or divest of ones we already had.

The second Strategic Belief was that clients themselves were changing. People buying and using our technology were still CIOs, but now that also included developers themselves, and more and more non-IT professionals who led marketing, HR, and other lines of business. Companies were using mobile, social, and data analytics throughout their operations, reinventing their companies from the inside out. They wanted products that were simple, intuitive, and delivered via the cloud. They wanted help with their own digital transformations.

The third Strategic Belief was that IBMers themselves had to evolve. To be essential to clients in this new era, we had to learn new skills. Not just technical skills but new ways of working, especially with each other.

My top priority was building belief in our purpose, the Three Strategic Beliefs, and in me. How and where I spent my first day, as well as what I said, would be symbolic. People would notice, talk about it, make assumptions about what my leadership would look like, what I valued, and what I expected of them. The last place I wanted to be was in my office.

That's why I was at our research labs in Yorktown Heights. I stood in front of the group, no slides, no charts. Just me and them. Using stories, I described how the Strategic Beliefs would eventually translate into technology and services that would help us be essential. I invited people to email me directly with feedback and their own ideas.

That same day, I sent each of IBM's senior vice presidents a handwritten letter describing three things I admired about them, like a maniacal focus on clients, insight about competitors, dedication to developing people, and refusing to be a prisoner of the past. In some instances I articulated ways I thought they could grow. I also received a lot of emails from people offering suggestions about what I could do to improve the company.

One of the notes I got was from an IBMer in research named James J. Wynne, who had watched the broadcast and, as he wrote me, counted how many times I took my glasses on and off during my presentation— apparently it was a lot. He went on to speculate in detail all the things that could be wrong with my eyes, prompting my behavior. I wasn't quite sure what to think and told a colleague, who smiled as he informed me that Dr. Wynne was a physicist at our Watson Research Center who helped invent LASIK technology. I shook my head in humility. I could never forget that IBM had its share of geniuses; it was a good reminder that a CEO is rarely if ever the smartest one in the room.

I got another email from my colleague John Kelly, an energetic intellectual with a scientific and strategic mind and a unique ability to simplify the complex. John was a senior vice president of research, and he offered observations about my day-one talk, and some advice:

> *The tone you set was different and refreshing. You know that you are open, collaborative and listen well, but you may not know how fast it permeated the place.*
>
> *We will go through tough times at some point. When we do, be tough but don't change who you are. What got you here will make you and us successful in the future. Keep a dual focus on the short term and long term. Different forces will pull you toward one or the other over time—resist.*

His words were prescient.

Over the next three months I visited more research labs as I traveled to city after city around the globe, holding town halls with employees, reiterating our purpose, and talking about our beliefs. I answered as many questions as people wanted to ask, and I shook thousands of hands. I also hosted client roundtables with more than two hundred CEOs and CIOs during my first six months. I genuinely wanted their candid counsel about how we were doing, and what we could do better. I heard from clients that loved us and from some so frustrated that they were on the verge of firing us. Many were going through their own transformations, and it was our duty to help them. I shared our Strategic Beliefs in the hopes that our clients might become as vested in our journey as we were in theirs. I also flew my seventeen senior vice presidents to Silicon Valley to meet with venture capital (VC) firms—I wanted them to see the competitive reality we were up against.

Being Essential and the Strategic Beliefs gave me and my colleagues a shared foundation from which to connect, work together, and build on—collaboratively. It also signaled the magnitude and difficulty to the journey ahead. I had learned from the PwCC merger that building belief is a process without end. Exhilarating in the beginning, the rigor is maintaining high levels of enthusiasm for a sustained period—especially when doubt inevitably creeps in, which it will.

Feedback I got during my first months was reassuring, constructive, and energizing. Many people told me what being essential meant to them personally, and they tied it to their lives. I felt like people were hungry for a purpose—a reason to come to work. Be Essential wasn't just some slogan from the new CEO. People also offered their views on how computing and clients were evolving, and how IBMers could, too. They also told me what was broken. In some corners of the company, a malaise had set in. I needed to hear it all.

Reflecting

Looking back on these two big events in my career, the PwCC merger and my early days as CEO, I hope I've conveyed how vital authenticity, honesty, cocreation, personalization, and foundational ideas are to bringing people along and earning followership. They allow us to bridge emotion and execution. Building belief is also a never-ending effort; it may jumpstart a change journey, but people who buy in can also get out at any time, especially when faced with the inevitable difficulties of moving to an alternate reality. Sustaining belief is the longer-term commitment.

As the next chapter shows, my nine-year journey as CEO and Chairman included choice after choice. Some easy to make, most very difficult. Some right, some wrong. Some applauded, some criticized. At almost every turn I found myself weighing opposing ideas, opinions, and values. Always trying to balance hearts and minds. My colleague John's last line of guidance—different forces will pull you toward one or the other—could not have been truer as I embarked on a path of transformation, especially as I came to understand the depth and magnitude of the change ahead.

8

Knowing What Must Change, What Must Endure

I'm in my office on the seventeenth floor of IBM's building in midtown Manhattan, where I recently made one of the most difficult decisions of my first year and a half as CEO: what to do with IBM's revered semiconductor business. I've listened to a lot of input and the conclusion I've come to will make some people very upset, and in a few minutes I have to deliver the news. I gather my thoughts and a few papers and head to the meeting. I'm thinking about how I'll explain the logic of my decision to my colleagues when I pass the small room next to my office and pause. We call this room "the library," and it's a tribute to the company's past. I don't come in here often, but now I feel compelled to go in, just for a moment. The library's walls are paneled with the same dark wood that lined the office of IBM's first CEO, Thomas Watson Sr. On one shelf, I see a black-and-white photo of Watson in that office with a sign that says "THINK," which was his motto—and remains IBM's. Standing in silence, I'm surrounded by more than one hundred years of history.

IBM gave birth to the modern IT industry, and it has lasted for more than a century by reinventing itself many times. The eight CEOs before me each steered the company through technological shifts, in some cases narrowly avoiding near-death experiences. Now it's my turn. Multiple factors have brought IBM to this next inflection point. But this one is very different from others. A convergence of technology trends—cloud computing, the rise of data, mobility, and social media—is redefining the tech industry, which is accelerating the pace of change everywhere. To survive and thrive in this new era, it's becoming clear that IBM must completely reinvent itself without losing its core identity.

Fortune magazine has described our challenge as existential. "IBM now finds itself competing with a slew of new and agile rivals, from Amazon (an online retailer) to Google (a search engine). Agile isn't exactly the word that pops to mind when thinking of IBM." The magazine cover featured a photo of me next to the headline, "Can IBM *Ever* Be Cool?" I cringed when I read it. The sentiment conveyed the intense pressure IBM is under to quickly become something different from what it is. But just how different? This nuance is always in the back of my mind, simmering.

The company's best days had always been when it had an underlying enduring technology platform—like the mainframe, the PC, or middleware—that a lot of institutions depended upon to run their business. To stay relevant, IBM now needs a new technology platform. We'll also have to rebuild our tech innovation engine and pipeline, and that means divesting of businesses that cost us more money than they make or are no longer core to our mission. Competing also means not just changing the portfolio of products but changing how we work. These new competitors are lean, fast, and have no legacy to enhance or protect. I'll have to move us to a flatter, more nimble existence and build new skills en masse.

Reinventing so much is a challenge for any organization, but especially one with $100 billion in revenues, a million-plus shareholders, well over 350,000 employees, clients in more than 170 countries, and a $100 billion pension. We have to do all this under the scrutiny of public eyes, with capital markets that have little patience and prefer to invest in companies with top-line growth, versus profits and cash flow. The fast-changing world also has implications for a global company as big and far reaching as IBM. There's a growing backlash against globalization, and more countries are opting to build their own tech industries rather than source beyond their borders. What's more, US currency will soon become strong for a prolonged period, and when the dollar appreciates, it reduces the global revenues and earnings we report.

I'm calm on the outside, but every day I wake up feeling the intensity and urgency to change in my very core. I have no doubt that the world would be different if IBM had never existed, or if IBM ceases to exist. My job, as I see it, is to be a steward for the company and to be in service of everyone with stakes in its long-term success. I want it to thrive long after my time at the helm, and I'm trying to do everything in my power to prepare the iconic company for another one hundred years.

Standing in the quiet library, I'm reminded of the legacy I promised to uphold as IBM's ninth CEO, and I think about what it means to uphold such a legacy. How much do you change? What shouldn't change? Leading IBM now will require more difficult choices about parts of the business to keep and build upon, what to add, and what to let go—even when it hurts.

For the years to come, IBM will be the last thought in my head before I sleep, drifting in and out of my dreams, and my first thought as I awake. I'd always worked hard. Now, work and life for me have become inextricably intertwined.

The Brain of Good Power

This good power principle is about bridging old and new to create something better.

Knowing what to change and what must endure asks us to think critically and solve problems as we take something that already exists and bring it to a new state. As such, I see it as good power's brain.

Change in any context and at any scale—be it personal, like switching careers; organizational, like transforming a business; or societal, like dismantling systemic bias—requires making hard choices about what things to preserve and what to reimagine. How do we decide? These difficult decisions can be made by thinking deeply about two basic questions.

First, *what* must change? In the case of a person trying to change careers, for example, the "what" may be your professional skills, accumulated knowledge, your network. All things in service of others that also reflect your character and personality. You don't ever want to change your "what" so much that you abandon your values or can't be true to who you are.

In the case of a company, the "what" is its portfolio of products and services that reinforce the company's mission and beliefs, and that are in service of clients and customers. If organizations don't change, they cease to be relevant, or may even cease to exist. But like a person, a business can't change so much that it loses its soul.

The second question is *how* do we change? For a person, the "how" refers to work habits you've developed, like being collaborative, or taking initiative, or being punctual. For a company, the "how" is the way work gets done. This is an organization's leadership, processes, behaviors, and most important, the workforce's collective talent, knowledge, and skills. The "how" is culture in action.

I've learned that the ways we work are as material as what we do or what a company produces. This seems obvious. And yet when moments of reinvention arrive, innovating the "how" can be overlooked in favor of focusing on the "what." Indeed, it's not enough to just tell people to deliver a different outcome. We have to cocreate a new way of working, give people permission to change, and create an environment that encourages and rewards new behaviors and skills—all at scale.

Transforming is not just about changing from one thing to another, or becoming X instead of Y, as alluring as that might be. Organizations or systems that have been around for a long time face inherent tensions in choosing how to integrate the old and the new. Those tensions include balancing expectations with reality, for one example, or weighing short- versus long-term outcomes, honoring past commitments while making new, future promises, or serving today's clients as we search for new ones. Transforming a really large entity also means reconciling the pace of change in the market with the rate and pace of change the organization can withstand. These and other tensions are hard to grapple with. That said, once we figure out what endures, even if it must be modernized, we have a platform from which we can bridge to the future.

As with prior principles, this one evolved through my own experience and reflections, culled from decisions made and lessons learned during my time orchestrating IBM's largest transformation yet.

Letting Go

Investing in IBM's reinvention demanded that I divest businesses that were losing money, commoditizing, or not growing. These were not easy decisions because they involved not only products but people. Yet only by shedding these businesses would we have additional capital to fuel the investments we needed.

IBM's semiconductor business was one business I decided we had to let go—at least some of it. We just had to figure out how. There was a lot of emotion tied up in IBM's semiconductor history. In 1964, IBM was the first company to commercially produce systems that had a design based on microminiaturized computer circuits, which today we call semiconductors, or chips. These integrated circuits are the brains of all computers, and they're very complex to produce, especially at scale. For almost sixty years IBM pioneered high-end chip design and production, leading the market with breakthrough technologies for ever-smaller, more powerful chips.

We'd always researched, developed, and manufactured the highly complex chips for our own products, and for a period we manufactured them for other companies' products, too. We'd won many awards and IBMers took a lot of pride in our capabilities. Now, though, we mostly manufactured our unique, high-end chips for our own products, and it had become incredibly capital intensive; we didn't have enough volume to run the operation at a scale that would make it cost effective. Also, producing the next generation of our chips would mean retooling two semiconductor foundries—the plants where chips are manufactured—at a cost of at least $10 billion, a massive investment. I knew we couldn't afford to allocate capital to modernize our chip manufacturing facilities because we needed to fund IBM's reinvention.

My conundrum was how to meet different needs and desires of multiple stakeholders. If I announced IBM was no longer going to make its own semiconductor chips without a clear plan for customers of our mainframes, it might please investors but also frighten hundreds of companies that relied on the chips in our systems, and it might freeze our whole systems business. We had to respect how the move affected clients by finding a way to keep our chip quality and supply intact before we announced anything. Balancing urgency, complexity, and market realities required collaborative new thinking, patience, and a willingness to tolerate the short-term pain of continuing to spend money to run the foundries while we figured it out.

One solution was to keep the mission-critical R&D work and divest the manufacturing. This was highly controversial for a few reasons. For one, the three phases of semiconductor production—research, development, and manufacturing—were an integrated process deeply embedded inside the company. Engineers often perfected design during the manufacturing phase. Some were convinced the end-to-end process was so seamless that, if broken up, the quality of the chips would suffer. We had people who couldn't—or wouldn't—even conceive of such an alternative.

I also had to navigate emotions. We had to divorce ourselves from history, say goodbye to something we'd birthed and nurtured.

After serious discussions, a few of us had agreed that IBM's semiconductor intelligence and science were what needed to endure, for ourselves and the world, not our physical production. I had tremendous respect for our engineers, but rather than accept their initial no, I set up a team to explore this alternative, led by two colleagues who had a lot of credibility with their respective teams, John Kelly and Arvind Krishna. John was in charge of all technology strategy and was considered a father of the semiconductor industry. He was also selfless, committed to doing the right thing for the company, so even though the ultimate decision might not have been an ideal outcome, he would bring people along. I trusted him.

I also trusted Arvind, who headed development and manufacturing for our systems and technology group. He was an incredibly bright technologist and also well aware that a lot of people would be very unhappy with him for disrupting their world. Managing different stakeholders and their emotions is different than managing products and technology. But I knew Arvind was the right and best person for the job. He would bring a logical perspective, without being emotionally tethered to the past. And very importantly, this would be a great stretch development assignment for him. I promised Arvind that I'd have his back no matter how angry anyone got.

"You only answer to me," I said.

For two months, the team came together to reimagine the end-to-end process in a way that wouldn't disrupt our current operations. We couldn't afford to lose a day of manufacturing. Heated arguments and bucking of some very smart heads took place behind closed doors, which was vital because conflict can breed progress as much as collaboration, as long as it's done respectfully.

The call I'd been waiting months for came just as I was about to get off a plane in the brutal heat of the Florida Panhandle for my annual Labor Day weekend visit with my brother. As I walked off the flight, I answered my phone and heard genuine excitement in Arvind's voice. The seemingly impossible change could in fact be done, he said, and then he went into the details about the solution they envisioned, with the caveat that we still had to find trusted manufacturing partners and get buy-in from a core group of engineers. I did worry talented people might leave in protest. But I was also prepared to let go anyone unwilling to help us transition, or whose opposition put the transition at risk. Taking no action put all of IBM at risk.

John helped lead the change. Together, he and Arvind worked with our controller, Jim Kavanaugh, to find the right high-end manufacturing partners and negotiate contracts.

Getting out of chip manufacturing was difficult, but it was the healthiest step for the company. The cost of maintaining operations would have sunk us. Instead, our essential R&D endured not just for the company but also for the world. Many countries would come to recognize semiconductor R&D as a highly valued capability and critical asset for national security. As John pointed out, "We kept the future and sold the present."

In 2020, the R&D team announced the world's first 2-nanometer chip. Today, the quality of semiconductor chips in IBM's mainframes is outstanding.

All told, between 2012 and 2020, IBM divested a total of $9 billion in annual revenue, representing five major product businesses; chip manufacturing was just one of them. I did all this knowing that it meant no growth for the company at a time when the investment world was clamoring for it, and knowing that it would take time for new products to replace lost revenue.

Shedding all those products and services was very hard work for the teams, but it was most painful for people whose jobs were upended. Letting go of products can be hard. Letting go of people is much, much harder, even when it's necessary for the overall health and survival of an organization. Whenever we sold a business, we tried to move people with it and protect their employment during the transition.

There were other times and reasons we had to let people go and I never took those decisions lightly. In fact, they were the toughest to stomach. I'd grown up with financial insecurity and understood a job is not just a source of income but a source of dignity. I always reminded myself that behind numbers were faces and families with financial obligations and dreams of their own. Always, I tried to make the best decision given the information available and knowing the company's long-term viability and relevance was at stake. As difficult as many of these decisions were, they were the right long-term choices. We preserved billions in capital that we redirected to new-era products that set the company up for long-term sustainability. Still, the pain was always there.

A good power approach to change doesn't settle for the obvious either/ or alternatives. It's willing to muster patience, sit through discomfort, and think through the impossible, holding the tension between two undesir-able, incompatible options until the situation can be reframed and a third alternative is found. Divesting the entirety of our semiconductor business or continuing to spend large amounts of money were both bad options. But reimagining our manufacturing process so we could partner with another company revealed a third and best alternative.

Even when I believed decisions were right, I would still feel their burden. It helped to talk through challenges with Mark after a particularly long day, but nothing erased thoughts of those who were angry, or whose lives were disrupted. I didn't dwell, but I never forgot. Living with that weight, though, is the nature of stewardship. I had to accept that.

Modernizing Greatness

Early in my CEO tenure, I'd called the CEO of Marriott, Arne Sorenson. We'd known each other since I'd run sales and marketing at IBM and Arne was Marriott's CFO. Our two companies were large clients of each other, too. IBMers often stayed at Marriott hotels, and IBM ran Marriott's massive mission-critical customer loyalty and property management systems.

I'd always kept a meticulous watch over our service of Marriott, from how we performed to which projects we won and lost. I felt strongly we owed them the best we could do, and I traveled often to Marriott's head-quarters in Bethesda, Maryland, which is how I came to know Arne well. He was affable and always clear, direct, and thoughtful in his comments, be they complimentary or critical.

I was calling Arne to find out how IBM was progressing on a smaller marketing software project we were bidding on against a number of new tech companies, and to make sure he knew all the reasons we were quali-fied to be awarded Marriott's business. As service oriented as I am, I'm also extremely competitive, and after I finished making my impassioned case, Arne said, "Ginni, hold on. Remember what I count on you and IBM for. Why do you care about this small marketing project? I count on you for some of the most important systems that run Marriott. Just be the best IBM you can be."

Be the best IBM we could be.

That insight reverberated as I made tough choices about how to reposition the company. So much had to change, like letting go of chip manufacturing, but I could never forget to keep and build upon the most valuable things that make IBM IBM.

To do that, I had to be honest about our present and future.

With the digital era moving so fast, the pressure on incumbent companies to be like all the shiny objects springing up around them is even more intense today. While enticing, it's not always right. My former colleague and astute strategist Ken Keverian put it this way: "Know what makes you great, because IBM would make a horrible Google, just as Google would make a horrible IBM."

I reflected on Ken's and Arne Sorenson's words—be the best IBM you can be—and leaned into an idea Thomas Watson Jr., IBM's second CEO, said decades earlier: if an organization is to meet the challenges of a changing world, it must be prepared to change everything about itself except the beliefs on which it bases all its policies and actions. I interpreted all their words to mean we had to reinvent the company but not stray too far from our core values.

So, who were we? What was that north star we shouldn't turn away from? The foundation upon which the hurricane of change could happen? Our essence?

Being essential was our unique strength.

Figuring out how "being essential" now translated into a technology roadmap and new products for this new era would be a process of discovery. I would learn that when we ventured too far away from our essence, we struggled and didn't reap the benefits of our incumbency. But once we know what makes us special, we can double down and adapt for the times we live in and modernize our greatness.

This is a valuable truth to internalize whenever trying to change any long-standing institution or process; focusing on what must endure provides a foundation for the change to come, and keeps intact things that already work. It's also a foundation that attracts followership and builds confidence.

At the same time I was trying to modernize our greatness, I was trying to be honest about what else no longer made us great.

Tackling Inhibitors

Since 2007, IBM had been adhering to a plan known inside and outside the company as the financial roadmap. The roadmap's key feature was its commitment to double-digit earnings-per-share (EPS) growth by specific dates five years out. For many years the company had met or exceeded its EPS goals through a mix of productivity gains, share buybacks, and growth of existing businesses, mostly via acquisitions and expanding into new geographic markets, while also maintaining and growing the dividend.

With the accelerating landscape of technology disruption, I came to see our EPS emphasis was not a sustainable strategy. We couldn't fulfill the roadmap's profit promises and simultaneously increase investments in new products. I was not alone in this thinking. In October 2012, the *Wall Street Journal* wrote, "From 2006–2012, nearly 40 percent of IBM's projected EPS growth can be explained by its lower share count. Granted, it is a good thing that IBM has returned cash to shareholders. The question is whether it can maintain share buybacks at the level it projects . . . something may have to give."

One respected investor told me, "Always run the company for the long-term owners, not the short-term renters." And yet there also was intense pressure from other investors to stick with the roadmap. Another investor mailed me a handwritten note on a bright-orange notecard urging me to "continue to buy back billions of dollars of shares."

I also had a keen understanding of how many individual shareholders owned IBM stock, in part for its dividend. I'd met and read endless letters about people who'd been put through college or bought a new house due to IBM. The reality, though, was that I had to reprioritize spending on investments in our future.

To make way for meaningful change, I needed to tackle the inhibitor.

In 2014, my new CFO and I announced the tough decision to leave the roadmap, alongside a long-term strategy to increase investments in what clients wanted and where the market was going, mainly cloud and artificial intelligence (AI), as well as cybersecurity and mobile computing. Repositioning capital allocation and increasing investment in the business would reduce our returns to shareholders. But we stayed committed to paying and increasing shareholder dividends, which we had done for so long.

The big unknown was when revenue from new businesses would outpace the erosion of revenues from businesses we'd divested and slower-growing ones.

I understood the magnitude of the decision, so I joined the live investor earnings call at the end of the quarter, a practice that wasn't routine for IBM CEOs. I didn't want our CFO to carry the message alone.

Reaction to leaving the roadmap was mixed. By week's end, the stock had dropped more than 10 percent because EPS was no longer guaranteed. There were also those who took a more farsighted, practical view. As an analyst from UBS told the *Financial Times*, "The roadmap is dead, which is a good thing. They've got to remake the company. It's a multiyear effort, there's still a lot of pain to get through."

Betting Big on AI

One snowy week in early 2011, months before I'd be named CEO, an IBM research lab in upstate New York was turned into a temporary *Jeopardy!* studio. I sat in the audience with other IBMers as the game show was filmed live, watching contestants Ken Jennings and Brad Rutter, two of the show's most successful players, and a computer named Watson. The real Watson was a big machine that housed artificial intelligence (AI) technology; it was situated behind the scenes, out of sight. On stage, Watson the competitor was symbolized by an animated screen sandwiched between Ken and Brad.

No one knew who, or what, would win the competition as each contestant answered questions from six categories that included Olympic oddities, final frontiers, and alternate meanings. I remember host Alex Trebek reading one of the first clues, "Four-letter word for a vantage point or a belief."

"What is a view?" answered Brad, correctly.

Watson took the lead, then got a bunch of questions wrong, to the chagrin of our engineers, who had created Watson's natural language capabilities in preparation for this moment. Eventually, Watson reeled off right answer after right answer. "Who is Franz Liszt?" "What is violin?" "Who is the Church Lady?" "What is narcolepsy?" When Watson's total earnings were almost seven times Brad's total, my colleagues high-fived.

Ultimately, Watson won, and the triumph of a computer over people spurred headlines like this one in the *New York Times*: "Computer Wins on 'Jeopardy!': Trivial, It's Not." The *Jeopardy!* episode illuminated the potential of AI, making the technology relatable and interesting to millions of people. AI's possibilities as well as its problems entered mainstream consciousness and conversations in ways they rarely had.

When I became CEO, building on and commercializing the AI technology behind Watson, as well as becoming a leader in cloud, were two big bets we would make to restructure and innovate IBM's portfolio.

Big bets are calculated, high-risk choices with the potential to dramatically improve the status quo. Big bets, unlike incremental improvements, usually require significant investments, as well as course corrections, because they can come with so many unknowns and complexities. Big bets' outcomes are not always black and white, win or lose, all or nothing. They can also deliver value in unexpected ways.

A market for AI technologies did not yet exist. We'd need to create it.

The promise of AI had captured imaginations since the 1950s. But building computers to think like humans proved overwhelmingly difficult, so much so that AI funding and research waxed and waned for decades, leading to long periods of dormancy called AI winters. Interest in AI revived at the beginning of the twenty-first century, and the wider world was exposed to it in 2011 when IBM's Watson competed on *Jeopardy!*

IBM's long-term aspirations for AI, though, were more ambitious than winning a game show. We believed we could develop AI technologies to improve all kinds of decision-making and solve problems people really cared about, in part by parsing the huge volumes of data that were too massive for humans and existing computers to handle.

We approached our AI development and commercialization from many dimensions, as should happen when making a big bet. If you believe in something, go all in, and I wanted the technology to permeate and benefit everything we did. We harnessed IBM's renowned R&D. We made and used AI tools to improve our own internal processes, like HR. We skilled our consultants to develop and implement AI applications with clients. Most significantly, we experimented with different business models to deploy AI, and we ultimately launched a specialized system we also named Watson, which we developed as a platform to underpin multiple AI applications for different industries.

Watson became the umbrella name for IBM's AI software offerings.

Not many if any companies were exploring the potential of AI to solve tough problems at scale. We had tested AI in various industries and saw its potential, and we created a division to focus on AI/Watson, led by Mike Rhodin. We chose health care as the first industry to invent and apply AI because we felt deeply about our obligation to use technology to address the world's most difficult, widespread problems. We saw AI's potential to make doctors even more effective by improving their rates of correct diagnoses, as well as improving access to quality medical advice for people in developing countries.

Our initial focus was helping doctors detect and treat cancer, which we described as a moonshot, because we knew it would be difficult. And difficult it turned out to be. As with developing many new technologies, much is learned along the way. Platforms are often rebuilt several times, and that's what happened with Watson. At first the system was too monolithic and too complex. So we course-corrected and built a modular platform. We also came up against a lot of challenges we didn't foresee, including factors beyond our control, like doctors' entrenched ways of working; the impact of the medical industry's fee model of paying for services versus outcomes; and the widespread disparity of data, whose collection and analysis is key to AI systems.

Among the biggest lessons we learned was that deploying AI, and not only in health care, is really about the people, not just the technology. To get real value, health-care practitioners have to reinvent how work is done. You can't just apply AI to current processes.

And you also have to build trust in the technology. Looking back at our AI journey, I agree with some of my colleagues who say that ten years ago the world wasn't ready to trust such an advanced technology to do such important work. A game show? Great. Cancer? Not yet, even though the systems we built often made fewer errors than human decision-making. People and even markets needed to be introduced to AI in smaller doses. Have it eased into their lives. Today, there's still due skepticism and AI needs proper regulation, but the technology has matured and so has the marketplace. Trust in AI is growing, but trust must continue to be built for AI to realize its full potential to augment humanity.

We knew that how we marketed Watson would affect the way people embraced AI. Back in 2011, there was excitement but also fear in the zeitgeist. Our approach was to make AI less of a threat by humanizing the technology, as Watson's appearance on *Jeopardy!* did. One TV ad showed IBM Watson chatting with Bob Dylan, analyzing his song lyrics. Our messaging hit a chord, but it also got away from us. In a sense it worked too well, creating high-profile expectations.

We were right to bet big on AI. But addressing its many issues at such scale proved incredibly complicated. There are reasons AI development had gone into hibernation so many times. Our health-care AI business did not grow how we originally envisioned, and that was a disappointment. We were doing something incredibly hard, but that didn't comfort me the days I learned we weren't making the progress we intended. I would allow myself to feel disheartened but not to give up. I insisted we find the ways, and muster the will, to forge ahead.

Ultimately, our AI efforts delivered meaningful, positive change. AI became a significant piece of IBM's business as clients adopted it to enhance essential operations like supply chain, finance, and HR, as well as boosting profitability. A retooled Watson became the foundation of IBM's AI platform, and our AI applications are deployed in thousands and thousands of clients. The attention IBM brought to AI also fueled a vibrant ecosystem of AI-related companies beyond ours, bringing AI out of its latest winter. For 2019, AI was still in its early innings when International Data Corporation (IDC) ranked IBM as the number one market share leader in the $3.5 billion AI software platforms market for the fifth consecutive year.

With AI, we were trying to innovate and create a new market. Our other big bet, the cloud, was different. Instead of making a market, we were playing catch-up to one that already existed.

Betting Big on Cloud

Because we were late to the cloud, finding our place took time, more than we ever intended.

A cloud is basically standardized computing that a company doesn't own or maintain but pays for as a service. In the early 2000s, companies began using cloud technology to run various systems. The first phase of the cloud was centered on the public cloud and was driven by consumer-oriented companies and applications, things like email, games, front-office tasks, and mobile shopping. The first public cloud company was Amazon, which essentially had been building a cloud infrastructure as far back as the 1990s; managing its infrastructure as part of its online retail operations became a competency that Amazon turned into a business with Amazon Web Services (AWS) in 2006. That same year, Microsoft began building its own cloud platform, Azure, which it launched in 2009. When I became CEO, IBM had various cloud products but had yet to build its own public cloud platform. Time was not our friend. As I said, other companies had a huge head start.

To scale quickly, we bought a public cloud company in 2013, worked to expand it globally, and hired more cloud talent. This gave us a solid public cloud foundation. But unlike our competitors, we didn't have a consumer business or end-user applications to drive our existing customers to our public cloud. This was an inhibitor, try as we may, that we couldn't do much about—we were who we were, an enterprise company.

We also discovered that the public cloud technology at the time wasn't sufficient for our corporate clients' mission-critical and more complex back-office applications. Moving our clients' systems to the cloud demanded more sophisticated features and tighter security than consumer-oriented, public clouds. We had to decide what it meant for us to be a cloud platform that supported essential, mission-critical applications.

I listened to many opinions. Every day felt like a sprint and every setback a frustration because time was at a premium. We were already late! I had more sleepless nights, but also some early-morning epiphanies, as we came to understand IBM's unique relationship with cloud technology.

We eventually arrived at the viewpoint that not everyone would move all their computing to several public clouds. In fact, if big corporate clients were to actually move their mission-critical and back-office applications to the cloud, three types of clouds were necessary: public, private, and a hybrid of the two. Finally, we knew where we needed to go, which was down a third path that didn't exist until we came up with it. It was a relief, and it was exciting.

Think of a private cloud as using all the benefits of a public cloud, but on your own premises, so it's potentially more safe and secure, although capacity is not unlimited. Because so many mission-critical applications already ran on our software, we understood this space well, and I again asked Arvind to take on a new responsibility and build our own private cloud. We quietly built one that clients could use with our IBM technologies. We quickly proved demand and need. We then set out to build the world's best open hybrid cloud platform. Hybrid connects a client's applications and data across their public clouds, private clouds, and on-premise systems—all with the utmost security. This provided clients with better economics; they needed fewer fragmented skill groups, and it gave them freedom to move work as needed for myriad reasons, like regulatory and security. The world of hybrid, we believed, was the foundation of the next phase of the cloud.

IBM clearly didn't lead the first phase of cloud, but we believed we could lead the second phase, given that 80 percent of the world's workloads had yet to move to the cloud. As the marketplace confirmed our assumptions, we gained enough confidence in a hybrid cloud strategy to make our biggest bet yet. In 2018, IBM made what was then the largest-ever software acquisition when we acquired Red Hat, a leading provider of open-source cloud software, for $34 billion. Long before the announcement I spent a lot of quality time discussing it with our board, and then months before we made it official, we spent time quietly collaborating, testing, and proving to ourselves that Red Hat could indeed become the cornerstone of our open hybrid cloud platform.

Phase two really allowed IBM to become the best IBM we could be. We had finally found our true home in the world of cloud, with hybrid cloud as our next enduring technology platform. It felt a bit like coming home. AI and cloud were not our only big bets, although today they are the company's core strategies. We also invested heavily to invent and build an era of quantum computing and to grow consulting and our cybersecurity capabilities.

These years of joy and disappointment taught me a lot about driving change at scale and the types of bets sometimes required.

In retrospect, I could see that whether making a market, or responding to a market, there are three things to consider. First, each requires different timing considerations. When responding to a market, there's a premium on things like scaling and speed; when making a market that doesn't yet exist, there's a premium on customer segment selection and readiness. Second, for any big bet to come to fruition, proof points are needed along the way to build trust and momentum. Third, both types of big bets are rarely straight lines, so you can't be afraid to course-correct and pivot. Grant yourself mistakes. But also know, the only mistakes you should ever regret are the ones you don't learn from.

All the efforts we took to reinvent our portfolio—staying true to our Be Essential core, letting go of businesses, tackling inhibitors, making big bets—were hard, strategic decisions to prioritize the company's long-term health and sustainability.

But transforming "what" we did was not enough. One of the most consequential lessons during this period was that "what" a company does is heavily influenced by "how" it does it. So, changing the "what" also requires changing ways people work. Even in retrospect, I'm not sure which was more challenging: revamping our portfolio, or transforming our culture.

Redesigning "How"

Two weeks before I became CEO, in 2011, my family had gathered at Annette's home for Christmas. I have five nieces and nephews whom I think of as my own children, and during family visits, I always carve out time to spend with each. For years, whenever I visited Annette, the youngest of her two sons, Mike, and I had a sweet tradition of holding "meetings" in the pantry, where we sat cross-legged and discussed very important matters like our favorite snacks and what kinds of games he was playing. That year, my nephew Mike had told me that he wanted an Apple iPad for Christmas, but his mom thought it was too extravagant for a five-year-old. Ah, but that is what aunts are for.

Christmas morning everyone was up early sitting around Annette's beautifully ornamented tree in our pajamas. Our family tradition is to let each person take a turn opening a present, which makes for a joyful but very long morning. Mike gave his mom a handmade pottery bowl, and I noticed he was getting a little restless watching everyone open one present at a time. I whispered that he should go ahead and open my gift. He ripped off the wrapping and when he saw it was an iPad jumped with joy, gave me a quick kiss, then grabbed that pottery bowl from his mom and put it on my lap before unpacking the iPad and running to the window, where he promptly took a picture of a deer standing outside in the snow and ran to my side to share his first photograph. I treasure that bowl, which still sits in my credenza. But I was just as grateful for my nephew's other gift: more insight into how IBM had to change.

Watching my young nephew in 2011 so intuitively take to the iPad alluded to the issue of consumability: IBM needed to figure out how to be an enterprise company in a world where user expectations were being set by consumer companies.

IBM created some of the world's most secure, trusted, and complex tech products for business. But our interfaces to those systems could sometimes mirror that complexity. Our clients—like most workers in the digital era—were coming to expect the technologies they used in their professional lives to be as easy to use as the technologies they used in their personal lives. We needed more products to be intuitive to interact with. Or, as I put it, consumable. We also had to produce those products at a much more efficient clip.

My first attempt to speed up our work was to use some tried-and-true blunt clubs. We reduced layers of management to spur quicker decision-making, and I constantly asked everyone to go faster, go faster, go faster. I sounded like a broken record, and people half-joked that "faster" was the only word I knew. "IBM's Chief to Employees: Think Fast, Move Faster" was even a *Wall Street Journal* headline based on a companywide talk I gave after a disappointing quarter. To the team's credit they sure tried.

As I reached out and talked to people around the globe and throughout the company, a reality became blindingly clear. Calling for speed without changing how work is done only exhausts everyone. You can't delegate complexity. It was really unfair, like telling someone wearing hiking boots to run faster without giving them running shoes.

This was a big lesson about leading systemic transformation: if you want people to change how they work, you (leadership) have to cocreate a new way of working and give people the right tools, permission, and processes to change.

So, what would it take to get our massive company to move more quickly and invent things in new ways? And fast? I put these questions to Robert LeBlanc, our then senior vice president of cloud, and Phil Gilbert, whose software company IBM had bought in 2010. Phil had an outsider's perspective and no problem expressing just how far behind IBM was at the time when it came to consumability of some of our products.

"If you think this is about making a difference with fifty people, let's not fool ourselves," he said. "Hiring a thousand designers might make a dent in the problem." To Phil's shock, I gave him the go-ahead to start hiring and come up with a plan to make much more than a dent. To Robert's credit, he made the trade-offs to fund the effort.

Phil's solution was to integrate design thinking into our culture. The highly tuned design thinking method starts with identifying and defining the real problems that users are trying to solve for, then working back from there, iteratively prototyping solutions in collaboration with interdisciplinary teams. This was not pervasively how we operated. IBM was, by its nature, more engineering-led, in that our engineers often started with solving the most complex problem and then worked their way back toward the customer. Phil's vision reversed this by embedding designers into thousands of product groups. Other companies had adopted design thinking but, in 2012, not at the scale we contemplated. Putting tens of thousands of employees through a generic online course wouldn't cut it. We all needed to learn via experience.

Phil and his team built a dynamic, vibrant studio in Austin, Texas. At that time, the space was unlike most of our offices with its transparent walls, desks on wheels, roving whiteboards, and group seating. Multidisciplinary teams were dispatched to the studio for weeks to learn how to apply design thinking's techniques to a real product or service. The design thinking team interrogated the teams, drilling into their assumptions and forcing them into situations that required gaining empathy for users, then letting that empathy inform how, for example, software is developed. Such outside-in thinking was a new muscle for many.

Weaving design thinking into the culture could be uncomfortable, and it took time. Only seven teams came through Austin the first year so the program could be fine-tuned and succeed once it scaled. After two years, people were calling Phil to reserve time at the studio for their groups. Soon, IBM began winning design awards.

It took grit to stick with such dramatic cultural change. By 2017, we had forty-four design studios in over twenty countries. We hired those one thousand new designers two years ahead of Phil's original schedule, and eventually we brought on five thousand new designers, who became part of an entirely new fifteen-thousand-person group dedicated to delivering modern, engaging products and services. We also trained tens of thousands more consultants in design thinking.

In 2014, Apple CEO Tim Cook and I also announced an exclusive partnership between our companies to build a new class of "consumable" enterprise applications.

Just as we needed to improve our products' consumability, we simultaneously needed to build offerings faster and speed up our response time to clients.

A new chief information officer we hired in 2014 helped us instill another method known as agile, which calls for removing layers of decision-making, but also bringing together small teams to experiment with ideas before going big. Agile teams rapidly test and refine ideas on tight budgets, correcting problems early so a new idea can come to fruition fast. At that time, this was a very different way of working for many IBMers, and a complement to the design work. I remember one Saturday, when I bumped into our new CIO while getting my daily tea at Starbucks. He told me he was knocking down walls, not just figuratively but literally. He had taken a sledgehammer to the walls in one of our office buildings so teams could occupy space in a more collaborative way.

I remember well what I thought in that moment. I'd purposefully hired some senior people from outside of IBM, hoping they would accelerate our time to new ideas. Some did it with grace and elegance; others broke some glass. Standing in Starbucks, I ignored the fact that he'd demolished an office in the spirit of making a larger point. I wanted people to try new things and not always ask for permission.

By 2019 more than one hundred thousand people were working in agile squads, and we had spent $1 billion in the preceding years remodeling as many office spaces as we could for collaboration. (This would prove quite fortuitous postpandemic, as people put a premium on returning to an office conducive to group innovation.)

Together, design thinking and agile provided the systemic work, behavior, and cultural changes we desperately needed.

There are many different methods to improve how people work. Organizations just need to choose what's right for them, because telling people to change isn't enough. We equip people to change by giving them the right tools. That said, design thinking and agile's tenets—cocreation; cross-disciplinary collaboration; iterative progress; empathy-driven problem-solving; an outcome-first, outside-in approach—are requisites for this era of consumability and speed, no matter what you are doing or changing. So much so that IBM packaged our custom approach to design thinking and agile into a client offering called the IBM Garage and drove the approach into the fiber of our work around the world. We executed thousands of IBM Garages, and they remain a hallmark program of IBM Consulting.

These good ideas couldn't have scaled without unwavering support from the senior team and many people throughout the company. Implementing each took time and patience as they rippled through our immense workforce over a period of years. Still, the clock kept ticking, and the competitor in me was constantly looking for proof we were making systemic progress.

Benchmarking

"Don't start this journey unless you intend to finish it."

This warning came from our chief marketing officer, Michelle Peluso, when we were discussing how to assess if our efforts to improve the quality of client experiences were paying off. Michelle was suggesting that we adopt a tool called Net Promoter Score (NPS). Until that time, we used phone and written surveys to measure client satisfaction, but these could produce biased feedback because we self-selected the clients and decided when to survey them. Feedback needed to be solicited randomly and more broadly to capture the most honest reactions.

Michelle was one of our key external senior hires—she'd been a White House Fellow, the global consumer chief marketing and internet officer at Citi, the CEO of Travelocity, the CEO of a startup—and she described NPS not as a metric, but a "religion." I came to understand what she meant.

The methodology was simple but strict. Basically, clients were asked just two questions: "How likely are you to recommend this product or service, on a scale of 0–10?" and "Why, or why not?" The questions were posed right after a client interacted with, or was using, a product—because these are the moments impressions get formed. Simple, right? It was more rigorous to quickly follow up with anyone who rated the experience as poor. Failure to connect with each disgruntled client increased their dissatisfaction and reduced our opportunity to make improvements.

Per Michelle's warnings, unless we were prepared to follow up every time, we shouldn't even bother asking the questions. This required more systemic changes in people's behavior, which meant changing the way we worked in other ways, also at a global scale. The first year was rocky as we integrated NPS into thousands of software and hardware products, as well as our consulting services, around the world.

Thousands of client responses flowed in daily. What really drove progress was analyzing that feedback data to identify problems occurring across business units. Every week, we reviewed the latest data and held meetings of NPS champions from around the company, who collaborated to solve pervasive issues so customers wouldn't keep tripping over the same things. Using data to go after the hardest problems was key to improving how we were in service of clients at scale.

I stayed abreast of every report and also personally inspected our progress in all sorts of ways. One day I walked into my office and brought up a new cloud application on my laptop. I launched the app, then decided to dial our customer support number for help, bypassing the chat option to speak with a live tech support expert. I described an issue, and the young man told me the problem was with the hardware and suggested a set of actions. I knew his suggestions were wrong (remember I'm an engineer) and kindly asked him to rethink his response or check with his more experienced colleagues. He held firm to his answer. I then introduced myself and of course he got worried that he'd done something wrong. I assured him not to worry. I was not upset with him. I was upset that he hadn't been trained properly. That was leadership's job.

A leader's job is to understand the reality by inspecting what's expected, then removing roadblocks. If we didn't measure progress, we wouldn't achieve our desired outcomes. We'd also done some benchmarking in 2012, and it convinced us of a positive correlation between high client experience and high employee engagement—engaged employees help deliver better client experiences. We'd stopped tracking engagement years ago. Now we brought it back with an employee survey that only polled three things: I'm proud to be an IBMer; for me, IBM is a great place to work; and I would recommend IBM to a good friend. Importantly, it also included one or two open questions: "What one word describes IBM for you?" and "What advice do you have for IBM management?"

Our own AI system analyzed the feedback, revealing common complaints and thus more things for us to change, like helping people acquire new skills, providing more performance feedback, reducing bureaucracy—all things we were trying to address through design thinking, agile, and other efforts. We didn't adopt NPS or employee engagement tracking lightly. It was tedious, but it was part of the rigor that systemic change requires. We became a better company because of it. By 2020, IBM's overall NPS score had a twenty-point gain, which catapulted us into the top quartile in the industry.

Learning and Teaching

Diane Gherson, our head of HR, once told me that the hairs on her arms tingled when I first discussed the extent to which IBM had to change its product portfolio. Only two out of ten IBMers had the tech skills and knowledge we needed for the company to move forward.

"This is it," she thought, and dug in for the urgent and never-ending journey to upskill and reskill the workforce.

At first, we were quick to hire people who had skills we lacked, en masse. We already constantly recruited new talent because the tech industry runs at relatively higher than normal attrition levels. What happened next was fascinating. A lot of new people came in quite confident that they would school old-school IBM, but they soon discovered that they didn't always understand the complicated nature of our clients' businesses and thus their sophisticated systems. I could actually see new hires' attitudes shift from disdain to respect as they realized that they had as much to learn as they did to teach. It was also rewarding to watch the reverse, as IBMers adopted new skills from their new colleagues.

Acquiring talent was just one path for a company as enormous as IBM. Building talent by reskilling tens of thousands of current employees was imperative, and we wanted the entire company energized to acquire new skills for a new era. In 2013, we made forty hours of annual education mandatory for every employee, and we provided multiple ways to meet or exceed that minimum. We created something called Think Academy, which included a compulsory online learning experience that took place the first Friday of every month, with a curriculum that cycled through topics key to our future—AI, cloud, cybersecurity—as well as our strategy, industry trends, and candid client feedback and appearances.

For four years I personally prepared and taught the first hour each Friday, amounting to fifty sessions! I wanted people to know just how important it was for everyone, no matter their role, to have the right skills and knowledge—starting with me.

I consider education a tool of change. I'd known that since I was young, when I helped my sisters with their homework while doing my own, and saw my mom go back to school. And I'd known it as a young manager when I made sure my teams got formal training. I'd always seen education as a democratizing influence, because no one is above or incapable of learning something. The streaming broadcasts were fun for me because I liked teaching, but I was also a student. Learning new things always makes me feel more confident. It's true to this day. And helping others learn is still one of the most genuine ways I build relationships.

But again, time was of the essence, and we had to accelerate our learning process. The most enduring lessons happen via immersive experience, especially for digital technologies. To help my leadership team embrace the cloud, for example, they each learned how to write code, and then competed in a code-off to see who could produce great cloud applications. To expose thousands of our people to the limits and benefits of AI, Jon Iwata, our marketing leader, brilliantly designed a companywide contest for AI-driven business ideas. All told, 8,361 teams from around the world vied to build 2,704 AI applications using design thinking, agile, cloud, Watson, and more. The only requirement was that their work solve a client problem, enhance a product or service, or improve how we operated. Judges chose fifty finalists to expand on their ideas with coaches. The breadth of ideas included AI apps to address autism; buy insurance; estimate nutrition from photos of food; detect defects in freight cars to speed up repairs; use virtual reality to visualize data patterns; and help kids being bullied.

The contest culminated in finalists presenting to me and several clients in a live-streamed event. Participation and viewership spread AI knowledge across the company and ignited excitement in its potential.

As the world and markets were changing, part of our responsibility was to be in service of our people by providing them with access to learning opportunities, unleashing the drive that exists in many people so they could create careers in line with their interests and timetables, while keeping up with the pace of change inside and outside IBM.

To give people control over their own ongoing education, we put transparency at the heart of an online learning management system we built. It allowed IBMers to plainly see the skills they had, and the skills they needed, and know if those skills were in high or low demand, abundant or scarce, and would be valued in the future job market. The AI-based, Netflix-like system recommended courses and offered personalized career guidance, arming people with information so they could acquire the right skills for their future. In fact, the HR team role modeled design thinking, agile, the use of AI, and cocreation at scale to build and deliver these capabilities. All told, we invested about $5 billion over ten years to revitalize skills and match people to new jobs and career opportunities.

The skills we needed people to learn weren't limited to technology. Leadership is also a skill that requires tools, so we came up with a framework to help our top 350 leaders orchestrate positive change in their areas of the business. The skills we articulated were meant to help leaders think and act differently. They included elements of design thinking and agile, as well as practices I'd learned over many years. Here are my favorites: Make decisions with imperfect data and intuition. Uncover root causes of a problem and attack its systemic barriers. Declare a position, then act quickly. Tap into diverse networks of ideas. Challenge assumptions. Seek and speak uncomfortable truths. Experiment, scale up, or let go. Cocreate and collaborate to deliver value. Think boldly. Seek feedback. And make the complex simple, and the simple scalable.

These seem easy, even obvious, but they're hard to practice at scale. We evaluated our top leaders against these new competencies, and some who'd ranked high in other leadership abilities for years ranked lower in the revised traits. They had to unlearn and adapt. To assist, we paired them with external executive coaches and brought them together in groups. Many took coaching seriously and dug in, but a few did not. We began to hold people accountable by connecting the new leadership skills to compensation and promotion decisions. When senior roles opened, I and the senior team personally looked over candidates and the quality of their transformational leadership skills. People realized that I was paying attention and that their careers could be impacted. That's how important it was to get leadership right.

These new competencies also factored into how we recruited, as we hired to acquire different leadership styles and for diversity of thought. One-third of my direct leadership team was recruited from outside the company, as were 20 percent of all executives. Some external hires were with us a short time, but all brought value whether they stayed for a chapter of the book, or the entire book, as I liked to put it.

Several big ideas emerged throughout our reskilling journey.

For one, people's ability to learn was only limited by their appetite to learn, their sheer willingness to grow, and their grit to keep at it. This affected how we recruited, compensated, and advanced people. We began to hire for, and reward, traits like curiosity and a propensity to learn, as well as defined skills.

I also became convinced that people should be hired and promoted based on their skills and knowledge, regardless of whether or not they had a degree from a four-year college, a credential that had become a dominant factor in assessing job applicants across industries. Over the course of the past decade, the overcredentialing of jobs—requiring a bachelor's degree for positions that didn't really require one—had become so widespread in companies that it was becoming a false barrier keeping millions of people from even applying for well-paying jobs. Eliminating that credential opened us up to new pools of talented candidates, many from underrepresented groups, which in turn helped diversify our workforce.

A third big idea was this: for individuals, a willingness and ability to keep learning had become the ultimate skill. For employers, a culture of continuous learning was the ultimate competitive advantage.

Moving On

I gave a lot of thought to the right time to retire. The traditional retirement age for CEOs at IBM was sixty, and I was almost three years past that. On one hand, the company had yet to demonstrate sustained growth. On the other hand, thanks to the unwavering dedication of all IBMers, I felt strongly the company was on safe ground because a new foundation was in place and growth would come. While there remained much more to do, I felt very confident that we'd developed the right next CEO to build on that foundation and continue the changes necessary to return the company to growth. In January 2020 we named Arvind Krishna as the tenth CEO of IBM. Arvind is a superb technical leader who's also authentic, values driven, and now had multiple experiences running businesses within IBM to his credit.

The company was not bigger than we were in 2012, but we were definitely better. We had our next enduring technology platforms—Hybrid Cloud and AI. Our $25 billion hybrid cloud business represented about 34 percent of revenues. Our consulting business was very strong. We'd divested $9 billion in annual revenue, and acquired sixty-eight companies, including successfully executing one of the largest technology acquisitions of all time, Red Hat. Necessary divestitures continued under my successor, including the divestiture of our managed infrastructure outsourcing business, which we announced in 2020 and was the largest to date.

Between 2012 and 2020, we invested more than $133 billion in R&D, acquisitions, and capital to prepare us to compete in a new era, while staying true to who we were. We'd reinvented almost half of our portfolio while keeping revenues about flat, net of divestitures and the effects of a strong US currency. Gross profits in 2020 were $36 billion on revenues of $73.6 billion. Our stock price had declined because we had not yet returned to that consistent revenue growth, but we had returned almost $43 billion to shareholders since 2012, growing our dividend more than 100 percent.

We'd also recentered ourselves and our products on the client experience and revitalized our skills and leadership. In 2020, eight out of every ten IBMers had contemporary skills for the future, having logged more than twenty-six million learning hours the previous year. We'd hired and developed talent we lacked, and almost half of the workforce was new to the company since 2015, including more than one thousand executives. Our employee engagement reached a record high in 2019, up seventeen points since 2014. And in 2020, IBM was rated number one in the customer satisfaction category of the Drucker Institute's annual ranking of corporate effectiveness, and ranked three overall.

IBM is a big company that's lasted a long time. It's been through periods of inflection that bridged the old IBM to a new one. Someone once asked me if I thought I had the good fortune or misfortune to lead IBM through this last period of inflection. I don't even have to think about it. Even with all the challenges and sleepless nights, I was incredibly fortunate. I had the rare privilege of working with hundreds of thousands of talented and committed people as we laid the cultural and technical foundation for the next phase of a truly great, enduring company.

I also knew that many of our decisions and efforts to transform IBM would not all come to full fruition during my tenure. Of course I wish they had, but I accept that that, too, is the nature of stewardship and systemic change.

Reflecting

The transformation IBM underwent during my years as CEO exemplified the power of we, and illustrated so many tensions inherent to knowing what must change and what must endure: balancing expectations with reality.

Weighing short- versus long-term outcomes. Keeping old and new prom-ises. Reconciling the need for urgency with the speed of change possible. As CEO, I had to constantly consider and hold conflicting ideas and plow through disagreement and discomfort to discover options that would secure a better reality for as many stakeholders as possible.

More personally, my own leadership style evolved as I straddled the emo-tional polarities of change: hope and fear. Optimism and caution. Frus-tration and excitement. I also tried to balance soft and hard approaches to leadership as never before, like making decisions with both empathy *and* logic, honoring our people *and* our mission, being personable *as well as* direct and demanding. I hoped my efforts to engage hearts and heads ener-gized people along the journey.

Along the way, though, a lot of us at the company realized that something else was at play. Knowing what to change and what must endure was not just a question for IBM. It applied to something bigger than our company. IBM's success and future were and remain intertwined with the success and future of the tech industry and the world at large. More broadly, how tech and nontech companies alike handle the promises and perils of technology and innovation.

In the context of good power, choosing to handle technology responsibly is a foundational issue that permeates how we're in service of others, how we build belief, and how we choose what to change and what must endure. Chapter 9, "Stewarding Good Tech," explores how I dealt with this issue as CEO, as part of and in parallel with our broader business transformation.

9

Stewarding Good Tech

I've only been CEO for a year and a half when something happens that will change the nature of the global tech industry. In June 2013, an intelligence contractor named Edward Snowden leaks classified government documents to the *Washington Post* and the *Guardian* newspapers. The documents state that the US government has been collecting data from several tech companies to track people potentially connected to terrorism. The program, called PRISM, conducts broad sweeps of internet traffic, making it possible for the private communications of American citizens to be collected and possibly viewed without a court order, amounting to warrantless surveillance. The leaked documents list several well-known tech companies as PRISM participants, implying they allowed the government to access their users' data without users' knowledge. The mere idea that the government has been conducting so-called backdoor searches causes outrage in the press and among the public. Some tech companies publicly deny their participation in, or knowledge of, PRISM. Nonetheless, people begin questioning just how private their smartphones, internet searches, information, and online conversations really are.

When I first hear the news about PRISM, I'm surprised but not worried. IBM has no connection to it, and we aren't among the companies named in the leaked documents.

This isn't my problem, I think.

Then the phone starts ringing. Foreign governments are calling. They're asking about their data on IBM systems—how we secure it, where we keep it, how we respond to government requests to access it, whether we are letting the US government see it. We already have contracts ensuring that we don't do this, but still they want to hear it from me. My erroneous assumption that IBM won't get caught up in PRISM fallout swings to disbelief as we get inquiries from organizations we've worked with for years, sometimes decades, asking about the security of our systems, and questioning our intentions and integrity. I think, *a company doesn't operate for a hundred years if it misuses data*. And while we aren't perfect, never by design or intent have any IBM clients' data been compromised.

My disbelief that IBM will get caught up in the fray morphs into anger and then concern for the consequences. But eventually it plateaus into calm acceptance. My team works hard to arm me with facts to support our words, as I take calls and then get on planes to reassure clients in person. All the while I keep my eyes on the news. Suspicions about the tech industry get worse; so do international attitudes toward US tech companies. Leaders in many countries tell me they're considering moving away from US technology, in favor of their national champions. Meanwhile, consumers are waking up to the fact that they don't have much clarity into what many companies are doing with their birthdates, addresses, health records, or overall trail of online behavior. Most people haven't been asking themselves, or anyone, really, who might be seeing and benefiting from their online data, and companies haven't volunteered many details. The internet still operates a bit like the storied Wild West, without a lot of rules and laws to protect people's safety, and without consequences for bad actors.

Months go by, and by early 2014 my team is debating what to do. We're not at the center of this problem, so we could lay low and hope to stay out of the heat. Or we can go on the offensive and speak more publicly to try to differentiate ourselves. We pick the latter.

Whatever we say can't be platitudes. We'll only be taken seriously if what we put out is clear, concise, and of course true. Our head lawyer,

Robert C. Weber, volunteers to write our beliefs and positions about data safety and security. We must be sure we can prove whatever we write with evidence. I trust Bob, a renowned lawyer with excellent business judgment and impeccable ethics, who won't let us settle for anything less.

On March 14, 2014, IBM releases "A Letter to Our Clients About Government Access to Data." It states that IBM has absolutely no connection to PRISM and does not put backdoors in its products or provide software source code or encryption keys to the NSA or any other government agency.

Writes Bob, ". . . If a government wants access to data held by IBM on behalf of an enterprise client, we would expect that government to deal directly with that client. If the US government were to serve a national security order on IBM to obtain data from an enterprise client and impose a gag order that prohibits IBM from notifying that client, IBM will take appropriate steps to challenge the gag order through judicial action or other means."

The full letter remains on IBM's website. To my knowledge, no other company has been this precise and public about their relationship—or lack of relationship—with PRISM.

Our clients appreciate and applaud the letter, but these won't be our last words on the subject of privacy. The PRISM episode has unleashed worldwide suspicion and distrust in technology, and it will continue to be a problem for every company. The issues are so much deeper than this incident.

The Muscle of Good Power

This good power principle—stewarding good tech—is about taking responsibility for the creation, application, and disruption of technology by making values-based decisions within a long-term context, addressing technology's upsides and downsides, and considering all stakeholders. Even businesses that are not tech companies and even people who are not tech professionals still use tech in some way. As consumers and users, we're in positions to make choices about how we wield it, and how companies make and manage it.

I've thought a lot about this, especially during my years as CEO. It was during that time that the world came to terms with harsh realities about the presence of technology in our lives. Important questions continued to be asked by consumers, businesses, and governments alike.

I believe society gives a business license to operate, and that license can get revoked if large swaths of society don't trust that business. We vote with our dollars as well as our voices. I'm not the first to say this, of course, but it needs repeating. If society is to flourish in our digital age, people must believe technology will lead them to a brighter future, not a darker place.

Even before PRISM, a collective lack of attention to the consequences of tech was eroding confidence in it, fueling a brewing war between what I came to call "good tech" and "bad tech." Good and bad tech refer to how companies are perceived based on their behaviors in the digital era. Every organization has the potential to be considered good tech or bad tech, even those that do not make or sell tech. That's because, today, every company uses tech in some way to go about their business. In short, every company is a tech company.

Technology the world is unprepared for, that goes unchecked, or that falls into the wrong hands can also hurt societies by harming minors, advancing terrorism, jeopardizing democracies, and widening socioeconomic divides. We must make trade-offs between enjoying tech's convenience and freedoms, and protecting the privacy, security, and well-being of ourselves and others.

I consider this the muscle of good power because it takes strength to do what's right for the long term, and to speak out and advocate for others. And like other good power principles, stewarding good tech requires dealing with explicit tensions. Weighing short-term rewards versus long-term ripple effects. Advancing upsides while publicly dealing with the downsides. Addressing self-regulations as well as government regulations. And not abandoning a greater purpose in the pursuit of personal gain or corporate profits.

As time went on, I would be asked for IBM's position on myriad related topics. I always tried to ground those positions in our values, and

I was thankful to be leading an organization long steeped in those values. Elsewhere, I could see decisions were inconsistent or very hard for leaders and organizations that did not have well-understood, embedded values to guide them, particularly if the decisions impacted their business models, profits, or growth.

As the list of issues and tensions demanding our/my position grew—be they from our employees or from governments around the world—I found it essential to declare a framework that reflected vital, values-based outcomes we would focus on. We would prioritize speaking up on issues associated with these values.

To steward good tech, I had us strive to: Be trusted. Be a champion and innovator for the highest standards of diversity and inclusion. Prepare society to thrive in the digital era.

Each person and organization can define their own framework, but I do believe these desired outcomes apply to all types of businesses, as stewarding good tech is not a technology issue; it is a values issue. That said, the bar is highest for those companies that make technologies the rest of us use.

Building Trust

For businesses and technology to thrive, both must be trusted by society.

Personally, I'm passionate about trust because I consider trust to be the foundation of strong relationships, and relationships give life meaning. We each define trust differently. For me, it's about intention. The intention not to harm others as we live our lives and do our work. The intention to hold confidences. The intention to live up to our promises, pledges, and responsibilities, and act consistent with our words. I freely admit, when someone breaches my trust by revealing a confidence, for example, or breaks a promise, or says positive things to my face and negative things to others, I'm hurt and can be very slow to forgive.

Trust isn't about acting perfectly or never letting anyone down. There are times we make honest mistakes, and times when trying to be in service of one group causes a disservice to another—the tension inherent to stakeholder capitalism.

One way to build (and rebuild) trust is to define and live our values.

In the aftermath of the PRISM revelations, I witnessed firsthand the benefit accrued to IBM as a result of having consistently acted in accordance with our beliefs and values. When I could use our values as the basis for my decision-making, on any number of issues, most times the path was clear. I remember when Senator Robert Portman from Ohio called me because he wasn't getting enough traction for a bill he'd been trying to pass for years. The "Stop Enabling Sex Traffickers Act," or SESTA, would hold liable companies whose online content knowingly facilitated the trafficking of children for sexual exploitation.

Senator Portman asked, "Ginni, if a company knows it's hosting a website for child sex trafficking, shouldn't that company be liable?" This sounded like common sense to me.

"Of course," I said. "If they do it knowingly."

Senator Portman pointed out that current federal law, written well before the internet existed as it does today, immunized owners and operators of websites and media platforms from civil and criminal liability. SESTA, and later a companion bill—the "Fight Online Sex Trafficking Act," or FOSTA—was intended to stop the use of digital platforms for hosting illegal behavior. But the senator was having trouble getting any companies to support it. The legislation would open a door that required companies to take more responsibility for content they knowingly hosted.

The bills' intentions reflected IBM's values as a company, as well as my own. I insisted that we actively support its passage, which influenced other businesses to join in, helping the bill to become law.

Of course, there were also times when trying to live our values can be murky.

When Donald Trump won the presidency in 2016, people who disagreed with him or his policies put pressure on business leaders not to engage with his administration. I wrote a letter to IBM employees noting that IBM

CEOs have engaged directly with every US president since Woodrow Wilson. I also wrote an open letter to President Trump expressing thoughts about how the government could help the country in contexts I knew best, including creating jobs in the digital economy. I then agreed to sit on the administration's Strategy and Policy Forum with other CEOs. Some people criticized the letter and the fact that I was part of the forum. Just as I had been appointed and agreed to serve on President Obama's Export Council and worked closely with that administration on the Trans-Pacific Partnership (TPP) Agreement, I looked at this opportunity as a duty to support the nation, and a decision of policy over politics. Not engaging with this administration would have been a missed opportunity to advocate for things we believed in. But there came a point when participation was no longer the right thing. I and other members of the forum agreed to disband when the president failed to condemn the racism of the Unite the Right rally in Charlottesville, Virginia, a choice unacceptable to the values I and my fellow IBMers held dear.

Deciding how and when to deal with government can be among the toughest tensions for business leaders to navigate, especially in today's politically charged environment. But if we want to influence issues that matter to our organizations and to the world, my feeling is that business needs to stay engaged, and have a seat at the regulatory table. And yet in these polarized times, just meeting with politicians of one party or another can be controversial.

My solution to take a policy-over-politics approach also reflected IBM's stance for decades. The company lobbies for public policies and legislation it believes in, yes, but it also maintains no political action committee to discreetly influence legislation. IBM assumes a nonpartisan posture. It's also one of the few companies that doesn't endorse or make political contributions to candidates running for office. Maintaining a nonpartisan posture allows us to engage with all elected officials.

It's also true that one company cannot advocate or stand up for every issue it cares about. Today, there are so many topics that businesses are asked to support or condemn. Most companies don't have the bandwidth to even understand the issues adequately. What's most important is that we be authentic and clear about what matters most, focus on that, and let our values be the lens through which we choose to engage or disengage. When our chosen issues arise, we raise our voices, roll up our sleeves, and get to work.

Underpinning Tech with Trust

I found the rising distrust in tech frustrating—in large part because our industry as a whole hadn't done nearly enough to earn trust. While the spotlight was not on IBM, I did want IBM to do something more substantial to hasten the public's trust in technology in general, not just in us, by issuing a strong position about how to underpin tech with trust.

I asked Chris Padilla, our vice president of government affairs, to build on Bob's 2014 letter and other data privacy principles IBM had released in 2017 and codify our beliefs and values more broadly around new technologies.

The first draft was written by some of our privacy and cybersecurity experts, and it was impressively thorough. But for a statement to have teeth it also had to be memorable and actionable, and it had to resonate widely. So I too took out my red pen. I worked with Michelle Browdy, IBM's new general counsel, who replaced Bob after he retired, to boil the technical language down to what became known as IBM's Principles of Trust and Transparency. It was intended to be used alongside our values, to guide our own efforts and offer a universal set of three principles for any company to consider.

The first principle was that the purpose of technology is to augment humanity. This means that the software and systems we create should be developed and applied in ways that enhance and make people better. The second principle was that data and its insights belong to their creator. Our view is that clients own all the information and insights they store, use, or cull from our systems. Protecting information is fundamental in a data-driven society. And while not all companies are in the data business, all companies can be data stewards. The third principle was to be transparent. That means the tech itself is free of bias and is explainable. When it comes to AI, for example, tech companies should be proactively candid about the purposes of the AI systems we create, as well as how and when AI is being applied, and who trains their AI systems. Transparency also means being honest about tech's potential harms, accidental or otherwise, and taking steps to prevent those harms.

After IBM released its Principles of Trust and Transparency in 2018, I became quite outspoken about stating and advocating for our beliefs. I gave speeches, talked with clients, and sat with heads of state in countless countries, ranging from China, India, and Brazil to Kenya, Egypt, and Colombia.

One of my memorable meetings was with German Chancellor Angela Merkel at her office in Berlin. I had prepared extensively for this meeting and was launching into IBM's positions on data privacy when Chancellor Merkel looked at me, smiled, and said with all sincerity, "Ginni, I already think of you as one of the good guys." As always, she too was well briefed. This was a high compliment, and I think her opinion was a reaction to our long history of consistent behavior compared to some others. It was nice to know that our track record over decades meant something.

Advocacy takes perseverance and a willingness to educate the public as well as lawmakers. A big part of my role as CEO was helping government officials better understand the industry, from AI to how different tech companies operated. Existing legislation tended to treat tech as one monolithic industry, applying the same rules to all businesses, consumer and enterprise, which had the side effect of stifling innovation for some companies, or punishing others unnecessarily.

In November 2018, I gave a speech to European Union officials in Brussels, Belgium, about the trust-in-tech crisis. I remember being purposely pointed on the need for more accountability. Some online platforms "have more power to shape public opinion than newspapers or TV ever had, yet they face very little regulation or liability," I said. "If there are specific companies that misbehave, steps need to be taken." What steps? "I would use a regulatory scalpel," I said, "not a sledgehammer."

New legislation needed to address the differences in how tech companies had evolved by applying what I called precision regulation. In the same vein as precision medicine, precision regulation doesn't treat the technology sector as one body by laying down broad-brush policies. Instead, regulations should account for differences in specific technologies; how those technologies are used; and their unique risk profiles. More targeted laws that focus on the most vital issues would hold companies responsible without risking or derailing the healthy growth of the digital era. In a sense, precision regulation targets how technology is used, versus the technology itself.

Of course, digital regulation is also linked to issues of world trade, and it's critical to build trust globally. This is why IBM participated heavily when it came to providing input on the Trans-Pacific Partnership. TPP also included the ability for like-minded countries to completely modernize regulations and protections around digital trade. This was long overdue, and my IBM colleagues and I worked hard to be sure the digital chapters of TPP were written properly. Even though the United States did not join TPP, it was good to see the same digital chapters we worked on adopted in the trade agreements between the United States, Mexico, and Canada. More work remains to find new ways to bring these regulations beyond friendly borders.

Using my platform to help build society's trust in technology and in IBM has been a mission, a passion, and one of the ways I tried to steward good tech.

A second way to steward good tech is to be a champion and innovator for the highest standards of diversity and inclusion. This means striving to make everyone feel like they belong, because they do.

Championing Inclusion

One night back in 2016, I received an email from a transgender employee who told me that she didn't feel comfortable taking a business trip to North Carolina because a new state law discriminated against the LGBTQ community. Once again I called my head of legislative affairs, Chris Padilla.

"Tell me more about what's going on in North Carolina," I said to Chris, who was cooking dinner for his family when he answered his phone. As he chopped lettuce, Chris explained that the state's Public Facilities Privacy & Securities Act, or House Bill 2, made it illegal for people to use public bathrooms that were designated for the gender other than the sex identified on their birth certificates. It was a bit more nuanced, but that was the discriminatory gist. Other states, like Texas, were considering similar bathroom bills, as they were known.

"Well, that's not right," I said. People should feel safe to be themselves in the places and spaces where they live and work. It's what allows them to be their best selves. "Let's talk about what we need to do."

That Monday, IBM denounced the law in North Carolina and began a campaign to defeat proposed legislation in Texas, which housed our second-largest workforce in the country. I personally called Texas Governor Greg Abbott and made it clear that if the legislation passed I would reduce IBM's investments in the state, which meant fewer jobs for Texans. The governor listened, then suggested I also call others in state government to share my position. Deciding to take a stand here was about taking a stand for inclusion broadly.

About twenty executives flew to Texas to meet with lawmakers. We also placed ads in local newspapers explaining our view to the public. We weren't just tweeting an opinion and hoping it went viral but taking a grassroots approach and communicating on many fronts. Other companies spoke out, too, threatening to reduce or halt their business in the state. Texas's discriminatory bathroom bills never made it to Governor Abbott for his signature.

IBM has a long history of standing up for equality and civil rights. A decade before the Civil Rights Act, the company wrote its first equal opportunity policy when it was opening plants in segregated southern states. At the time, our CEO, Thomas Watson Jr., unequivocally stated that IBM would not comply with sanctioned segregation. "It is the policy of this organization to hire people who have the personality, talent, and background necessary to fill a given job, regardless of race, color, or creed," he wrote in a public statement, which was perhaps the first corporate mandate on equal employment in US history. Subsequent generations of IBMers have worked to advance that mandate.

Stewarding good tech means always raising the bar on being a champion and innovator for the highest standards of diversity and inclusion.

Why did I decide to act so swiftly and resolutely on an issue like this despite the political risks? Even before becoming a CEO, I felt I had a responsibility to make the promise of inclusion a reality for more people, inside and outside the company, and in different countries.

Why did inclusion matter to me personally? I understood that I was a woman in a field and industry dominated by men. My way of advancing—and breaking so-called glass ceilings—was to do my best, work hard, develop others, and keep learning. I also see myself as the beneficiary of people and policies that made concerted efforts to include someone who might be left out, left behind, or discriminated against. I had a mother who accepted people for who they were. I grew up around neighbors who cared about the less fortunate. I had access to decent public education, as well as a private university due to academic and financial scholarships. I also was employed by companies and worked for managers that, for the most part, did not hold me back because of my gender.

There's no doubt that the inclusive attitudes where I spent my professional life influenced me. The company hired its first Black and female employees in 1899, and its first professional female employees in 1935, the same decade it established equal pay policies for men and women. The company named its first woman executive in 1943. Throughout the seventies and eighties, IBM was at the forefront of hiring and promoting underrepresented minorities and women—again, I consider myself a beneficiary of those efforts. Granted, IBM had a reputation for uniformity in dress and presentation, as many corporations did. But for the most part I elected to grow my career in a culture that made conscious efforts to value all people. When I was a young manager back in the eighties, my performance reviews graded me on how well I provided equity of pay, recognition, and promotions to people in my unit, as well as how I accelerated the development of minorities and women, and how successfully I focused on minority hiring. We didn't call it diversity or inclusion back then, but by making even first-level managers like me responsible for it, the imperative took hold in my young psyche, influencing my future leadership.

I matured into my leadership roles determined to carry on the tradition by embedding inclusive values and efforts into how we worked. As proof of that progress, IBM received the prestigious Catalyst Award in 2018 for Advancing Women and Diversity in Business, making IBM the only tech company to receive it that year, and the only company to receive the award four times since the award's inception in 1987. By the time I retired in 2020, the company had achieved best-in-class inclusion scores and record diversity across all representation groups, including being one of the leaders in the tech industry with the most women in executive positions. Eighty-eight percent of our employees said they could be their authentic selves at work. These are achievements I'm especially proud of.

People ask me if there was a silver bullet to the company's track record on diversity and inclusion. My answer is that inclusion is not one thing, but a choice we make again and again.

We must authentically believe, in our hearts as well as our heads, that inclusion creates better products and makes companies more competitive.

Research has found, for example, that the demographics of engineers who create AI play a role in the AI's predictions. We address bias in technology by populating innovation teams with people who reflect a mix of races, ages, and gender, as well as a variety of viewpoints. Creating such diverse engineering teams requires hiring and promoting from broad slates of qualified candidates. But we will only do that if we authentically believe, as I do, that inclusion is not only the right thing to do, but also makes our products and our company better.

I also think that companies must constantly raise the bar on their own inclusion efforts and outcomes by asking how to make it possible for more people to participate and stay in the workforce productively. People are different from one another in endless combinations of ways—from our bodies, backgrounds, and stages in life to our learned skills, innate challenges, and how we problem-solve. We are all our best selves when we are our true selves. Workplaces that provide space for our differences to exist allow more people to share perspectives and shine.

There are so many ways to make environments more welcoming for all. We can create and fund affinity groups. We can continue to build our own awareness through open discussion. We can make it easier for new mothers to come back to work by paying to ship a woman's breast milk back to her home for free when she travels, which IBM began doing in 2015. We can create returnship programs for those who must rebuild confidence to reenter the workforce, which IBM did with great success. We can ensure every slate of job candidates is diverse. We can reassess all our job requisitions and remove false barriers, like requiring a college degree when one is not required to begin a position. We can consider the unique ways people learn, then identify roles in which people on the autism spectrum, for example, can excel. We can and should continue to push the boundary of the definition of inclusion. In today's world, an inclusive environment is also one that tolerates differences of political opinion.

I would also never forget that addressing issues of diversity and inclusion around the world requires understanding a region's cultural context, and in some cases meeting countries where they are in order to get them to progress to where we believe they should be. In 2013, Japan's prime minister Shinzo Abe proposed adopting Womenomics, a concept of how and why to close gender gaps that was developed by Goldman Sachs. Research suggested that by closing the gender gap in Japan, the country's GDP could increase by up to 15 percent. IBM had also been very committed to improving its own workforce diversity in Japan. As a strong sign of support to the country, and to further our own efforts, I cohosted a conference in Japan with Prime Minister Abe's wife, Akie Abe, in 2016 for almost one thousand Japanese women. I also enlisted the IBM board of directors to join panels and share their global experiences. What a statement and what encouragement that gave to many, including the men in the audience. My point is to never stop innovating ways to include more people.

Being accountable is also essential. After the PwCC acquisition, I noticed for quite some time our gender diversity wasn't improving in some countries, even after the local offices had merged operations. I remember flying down to one of our offices in Latin America and asking to meet with all the women aspiring to be partners. We were in a conference room, in a circle. I began by asking the women about their careers and credentials and then to please tell me if they felt that they had been passed over for deserved promotions. I was grateful they felt comfortable enough to be candid. These were indeed qualified women. I went back to the regional leaders, all male, and told them I had run out of patience. All hiring would be stopped until they had greater diversity representation in the senior team. In this case, the stick versus the carrot worked, and to this day Latin America has one of the best diversity results in that business.

As CEO, with the board's support, I also changed our executive compensation so bonuses would be adjusted higher or lower depending on whether or not a leader contributed to our progress on diversity and inclusion.

Organizations should define specific targets to track progress. If you believe people should be paid equally for the same job and performance, for example, audit compensation annually to be sure there is equal pay for equivalent roles across different representation groups. When deltas exist, adjust.

While good power promotes inclusion at scale within an organization, that alone is not sufficient. Employers have a responsibility to ensure that the future doesn't belong to the few but to the many—even those beyond its walls—and to ensure that large parts of society are being prepared with the right skills to thrive in the future. This belief has taken me on a life-changing journey that is going beyond my years as CEO—although it took root at the beginning of my tenure.

Preparing Society

In 2012, IBM couldn't find enough qualified people to fill hundreds of cybersecurity roles. The candidate pool simply wasn't big enough. The skills shortage wasn't limited to cybersecurity, or to IBM, or to the United States, or even to the tech sector. All companies were struggling to fill tech-related jobs. And yet millions of people, many from underserved, lower-income populations, were having trouble finding good-paying jobs because they didn't have the skills or the college degrees that employers wanted to hire. I referred to this growing mismatch as the digital divide.

We addressed the problem, in part, by recruiting nontraditional candidates, mainly people who didn't have the four-year degrees our tech jobs usually required, but who did have skills to begin a technical career. One place we sourced this talent was a unique high school that IBM confounded in Brooklyn, called P-TECH, which stood for Pathways in Technology Early College High School.

At P-TECH, students dual-enrolled in high school and college and took a combination of courses in STEM fields (science, technology, engineering, and mathematics). Classwork was paired with hands-on work experience and paid internships, and students could graduate from P-TECH in four to six years with a high school diploma and an associate in applied science degree. The school was free to all who applied—you didn't have to test to qualify—and graduates often landed good-paying jobs at local businesses that provided mentors and internships.

IBM designed this first-of-its-kind program and, in 2011, colaunched it inside a Brooklyn high school with the New York City Department of Education and the City University of New York (CUNY). When I became CEO that was the only P-TECH school, and many of its students began working for IBM as interns, apprentices, and eventually some as full-time employees. Their success, and P-TECH, would forever change my and my colleagues' views of talent development.

Around the time IBM began hiring P-TECH students, I had a related enlightening experience.

I've been fortunate to meet many heads of state throughout my career, and the topic that almost always comes up is jobs, which is the universal currency across countries. Specifically, government leaders want to know how companies like IBM can create more economic opportunity for more of their citizens.

In 2014, I met with the former president of Israel, Shimon Peres. For almost three hours we sat in his office, our conversation meandering from our lives to politics to the global economy. Peres had led a long life of public service after emigrating from Poland to Israel with his family as a child. As foreign minister, he won the Nobel Peace Prize in recognition of his efforts to pursue peace with Palestine. He was in his nineties, and the day we spoke I found him contemplative and insightful as we talked about building work-forces around the world. We were discussing the continent of Africa, where IBM would open up several new research centers, and one thing Peres said really struck me.

"Companies do more to develop countries than governments, as they know no boundaries."

I took him to mean boundaries literally as well as metaphorically. Governments aren't known for innovative market disruptions beyond their borders. Companies, however, bring new things into a global marketplace, seeing fewer limits of possibility and place. Companies birth new eras and bring innovation and new jobs across geographic borders.

During my early years leading IBM, I was beginning to clarify the belief that all of us have a responsibility to prepare society to thrive in the digital era by training people for the very jobs being created, at all stages of their careers. Unfortunately, we all need to do more on this front. Decades of widening social and economic inequities, heightened by the financial crisis and great recession of 2008, have raised fundamental questions about whether capitalism is working for most people. So many folks are worried about tech's effects on their financial security, fearing technologies like AI will lead to mass unemployment as the jobs and skills they have become obsolete. And because companies tend to coalesce in big cities, people in rural areas have little or no access to new jobs being created—although this may improve slightly as more jobs migrate online postpandemic. Even so, other barriers prevent access to employment for millions, like the trend to fill most tech jobs with candidates that have at least a four-year degree, even when a college education isn't required to do the work. These and other systemic hiring habits are leaving millions of people out of the digital economy.

People can't work unless they have the skills that employers need. When masses of people are unqualified for good jobs, they get left behind and lose faith in their potential to improve their lives. They also lose faith in "the system" to meet their most basic needs, which is why systemic change is so crucial. If vast numbers of people don't see a better future, everyone suffers—including business itself. There must exist employment opportunities for the many.

In 2016, I wrote an op-ed in *USA Today* about how disruptive changes in technology were creating dangerous situations around the world, one in which millions of people were or would soon be unemployed and unable to find work even as millions of good-paying jobs were going unfilled because there weren't enough qualified workers.

"Lasting job creation will require an understanding of important new dynamics in the global labor market," I wrote. "This is not about white collar vs. blue collar jobs, but about the 'new collar' jobs."

At IBM, a team and I coined the term *new collar* to distinguish a new category of digital-era workers from the stereotype of manual labor, hourly wage jobs associated with blue collar workers, and the managerial, administrative roles of white collar workers. New collar jobs and hires bring a range of contemporary and needed technology skills to almost every position, but the jobs do not require a four-year college degree. As such, they do require new approaches to education, training, recruiting, and advancement.

Adapting to this new collar reality is the joint responsibility of governments, businesses, educational institutions, and individuals. We have a shared stake in the outcome: more good-paying jobs bring economic opportunity for more people, and economic opportunity is an equalizer that creates healthier, happier, safer communities.

Preparing society for the digital era by helping more people access education and employment opportunities may be the most vital pillar of stewarding good tech, and there's so much more that can and must be done.

Stewarding Corporate Responsibility

In 2019, I was sitting on a stage in New York City with the CEO of Johnson & Johnson, Alex Gorsky. I'd gotten to know Alex well over the last decade, as we grew our careers at our respective companies. Alex was a big believer in values-based leadership, which was in part why we were on stage together. We were being interviewed—grilled, really—by *New York Times* business journalist and author Andrew Ross Sorkin at the annual DealBook Conference that he hosted.

"When this announcement first came out," Andrew said to the audience, "I literally sent them an email and said, 'We've got to start the day with this conversation because it feels like there's a sea change taking place in business, I think. We'll see if there's *really* a sea change taking place in business, but this is what you did.'"

He went on to explain why Alex and I were there, as representatives of the Business Roundtable (BRT), an association of CEOs of America's leading companies. The BRT had just released a controversial statement, titled "The Purpose of a Corporation," that basically said CEOs of 181 US companies committed to lead their businesses for the benefit of all stakeholders: customers, employees, suppliers, communities, and shareholders. The statement was a refreshed, modernized version of the BRT's long-standing position that corporations exist principally to serve shareholders. I agreed to corepresent the revised statement, along with JPMorgan Chase CEO Jamie

Dimon and Alex, who led the BRT's work on the revision, because I felt it represented how IBM operated, and how I was taught to lead it.

"I will note that shareholders was last on the list," said Andrew, referring to the five stakeholders. A common criticism was that the revised statement devalued shareholders. I pointed out that the relationship between each of the stakeholders was "and," not "either/or."

"We don't live in a binary world. None of us manage in a binary world . . . you have to have shareholder return, and then part of the virtuous circle is all those other constituents," I said. I've always believed that commercial value and societal value are not mutually exclusive. Yes, the pursuit of revenue and profit is essential for any business to survive and thrive, but such pursuits are never in a vacuum.

The BRT statement was considered a big deal at the time, cheered by many employees and consumers, and provoking editorials and panel discussions debating whether the practice of shareholder primacy over a stakeholder-based economy was contributing to widening economic inequities. As Andrew said, there was a lot of critique. Some accused the BRT of rhetoric not backed up by enough action. Others were philosophically opposed to the idea, arguing that the attempt to balance the needs of multiple stakeholders overreached any company's concern. The truth is that the statement expressed philosophies many companies already held and practiced.

"What the Business Roundtable did, which is very important, is to canonize what has already been the prevailing practice at great companies like IBM and PepsiCo, Regeneron, EY, and Disney," Yale School of Management professor Jeffrey Sonnenfeld said on CNBC. Jeff has spent four decades encouraging companies to also act on behalf of society, and he used a key phrase, "prevailing practice." In the end, the BRT statement was really about leaders acting consistent with their values over long arcs of time.

The BRT statement was also symbolic. Systemic change is triggered and sustained by multiple forces, and such a public statement from major corporations was a forcing function for all businesses to reassess their contributions in the broader scheme and consider how to be in service of more people, not just a few.

It's been more than five years since the BRT statement. Has there been a sea change, as Andrew wondered? Are businesses making progress being in service of multiple stakeholders, versus just one or two? The answer is yes *and* no.

"The Roundtable's action showed how pervasive the movement had become," wrote *Fortune* magazine longtime editor in chief Alan Murray in his 2022 book *Tomorrow's Capitalist*. "Business was changing, in response to the needs of society, and under pressure from a new generation of employees, customers, and investors. History had taken a turn."

And yet, there is so much more to be done. Economic and social inequities are growing in severity and consequence. Those of us in the business community must continue to find new and creative ways to address various issues.

Reflecting

Today more than ever, capitalist societies find themselves at an interesting, even precarious, point. A crossroads. That's why I consider stewarding good tech so foundational to good power. Its tenets—building trust, championing inclusion, and preparing society—permeate everything we as leaders do. The choices we make in these areas will define our shared future, for better or worse.

The biggest tension of stewarding good tech is, I think, weighing short-term rewards with long-term effects. Negative consequences like loss of personal privacy or economic exclusion will be less apparent and take longer to manifest than immediate gains like a blockbuster IPO, or the admiration of peers, or launching a new app. Stewarding good tech is about recognizing our power over technology, using it wisely, and choosing to play the long game. This brings me to the other foundational element of good power: our ability to weather the challenges of change by summoning resilience.

10

Being Resilient

Just as my siblings and I have our own memories of our father's abandonment, we have our own take on how its aftermath affected our lives.

Joe cried the day our father left, but he never cried for him again. He looks back and sees a fourteen-year-old boy who suddenly had to be responsible for himself. So he focused on doing the best he could at the tasks in front of him, like staying up until 3 a.m. to finish homework, and excelling at varsity sports. Joe believed that the worst person he could let down was himself. His tenacity was compounded by his competitive spirit and natural analytic abilities.

Joe graduated Dartmouth College and joined the commodity trading firm Louis Dreyfus. He found a mentor and by twenty-nine was president of Louis Dreyfus's cotton company. He spent forty years buying and selling cotton all over the world, growing the business sixty-five-fold into the world's largest cotton company. His work is intense and high risk, yet he thrives under the pressure. Joe will tell you he sticks with it out of passion. He will also acknowledge that our father's absence left an undeniable void, and one way to fill it was through accomplishment.

Annette recalls being an eight-year-old who had to navigate a household of busy older siblings and a busy mom. She, too, needed to be self-sufficient.

Yet the departure of our father left its mark on her as she yearned for his time and attention. She harbored a desire for significance. She found that significance by excelling at her schoolwork, leading student council, and competing to win in contests like the Fourth of July bicentennial essay contest, earning her the role of master of ceremonies. From a young age, Annette was driven to do things that mattered, especially helping others. She, like me, entered Northwestern University intent on being a doctor, until a biochemistry professor suggested she study what she loved. Annette went on to earn an undergraduate engineering degree in computer science, and later an MBA from the Kellogg School of Management.

She joined the management consulting firm Accenture in 1986 (then a division of Arthur Andersen), becoming one of the firm's youngest partners, with a love for emerging technology. Ultimately, she rose to the very top of Accenture, as the chief executive of strategy and consulting. Along the way she dealt with hurdles professional and personal, including a crisis of confidence when she considered returning to the workforce after several years at home raising her children. Annette retired from Accenture in 2022, the same year she ranked number one on the list of Top 25 Women Leaders in Consulting. Today, she will tell you that a main source of her sense of accomplishment and significance, aside from her wonderful sons, is helping others return to work by acquiring new skills and overcoming doubts.

Darlene, who was the youngest when our father left, was less influenced by his leaving than her older siblings. She mirrored what she saw us do: study, compete, go to college, work hard. Playing board games and sports bred a constructive competitiveness; Dar got joy not just from winning but from outstrategizing or outskilling a worthy competitor. A varsity softball player, she would practice pitching for hours, and she loved being up at the plate with two outs in the ninth inning. The sport also instilled a team-first mentality. Darlene earned a full-ride scholarship to Ohio State, and then later obtained her MBA from Georgia Tech.

Dar's tenacious, collaborative nature propelled her twenty-nine-year career at the Coca-Cola Company, where she eagerly took on roles others
shied away from, turned around failing business units, and became Coke's
first female chief procurement officer. Darlene also served as president of
Coca-Cola in Canada and for the Northeast United States. In 2022, she
left Coke and was named CEO of a multibillion-dollar consumer goods
company. Today, Darlene will tell you that growing up without having
much made her resourceful and appreciative of her family; she grew into
a problem-solver who values people. As a gay woman, she will also tell you
that our family's unconditional love and acceptance provided her lifelong
psychological safety and the courage to be her full self.

Can you tell how proud I am of my siblings? They might as well be my
own children.

The four of us sometimes reflect on how far we've all come—we are both
thankful and amazed at how our lives turned out. And yet it wasn't luck
that propelled each of us to transcend a tragedy in our childhoods and forge
ambitious paths. The singular characteristic that describes us is resilience.

The Spirit of Good Power

Resilience has allowed me to forge ahead when faced with disappointing
setbacks, conflict, crisis, and critics. In my experience, resilience results
from a number of factors, but two in particular—relationships and attitude.
Both are under our control.

The right relationships provide perspective, meaning they help us judge
something's importance, or see something from another, perhaps broader,
angle, which is essential for forward progress. Relationships also fuel our
energy and are a source of growth and support.

Attitude is how we choose to deal with the many challenges we face in
a crucial moment of decision-making but also over time. The most difficult goals take a long time to come to fruition, especially for large systemic

change. A leader's attitudes—optimism versus fear, calm versus panic—will shape their organization's attitude.

Resilience manifests in emotions that have the power to lift us, which is why I consider it good power's spirit.

So much is at stake when we strive to create positive change for ourselves and our teams but especially at scale. The higher our goals, the harder the climb. Obstacles along the way will be episodic as well as constant, and we don't want to let a crisis derail our plans or the steady buzz of critics shake our confidence. In essence, being resilient comes down to choices we make.

Nourishing Relationships

Genuine relationships provide me with perspective, and perspective lets me see things from a wider lens and creatively solve problems.

I tried to build a broad array of relationships throughout my career. My most treasured relationships are with my family and friends. Just knowing that they're in my life and that they support me keeps me grounded. I've long said there's no such thing as a bad ending because I have family. My bonds with my siblings are strong because of our shared history, but more so because we stay engaged in each other's lives. Although incredibly busy, Annette, Darlene, Joe, and I routinely text and call to tell each other good news, and to seek advice and moral support. We listen without judgment, encourage each other, and come together in times of need as well as tradition (and still argue a bit, too).

Years ago we established rituals that we stick to. For twenty-five years, Mark and I hosted Thanksgiving at our house; when I just couldn't do it any longer, Annette took over. I'm not much of a cook for two, but I've mastered the art of Thanksgiving dinner for forty-five, replete with my grandmother's stuffing and homemade cranberry sauce. Each Christmas, someone bakes Grandma Mary's cookies from the same recipes she followed in her kitchen above the lamp shop. Every Labor Day weekend, I visit Joe and his family in Florida.

Outside of family, I have longtime friends whose presence is a constant source of stability and fun. These are women I met at college and early in my marriage. They aren't connected to my professional life, although they know all about it. Our careers are quite different. Some chose to work, some chose to stay home to focus on family, some both. None of that matters because when we're together, I'm just Ginni. These friendships have lasted because of the quality of our time together, not the quantity. These are the women I vacation with, reminisce with, and whose milestone celebrations I prioritize. Our interactions are an oasis of joy and unconditional acceptance.

Right after I became CEO, a mentor told me to look around and identify the genuine, deep friendships I already had. People who liked me before I had positions of power. "Those are the ones you need to keep close," he said. "Many others will only want to know you because of who you are today."

Mark, my very significant other of more than forty-five years, has always been the most important relationship in my life. Where to begin. I'll start with this: it's misleading to assume that ambitious goals can be achieved without tremendous amounts of time and dedication. Mark never resented the time and dedication my career required, and as a result I can't imagine my professional journey without him.

For me, so much of his support is just his presence. Mark is as playful, curious, and street-smart today as he was on our first date. We are different—he says that I'm a type A and he's a type Z. By staying true to himself, Mark makes it easier for me to be true to myself. Early in my career that meant I could keep working when my coworkers played, literally. For years Mark was my proxy on office sports teams. He's a talented athlete—I'm not—so I doubt anyone was upset that he showed up for softball games instead of me. Mark has also played countless rounds of golf with my colleagues and clients, and for decades he joined me at business events, my jovial plus-one.

Mark's humor lightens me in times of stress. I once overheard my assistant say, "We always know when Ginni is talking to Mark on the phone because she's laughing." At home, he'd listen to the dilemma of the day with interest and insight, and he could give me perspective even when it meant pointing out my shortcomings, but without harsh judgment.

No one takes greater pride in me than my husband, and he has never been jealous of my career, perhaps because he achieved his own definition of success in his. Was I just lucky to have found and fallen in love with Mark? Did coming from single-parent homes propel each of us to work harder to preserve our own marriage? What I do know is that our relationship has benefited from intention and sacrifice. And a boatload of patience.

For years I maintained our home base in Detroit instead of relocating every time I was promoted to a new job. That allowed Mark to stay in the city and at the job he loved and be near his own family and friends. I'm grateful that IBM allowed me to do that. But it also meant I became a global citizen by traveling extensively. When this pattern became apparent, Mark and I promised never to spend more than two weeks apart. We stuck to it. He'd fly to meet me for a weekend, or I'd return to Detroit late on a Friday. Once, I returned home to discover that Mark self-installed a putting green in our basement, including three holes he'd jack-hammered into the concrete floor. When I deigned to question his decision, he said without a trace of sarcasm, "Hey, you have to be present to vote." *Fair enough*, I thought. That's when I realized that I had to stop caring about certain things that I couldn't or wouldn't make time for, like what breed of dog we got, or even that we got a dog! Over time Mark's solo decisions escalated. He even bought a new house that I never saw in person until we moved in. I learned early on that my husband could relieve me of great burdens; I just had to let go, and let him do things his way.

About seven years into our marriage we were driving on a highway, when Mark suddenly asked me, "Do you wish we had children?"

"I don't think so," I said. "Do you?"

"I don't think so either." Then we talked about why we both felt that way. We'd each come from single-parent homes, albeit under different circumstances, and while we were keenly aware of our respective mothers' strength and love, their struggles were also etched in our memories. Personally,

I really did feel that my younger sisters would forever be my children. Whatever maternal instinct I had felt very satisfied. Joe and Annette had already started their families, and I adored my nieces and nephews. So while Mark and I both love children, we decided we'd be great aunts and uncles.

I share this very personal decision for a reason. I don't want anyone to conclude that having the time to become or to be a CEO and having the time to be a mother are mutually exclusive decisions. They were not and are not. To me these are independent personal decisions we each make. Many of my colleagues are wonderful mothers and parents. That said, I know that our decision certainly made it easier to spend time on our relationship and our professional lives. As one of the few women who did not have children, it made me even more acutely aware of the challenges working families had.

So many of the women I worked with had children, and I know via their and my siblings' experiences with their families that the demands on people's time and emotions can be exponentially higher. I have so much respect, empathy, and admiration for working parents, and it has informed many of the employee programs that IBM offered during my tenure. I equally respect those women, and men, who left the workforce to stay home with their families. Empathy and respect are the point.

Back when I became head of IBM, the *New York Times* ran an article headlined, "A CEO's Support System, aka Husband." Most of the piece was about the outsize support that business leaders get from significant others. The article noted that the overwhelming number of American CEOs are married. All I can speak to is my experience. There's no doubt that Mark's dedication to our home life as well as to my own career made it possible for me to avoid distractions, to focus, and to be more resilient.

Like family, our most essential relationships are also behind the scenes, invisible to most people but sources of nourishment for us.

The first time Janice Cafmeyer and I met, in 1982, we saw each other as competitors. We were systems engineers working in different Detroit offices, and our first interaction was at a meeting of employees that IBM dubbed "high potentials." We were two ambitious young women equal in title and talent who looked a bit alike, although Janice was two years younger and I was six inches taller.

Our careers developed in parallel. We both joined the consulting unit IBM started in the early 1990s, and together we worked on difficult assignments, learning about the art of business consulting, and learning about each other. Over time, we stopped being competitive and treated each other as respected peers. Even partners.

The nature of our relationship veered when I was offered the role to lead our regional consulting team. When I got the call about the job, I remember turning to Janice and saying, "I think we just got promoted." I couldn't imagine moving on without Janice. From that point on, we settled into a mutually beneficial relationship that Mark described as Batman and Robin. For more than a decade, Janice supported me in various roles, from the PwCC merger to my first year and a half as CEO.

Maybe the best way to describe her role was as chief consultant—for IBM and for me. Her assignment was not to serve me as much as to be in service of IBM's clients. As I took on more internal responsibilities, I never wanted to stop paying attention to clients. I could count on Janice to ensure we were fulfilling our promises, working with them and with teams. She executed without ego and showed respect for everyone. I always appreciated *how* Janice did her job as much as *what* she did.

Her unvarnished feedback also told me what I needed to hear, even when I didn't want to hear it. Other times a brief, reassuring email from her reminded me not to second-guess my choices. We could frustrate each other, to be sure. But with straight talk we found our way through. I could say, "Don't roll your eyes at me!" She'd say, "Enough already!" We all need someone to tell us enough already.

Over the years Janice could have accepted many other opportunities, where she surely would have also excelled. Some people urged her to "leave Ginni's shadow," as they put it. But Janice didn't see it that way. "I'm in her light," was how she replied.

When I was appointed CEO, Janice graciously delayed her retirement by a year as I settled into my expansive new role. She would have stayed on permanently if I needed her; she told me that, and so I never asked. Janice was a gift to me. Not asking her to reprise her role was my final gift to her.

Another crucial relationship has been with my assistant for more than twenty years, Aimee Burns. I trusted Aimee not just to keep confidences but to make decisions about one of my most precious assets—my time. A strong assistant like Aimee must understand context to decide on the fly how to prioritize the urgent from the important, and Aimee has impeccable judgment. Her intuition also sets her apart, as does her calm demeanor. Aimee dedicated endless hours to me and IBM, while also raising three wonderful daughters, including twins. I'm forever thankful for her blend of professionalism and grace.

I had so much more than an assistant, a "Robin," and a spouse—I had Aimee, Janice, and Mark. Their steadfast support allowed me to work with a clearer head and right-sized confidence.

Forging Bonds

I think back to my early years when I realized the value of networks—supportive communities that we nurture through genuine interest in people and by sharing what we know. Networks are built over time by what we give others. In time, they also give back. These are not just relationships, but relevant relationships. My network expanded to include leaders in business, academia, government, media, and entertainment, all around the world.

It's hard to articulate the invaluable perspectives I received from these people, and it's amazing how many times people appeared with advice or support at exactly the right moments. I've always tried to do the same for others.

I especially think about the bonds I formed with other women CEOs. Each has great strengths I learned from. GM's Mary Barra is authentic to her core. PepsiCo's former CEO Indra Nooyi stands in her convictions. DuPont's former CEO Ellen Kullman has great resilience. Lockheed Martin's former CEO Marillyn Hewson is purpose driven. Xerox's former chief Ursula Burns impacts the larger community. The list goes on. It's so important for women to support other women, and I came to trust and admire these colleagues. We remain friends even as our titles change, which speaks to the genuine nature of our connection. It was never transactional.

If relationships with relevance fuel resilience by offering new perspectives and support, the broader and more diverse the array the better. For years, I found that the best way to establish and maintain relationships is through respect. Every time I embarked on a new endeavor or job, I tried to begin by showing respect to the people I'd be working with. Going around the room citing people's qualities, as I did with the managing directors, became a ritual I stuck with for years, in various forms.

During my years as CEO, I spent one-on-one time with each director on the board to get advice and counsel. Boards represent the shareholders, and a wise person told me that when it came to a CEO's relationship with a company's board, trust is built by the drop and withdrawn in buckets. As I said, I was lucky to have such a distinguished, experienced, and wise board.

Endless small gestures also reinforced my relationships over time. For example, on my first day as CEO, as you may recall, I sent each of IBM's senior vice presidents a handwritten letter. Another time, I sent a letter to the eighty-five-year-old mother of a retiring colleague, describing her son's many career accomplishments; I knew he and his mother were close, and a letter like that would mean more to him than any other gift. At company events, when hundreds and hundreds of IBMers stood in line to shake the hand of their CEO, I'd stand there for hours, too, asking each person what they did for us and thanking them. I insisted on staying until every hand was clasped. I also remember privately meeting with families of our employees who had been aboard Malaysia Airlines 370 when the passenger plane disappeared over the Indian Ocean in 2014. What we do when no one is watching is sometimes the most significant thing we can do.

Strong professional relationships are steeped in respect, empathy, and authenticity. And when people feel seen and appreciated, they remember, and they will use their most precious asset, time, to share their views and perspectives with you.

I can't write about relationships without a few thoughts about loyalty.

Our family situation growing up bred a sense of loyalty among my siblings and me. We've wondered if our penchant for loyalty is a reason why we've each spent the majority of our careers at a single employer. It's hard to walk away from relationships we've built with organizations and with people. My own resilience at IBM was buttressed by the dedication of my direct team, and thousands who played vital, non-client-facing roles, from executive communications to finance to administrative support. When we're loyal, we stick. We also work differently. "I don't want to let you down" is how I feel about my siblings as well as the people I work with. It's a refrain people often say to me.

Loyalty, however, can also blind us to difficult realities, and again waste our energy. There were times I waited too long to replace people who weren't effective in their jobs because of my commitment to give them the benefit of the doubt or yet another chance. I had to grapple with the question, "What do we owe our professional relationships?" My answer, and my learning, is to remind myself that a mission is bigger than any one person—and a leader's loyalty is to the mission.

My final thoughts on relationships are about the one we have with ourselves.

By now you surely know that working hard and working a lot of hours has always been my default and my choice. I enjoy it and always have. But it's also true that I underestimated the importance of time away from work to build resilience. Consciously carving it out was something I learned to do over time. As I've written, there was a period in the nineties when I worked so much that I wasn't eating well or exercising. I finally realized that to have the energy to do all that I wanted to do I had to be healthier. It took a lot of discipline, but I started exercising. At first I read emails while cycling on weekend mornings—that was time I could control. Over the years exercise became a daily ritual, and with that my energy as well as my confidence both spiked.

Taking time away from work helps us be our best selves. Current generations seem much more in touch with this philosophy than I was. The pandemic also prompted a lot of people to rethink how much time and energy they dedicate to their jobs. The only person who can create any type of balance for you, is you. Most companies and managers will take whatever you are willing to give. So have confidence and conviction that setting boundaries is necessary. The people and processes around us adapt to our choices, as long as we continue to bring value to our jobs.

The time we put into relationships with ourselves and others is ultimately about quality, not quantity. I think that how we show up, not how often, matters most.

Responding to Challenge

When it comes to handling setbacks, I was raised not to see myself as a victim of others' actions, and to take responsibility for my own, as uncomfortable as that might be. Baba, Grandma Mary, and my mother all lost their husbands, each for different reasons. Their losses could have translated to an unhappy home life, but they carried on with decency. I grew up seeing them not as victims of tragedy, but as survivors who controlled their own fate. Their attitude and subsequent actions led me to believe that I could choose how I reacted to life's challenges, large or small. My golden rule has long been, "There's always a way forward, so put all your energy into that. Tomorrow can always be better than today."

Attitude is about the choices we make when faced with chaos, conflict, setbacks, and critics.

So much in my working life is beyond my control, so I try to control what I can. Prepare for a meeting, check. Rehearse the presentation, check. My appearance is another variable I can control. I'm most confident dressing like me, not dressing to fit in. Over time I found my own definition of professional attire, and my clothes got more stylish and colorful. Bright blues, yellows, greens, and pinks. People commented that I was so fashionable, but fashion wasn't my intent. I just wanted to feel myself, and feeling myself made me confident so I could focus on all the other variables I could control! Same for my hair. I've worn thin headbands for as long as anyone can remember. The headband has gone in and out of style for years, but I stick with it because it's the easiest way to keep my hair out of my eyes. Feeling comfortable in my body helped me function amid chaos.

When it came to conflict, I opted to follow my colleague Bridget's example and run to it.

Conflict sticks with us if we let it brew, hovering in our minds and sapping precious energy as we inevitably revisit a situation over and over. If, instead, we choose to see conflict as an opportunity to improve a situation, we'll be better equipped to face it and resolve it. Running toward conflict takes courage and often humility, but it's more productive.

I have faced conflicts that were interpersonal and situational. For example, IBM ran toward the international conflict over data security and privacy. Rather than hide from the global debate and try to keep our name out of it, we openly declared our privacy policies, and I publicly argued for better regulations, as I've written.

Any global tech company must address various conflicts between countries, especially around issues of national security and ownership. IBM's history goes back further than most. We were the first truly international tech company, with a presence in dozens of countries years and even decades before Google, Microsoft, Alibaba, Tencent, and others existed or became global brands. The issues we have faced on the international stage have only gotten more complex. As the ninth CEO of IBM, my approach was to face conflict on the international stage head on. Sitting down with presidents of many countries was about clearly communicating the issue at hand as we saw it, including issues of nationalism and protectionism. I always framed the conflict in terms of the other's agenda, and instead of just lamenting the issues between our countries, we usually made progress.

While I faced conflict directly, it also helped to compartmentalize.

IBM is a huge company, so naturally there were times when conflicts in the form of crisis rained down on us, and on me, all at once. In the life of any leader, a crisis and everyday to-dos are often separated by mere minutes. Over time I learned how to move through vastly different topics and conversations, not letting emotions or information from one meeting spill into the next, and to be equally present for everyone. My tactic is simple: I compartmentalize. Some of the best leaders I know do this. You'd never guess sitting across from them that, for example, the government had just denied permission for a large acquisition, or a product launch risked delay. My approach has been to take one crisis at a time, be clear on a plan forward, then put it in a mental box and focus on the next issue—until it's time to revisit the crisis.

I've also reminded myself that, as a leader, my reactions to setbacks cascade to others.

Prior to becoming CEO, I distinctly remember being in Beijing, China, fuming in my hotel room. At the time I ran a business that needed to acquire a certain company. My team and I put our hearts and souls into rallying support for the purchase, but it wasn't approved by the committee that decides how to allocate capital across the enterprise. To say I was upset was an understatement. I spent a good hour steeped in anger, debating how to relay the bad news to my team. I could bemoan the company's priorities and blame the committee for making a decision that would cause us to miss our performance goals. Or I could calm down. Tell the team I was frustrated. Explain why the decision was made. Then express gratitude for their work and put all the focus on finding an alternate way forward. I let the emotion drain out of me and I chose the latter.

Before I became CEO, most setbacks I experienced occurred in the confines of IBM. But leading the public company put setbacks in the public domain, and squarely on my shoulders.

I remember the day after we announced that IBM was leaving the financial roadmap, in October 2014. I was scheduled to speak in front of two hundred CEOs in Boston, part of a program for Boston College's Carroll School of Management. My keynote was planned for months. The morning of the speech IBM's stock dropped and the company was a hot topic in the business press. I could hear a cacophony of hushed chatter as I walked across the stage to the podium. I was acutely aware of the elephant in the room, so I addressed the events of the past twenty-four hours head on. I can't recall exactly what I said, but I owned the news, and I sensed a lot of relief and empathy in the audience. We had a good session—the elephant had exited the building.

I tried to accept setbacks with grace and move on. Even when they were splashed across the day's top headlines. Sometimes critiques were warranted and I read them with an intent to learn. But sometimes the coverage felt exaggerated and magnified.

Once, another woman CEO reached out to me in frustration.

"Do you notice that when one of our companies has a struggle, some media calls us out by name?" she asked, somewhat rhetorically. "And yet when a male CEO's company is having trouble, it's often the company's issue, not the CEO's." This was a bit of a generalization, but I understood her point: at times failure is more personalized for women.

A few years ago, I was asked to speak to a class of MBA students about leading through crisis. The professor began the session by asking me what it takes to be in the hot seat for the long run.

"You had a really hard tenure as CEO," he said. "The world was not always kind to you." I was taken aback because I never thought "the world" was not kind. There was much more to IBM's transformation story than what was expressed in some headlines.

Society wants leaders to be authentic and to own mistakes, and yet people can be quick to punish imperfection and pounce with opinions, sometimes with incomplete, little, or unvalidated information. Ignoring critics isn't the answer. I can step back and ask myself if critics have legitimate points, and what if anything we might glean from their perspective. I still do this. But I also try not to absorb criticism too emotionally, even when it's public, personal, false, and magnified for affect. Critics may inform me, but they don't define me.

Conviction is also a foundation of attitude and resilience. During IBM's transformation, I always believed that we were taking the right and very difficult actions to ensure that the institution of IBM endured for decades.

This helped propel my confidence and optimism when IBM's stock price didn't yet reflect our true value. I knew so much inside the company had to change, as I've written. And every day I saw progress that my colleagues were working so hard to achieve. So many milestones never made the news—becoming agile isn't the sexiest headline—but I knew the truth: we were building a better company. So, we needed to honor those milestones. Transformations of all kinds need to be celebrated, not just endured.

When my nephew was about ten years old, he turned to me and asked me, "Auntie, does it bother you when people are mean to you or IBM on television?" I looked at him and said, "We're doing what must be done."

During the years transforming IBM, it was vital that our global workforce saw a CEO with calm conviction and confidence in the future, as well as concrete plans. I knew that how I comported myself affected how thousands felt and behaved—especially when others doubted us. With so much at stake, I called upon my own resilience, as well as my life's work, to rise to the challenges.

When I retired from IBM, a client shared a quote that she said reminded her of me.

Fate whispers to the warrior, "You cannot withstand the storm."

The warrior whispers back, "I am the storm."

PART THREE

The Power of Us

Changing Our World

So many of us hunger to make a meaningful difference in society, but how do we create positive change in a world where so many problems seem unsolvable? One way is by looking at big problems as big systems to be transformed.

Scaling good power is the ambition of part III, and the lessons and insights I share come from my multi-decade journey championing what I later came to call the SkillsFirst hiring and training movement. It's a story that parallels my life, but mainly my years leading IBM, when work to reskill the company revealed a truth to help improve our world: societies that value lifelong learning and skills over just degrees open the workforce to millions of underrepresented people. This is a huge mindset shift for individuals, businesses, educators, and governments.

How do we make systemic change? Many levers must be pulled. Multiple needs must be met. The desire for change must become a movement. Good power at scale can help build belief in a movement; cocreate new solutions; let go of what's wrong; and modernize what's right.

SkillsFirst is my mission, but you have your own. I hope my efforts trying to create positive change in the world inform yours, because we can't make real progress without "the power of us."

11

Envisioning a Better Future for More People

Connecting the dots of history can help us see the future.

Today, when I think about what's possible for our world, I travel back in time and see my mom and how my journey from "me to we to us" unfolded from my youth.

My mother has always been smart—she just never had any education past high school. She needed the chance to learn and apply herself to get a good-paying job and rebuild our lives. When she started attending night classes at the local community college to learn computers, she struggled being in a learning environment; it had been almost twenty years since she sat in a classroom! But she got with it, and eventually got a better job in a small office that paid more money. I remember her buying new outfits so she could dress more professionally, and her coming home and telling us about the things she did and the people she met. Her eyes got wide and she might smile recalling something funny someone said that day. It was like my mom discovered a whole new world existed. Work became more than a chore and a paycheck. It gave her life added dimension and meaning—it gave her dignity. As her daughter, I witnessed how just a few new computer and bookkeeping skills boosted her self-confidence and gave our family more stability, and how those skills eventually led her to a career leading administration for the sleep clinic in a major hospital.

I also see myself going off to college. If I hadn't studied like crazy in high school, and if Northwestern University didn't have a policy of admitting applicants first on academics, not on our ability to pay, I never would have gotten in. Northwestern's duty to equity—admit who is qualified and then figure out tuition—gave me access to new people and new opportunities. I got some money from the school, and I qualified for government loans designed for students like me. If General Motors didn't have a program that gave scholarships and internships to diverse students at Northwestern and other top schools, I likely would have graduated with an overwhelming amount of debt, never worked for GM, and not found my way to IBM and the incredible career I had. One university and one company's beliefs that more people should be able to access skills and a good education and good employment jump-started my journey. When one door opens, more doors open.

Reflecting back on my roots revealed seeds of truth that informed my life. By the time I began working I understood that lack of access, not aptitude, was a barrier to a better life for a lot of people. I also realized that education doesn't have to stop once we leave formal school. I recall the hours I stayed past quitting time at GM to teach myself about software, or the time I went to a client's office on a Sunday with Mark and his TV and hot dogs in tow, or when I showed up at a mainframe installation before the field engineers to study the manuals. Some might roll their eyes and say I worked too hard. But I didn't want to look stupid in front of people. And given I was often the only woman in the room, skills and preparation were my shield and confidence. Plus, I just liked learning.

It was my boss Pat O'Brien who taught me that helping others learn was part of a leader's job. I had education plans for everyone who reported to me, and I was personally involved in their training. I enjoyed teaching. Just like I did with my sisters at our kitchen table, it was my way of caring. I was also accountable for equity of people's pay and promotions. Growing my career at IBM, I could see how skills and equity were inextricably linked. I also saw the value of apprenticing as a consultant to learn new business skills for which I didn't have a formal degree. I internalized the idea of just how vital ongoing learning is, for people and for organizations.

By the time I became CEO, my beliefs about the importance of access and the value of being a consummate learner were firmly set. Their influence permeated those years, which turned out to be a good thing. The world of technology was changing at a dramatic pace not seen before, and the nature of work was evolving, too, creating jobs that demanded new skills. At the same time, economic inequality was widening. The digital divide was in desperate need of bridges—so was our ever more polarized world.

Paving a New Pathway

I was frustrated.

It was 2012, my first year as CEO, and IBM was having trouble finding qualified job candidates to fill hundreds of open technology and cybersecurity positions, despite the nation's high unemployment rate. This was not just our problem but an industry problem and even a national security problem. Lack of cybersecurity expertise is a threat to companies and countries. Building cybersecurity and tech talent was a mission bigger than one business.

I remember asking myself, *Why was there such a mismatch between the demand for tech talent and the supply?*

About the same time IBM was looking for tech talent, a ninth-grade student in a lower-income community in Brooklyn, New York, hacked into his high school's computer for fun, and got caught. His principal, a wise man named Rashid Davis, remembers sitting in his office looking at the bright, brash student in front of him. Gabriel Rosa was the oldest of five kids. His father had emigrated from the Dominican Republic when Gabriel was young. Rashid had some choices. He could either expel the young man, who had an obvious penchant for technology, let him off the hook and go back to class, or pause and consider an alternative. After a few stern words, Rashid told a very relieved Gabriel he wasn't going to suspend him.

"We need to channel your energy or you're going to find yourself in trouble," Rashid said. "If you can stay in school and build on this talent, it will be a different world for you." Rashid assured Gabriel that if he hunkered down for the next six years, he could graduate not just with a high school diploma but also an associate degree, at no cost to Gabriel or his family.

Gabriel joined P-TECH, that first-of-its-kind six-year program that IBM designed and helped found. P-TECH operated inside Gabriel's existing high school. Attending P-TECH by dual-enrolling in high school and community college was likely his best pathway to debt-free higher education— and a good job if he graduated. With guidance from Rashid, Gabriel was soon learning skills in programming and mobile app development.

Why was Rashid so confident this was the right course for Gabriel? Rashid was P-TECH's brave pioneer principal, the role model and lead voice within the educational community on the endless possibilities the P-TECH model unlocks.

I was introduced to P-TECH, Rashid, and that Brooklyn school by IBM's leader of corporate social responsibility, Stanley Litow, a dedicated and determined man who envisioned and then spearheaded the unique program, which, as I mentioned, mixed high school and community college courses in STEM fields and paired classwork with work experience through paid company internships. Stan explained to me that too many community colleges are failing students. Fewer than 40 percent of enrollees complete a certificate or even graduate within six years; the percentage is significantly worse for lower-income students and people of color. In addition to low completion rates, many community colleges are also underfunded, and their enrollment is declining. And too often the skills students do get aren't what the job market is looking for. But a school like P-TECH focused on building employable skills.

As IBM began employing P-TECH students, it was inspiring to have them fill some of our talent needs, while simultaneously giving young people access to quality education, marketable skills, and better jobs. P-TECH was a win-win at the intersection of what's good for a company and good for a community, and the concept was beginning to garner interest from some cities and states.

But wasn't there an even bigger win? To steward good tech, it was our duty as a global company to prepare people around the world to thrive in this new era of technology. I asked myself, *Are we proving a new way to tap into diverse pools of talent? Is our experience with P-TECH showing us that many good jobs can be filled by people without four-year degrees? What if P-TECH could have a positive impact beyond IBM's offices in New York, and even beyond our own business? Beyond the United States?* We had to push forward and test our limits. So I committed to making P-TECH more than a one-off corporate social responsibility (CSR) initiative. It became a world-wide business imperative as we committed to help P-TECH scale to more states and countries. Supporting P-TECH became a responsibility of IBM's line business units, in addition to HR. IBMers in cities around the world gladly spoke to P-TECH classes and e-mentored students.

In 2013, during President Barack Obama's State of the Union Address, he described P-TECH while the world listened. "We need to give every American student opportunities like this," he said, challenging Americans to "redesign high schools so they better equip graduates for the demands of a high-tech economy . . ." It was great PR! The next morning, more governors started calling IBM to find out more.

I vividly remember when the president visited the school to see it for himself. We were walking down hallways lined with posters of students' bright smiling faces, with captions like "college and career ready."

"Where's the computer lab?" he asked me. I explained to the president that P-TECH first taught students critical skills like problem-solving and how to work in teams. Hard skills like programming were the least of the problems; many of those could also be taught later by employers.

In each location a P-TECH school opened, other companies got involved by mentoring and helping the high school and community college identify skills and curriculum students needed to learn to be employable. Those companies also provided paid internships, and a chance to get a full-time job. Students weren't guaranteed employment, but P-TECH graduates were prioritized when recruiting. Eventually, the P-TECH model opened in over three hundred schools in twenty-seven countries, including more than two hundred in sixteen US states. The program now has a total of two hundred college partners and six hundred business partners, and so far has produced a pipeline of more than 150,000 students.

In 2014, Gabriel Rosa landed a paid internship at IBM during his junior year, and in June 2015, he graduated with a diploma, an associate degree, and a full-time position at IBM. He was promoted many times over and became an IBM software developer.

The talent search that led IBM to recruit from P-TECH revealed to me how innovative forms of education can bring more people into the workforce. The vast majority of P-TECH students earned at least an associate degree, and many go on to higher education. Alyssa Sandy was thirteen when her mother moved their family to Brooklyn so she could attend P-TECH, where she learned that she loved writing code and was quite good at it. After graduating, Alyssa attended East Carolina University on an athletic scholarship, where she wanted to combine her love of coding and design, earning a bachelor's in university studies with a visual design concentration. She then earned a master's certification in website development, and in 2022 she attended Elon University to obtain a master's degree in interactive media. Another former P-TECH student is on track to be the program's first graduate to earn a PhD. ShuDon Brown was born in Brooklyn, graduated P-TECH in four years, got her bachelor's in business analytics from William Peace University, then earned a master's while working for IBM. In 2022, ShuDon was pursuing her doctorate in leadership studies at North Carolina Agricultural and Technical State University while still full-time at IBM as a robotic process automation leader.

P-TECH is proof that zip code or postal code do not determine someone's aptitude, and that public-private partnerships between governments and business can often solve problems better and faster than either entity alone.

Jobs are the silver bullet that makes P-TECH so successful. To paraphrase what Shimon Peres told me, jobs are currency, and at P-TECH the potential of paid internships and employment for students keeps administrators and teachers incentivized to teach marketable skills. The prospect of a good job also motivates students to study subjects they might otherwise have overlooked, and it also motivates parents to stay engaged. Likely employment is an incentive to graduate, and one reason that P-TECH's completion rate of associate degrees is 400 percent higher than the on-time national community college graduation rate in lower-income communities in five states— New York, Colorado, Texas, Connecticut, and Maryland. A virtuous circle.

But more than anything, P-TECH opened my eyes to the fact that society as a whole—and by that I meant educators, businesses, and governments— wasn't preparing enough people for the digital era.

The power of us was beginning to unfold.

Paving a Second Pathway

It was 2011, and Tony Byrd wasn't in college and didn't have a job. At eighteen, he'd graduated high school and spent his days playing pick-up basketball and lounging around his house. He and his two older sisters had been raised by their mother, Jennifer, who had supported their family by working her way up from a cashier to a manager at an IBM cafeteria in Raleigh, North Carolina.

One afternoon, she called Tony from work.

"It's time you did something," she told her son.

Less than a week later, Tony had a job at the coffee shop on IBM's corporate campus. He was a hard worker and most enjoyed chatting with his customers, the IBM employees who flowed in and out for their daily drinks. He knew their names and their favorite sports teams, and he often asked people what they were working on. He imagined it would be nice to work for IBM, somewhere other than the coffee shop.

His customers got to know Tony, too. After his daughter and son were born in 2014, Tony had tried to take a few community college classes in computer science in the hopes of getting a higher-paying job to support his family. But he didn't have time for school, family obligations, and a full-time job.

One day in 2017, one of his favorite customers told Tony she thought he'd be perfect for a new apprenticeship program IBM was launching. She urged him to apply for one of seven full-time spots.

"You'll be paid to learn," she said. He'd be trained as a software engineer through a mix of on-the-job experience, structured coursework, soft-skills training, and coaching. It could qualify him for a higher-paying entry-level job in tech and put him on an upwardly mobile career path. Eager but nervous, Tony applied but wasn't accepted. His customers believed in him, though, and encouraged him to try again, so Tony stayed at the coffee shop, waiting to apply again a year later.

The age-old method of teaching people skills of a trade via apprenticing is perhaps the single greatest talent opportunity we've encountered in our economy in a long while—and we're squandering it in the United States, stuck in stereotypes. Modern apprenticeships have evolved far beyond plumbing and construction into full-time, paid positions in tech, health care, finance, and other fields through a mix of courses, hands-on experience, and mentoring.

European countries have benefited from apprenticeships for decades; for many countries vocational training paired with apprenticeships is a main path into the workforce. The United Kingdom has fourteen times more apprenticeship programs than the United States on a per capita basis. Germany has nineteen times more. In fact, several great IBM leaders were a product of these systems. Our next-door neighbor, Canada, has caught on with eleven times more. Many Swiss CEOs began careers as apprentices, and Swiss businesses respect it as a legitimate, honorable pathway.

"In Switzerland, apprenticeships don't define you; they prepare you for life," says Suzi LeVine, the former US ambassador to Switzerland and

Liechtenstein, and a vocal leader of the apprenticeship movement in the United States. Here, apprenticeships still carry stigma. The country lacks the private sector's will and the public infrastructures to fuel wide adoption.

I'd apprenticed many times during my career, and I knew the value.

In the mid-2010s, IBM decided to expand our apprenticeships to further widen our talent pipeline and diversify our workforce. We quickly discovered just how far the United States lags behind other countries. Apprenticeship models already registered with the US Department of Labor (DOL) didn't reflect contemporary tech skills and jobs. In fact, there were so few registered tech apprenticeships that we had to create our own, starting with software engineers and mainframe developers. We worked closely with the DOL for a long time to ensure each program met high standards and could be credentialed. We didn't keep them proprietary but made them public so other companies could use them, even our competitors.

The first new cohort of our modernized apprentice program started in 2017 and got rave reviews from managers. The second cohort formed in 2018 and was a group of thirteen people that included mid-career professionals, a former FBI agent, a nurse, and Tony Byrd, who bid goodbye to the coffee shop to become an apprentice as a software engineer. He was given a laptop and assigned a manager as well as a mentor. Tony took more than two hundred hours of coursework in person and online and completed two thousand hours working with project teams, shadowing engineers, and programming. He got experience writing and in collaborative teamwork and adopted other soft skills that built on his already inviting communication style. By 2019, mastery of twenty-eight competencies as well as his coding skills earned Tony a certificate in software engineering from the US Department of Labor. He networked with people he'd come to know through the coffee shop and on the job, and he landed a full-time role at IBM in customer service, helping clients who were building APIs, or interfaces, to IBM's cloud platform. One of Tony's managers is the woman who first encouraged him to apply to the apprenticeship program.

Within a few years IBM had created modern professional apprenticeships for twenty-four different roles. By 2022, programs in sixteen states had produced a talent pipeline of more than five hundred individuals, 90 percent of whom became our full-time employees. The group included people with and without college degrees, ranging from teenagers to grandparents with all types of previous job experience. Apprenticeships truly were the ultimate "learn-and-earn" vehicle.

IBM had looked at something familiar in a fresh way. A few other companies were looking, too.

Aon, a global professional-services firm, was among the first large corporations to embrace professional apprenticeships. In 2017, the company built a regional network of employers in its US headquarters city of Chicago and partnered with City Colleges of Chicago to create two-year apprenticeship programs. The apprentice roles in HR, IT, finance, and the insurance business provide full-time salaries, benefits, on-the-job training, free college tuition, and guaranteed job offers after completing the program. By 2021, the Chicago Apprenticeship Network had grown to fifty-seven employers and over one thousand apprentices. That same year, the company committed an additional $30 million to expand the program to six new cities, from New York to San Francisco. Aon's retention rate for its apprentices continues to increase each year, and is greater than the retention rate for its entry-level employees.

Greg Case, the CEO of Aon, is as passionate about new pathways and new pools of talent as I am. We both see the opportunity to impact society. "The question is not if apprenticeships work, we know they do," Greg has told me. "The question before us is how we can bring them to scale."

For apprenticeships to gain traction, business leaders must drop our competitive defenses and adopt a spirit of co-opetition, working together to cocreate models for an array of common occupations. Company-specific programs prevent apprenticeships from scaling, as too many businesses see them as a proprietary advantage rather than a way to raise all boats. Governments do invest to incent the public sector to use apprenticeships, but shockingly, the federal budget for apprenticeships is a paltry $200 million, which includes grants and oversight. Once governments and more businesses see apprenticeships through the lens of status, not stigma, they'll go to extraordinary ends to capture their value.

When I met Tony again in 2022, he also told me about his children, Julianna and Anthony Jr., who were seven and eight. He was a role model for them, and his plan was to keep growing his career, maybe manage several teams one day, or even go back to school.

"Did you ever feel funny not having a college degree?" I asked him.

"I know I don't need school to be successful here," he told me. "It was good to get that reassurance that not everybody here has been to college, but if I do want to go back to school, I can go forward with it and know that I have support."

Paving a Third Pathway

Around the time my sister, Annette, was contemplating resuming her career and going back to work at Accenture after several years caring for her family, she and I were having one of our catch-up conversations. I listened to Annette muse about how her industry had changed since she'd stepped away, and I listened to her wonder if her skills were still current. At first I laughed. Annette is so talented. She has an engineering degree and an MBA, and she had built some of the most advanced digital solutions in the world. What on earth was she worried about?

Shortly after our chat, I was doing a routine review of IBM's engineering talent to see if we were meeting diversity goals, which included increasing and promoting women and other underrepresented groups across all our technical roles. Because I'd been talking with Annette, I asked my colleagues to find out how many of our female engineers had left IBM for personal reasons but not returned, and why. The results surprised me. It turned out that many had left to care for family but didn't return because they didn't have updated skills, and/or they lacked confidence. So often women are more critical of their own abilities than anyone else's, and I remember being sad at how easy it was for bright, accomplished people to assume they couldn't catch up to a world they feared had passed them by—when all they needed was a skills refresher, and a little boost of confidence.

In 2016, IBM began experimenting with a new program to help bring women back into the company. We called the three-month tech reentry program *returnships*, and we invited people who had left IBM for periods as long as ten years to come back and take some educational courses as well as begin working with a team. Most of the participants were women, because women are most likely to leave the workplace to care for children and aging parents. The first program paired eight returning employees with experts in a given technology, as well as a mentor. People could stay one day, or three months, whatever it took to feel confident to return to work.

We quickly learned that, more than tech skills, people coming back needed to learn new ways of working, too, like design thinking and agile. So we tailored each returnship to address a variety of areas through classes, live projects, and opportunities to earn digital credentials. The returnship was paid, but it did not guarantee a job. It also was a chance for people to renew internal networks, as well as rebuild that self-confidence. Participants could interview for new roles and, if hired, come back full-time, or with flexible schedules. In 2022 alone, about 150 people had participated in IBM's returnships in eleven countries, with a majority being hired by IBM full-time. I was so happy. What a victory, getting women with technical talent back in the game.

IBM's journey with P-TECH, apprenticeships, and returnships throughout the decade heightened my belief in the value of building new pathways to good jobs, and my belief in experiential learning. We absorb so much by doing. It also reinforced for me and my colleagues that a traditional degree isn't required to excel and succeed at a good, upwardly mobile job. Building and scaling more pathways energized me because they're in service of a company and in service of underserved populations, and thus society. They also offer real solutions to the real problems of unequal access to education and employment and widening economic divides.

Tapping Everyone's Potential

Stories of people like Gabriel, Tony, and even my sister Annette tell a larger story of systemic problems to be solved.

Since the late 1970s, median earnings in the United States have stagnated relative to the rise of worker productivity, which was up 66 percent. While average compensation has generally kept pace, the median compensation—income for the majority of workers—is only up 9 percent. This gap between productivity and earnings is often referred to as "the great divergence," according to an MIT study, *The Work of the Future: Building Better Jobs in the Age of Intelligent Machines.*

For me, this data confirms why so many people can't see a better future for themselves. They feel left out of economic prosperity because they have been.

In the United States, unequal distribution of income can in part be explained by the polarization of jobs. As the percentage of low- and high-paying jobs in the workforce have each increased, the percentage of medium-paying jobs, those in the middle, have decreased. In other words, middle-income jobs that for decades after World War II allowed millions of people to join the middle class have been hollowed out. They simply don't exist anymore, having disappeared over the course of my lifetime. Economist and the MIT study's coauthor, David Autor, calls the thinning middle between high- and low-paying jobs the barbell effect.

There's a definitive connection to education.

The average rise in compensation—all those high-paying jobs at one end of the barbell—is largely the result of sharp increases in pay for people with college or higher education. Meanwhile, people with some or no college have seen no to modest income growth. In essence, the reduction of those middle-income jobs has pushed non-degreed workers to lower-skilled and lower-paying jobs, with little opportunity for advancement. All the higher-paying jobs go to people with higher education. This widening earnings gap between people with and without four-year degrees has been a major driver of overall earnings inequality, and it's pronounced among Hispanics and Blacks.

Looking at the data, it's tempting to think that obtaining a college degree is the only key to higher pay and better livelihoods for more people. Not so. While college is the right route for many, it's definitely not the sole, or even the most effective, solution to help bridge income inequality for everyone.

First, there isn't time. Approximately 62 percent of people over age twenty-five in the United States don't have a bachelor's degree or higher, according to the Census Bureau's Current Population Survey. So many people need better jobs now, and technology is changing so fast, that neither they nor businesses nor economies can afford to wait for millions of people to go to college.

What's more, college degrees aren't even necessary to succeed at many higher-paying jobs available today. And yet for more than a decade, employers have been adding college degrees as a minimum requirement for jobs that once didn't require them, yet nothing about many of the jobs had materially changed! This trend is known as overcredentialing, or degree inflation, and it happened because we employers use a degree either as a proxy for ability, or as a quick way to automatically filter thousands of résumés. The side effect of overcredentialing is a false barrier into the workforce for millions.

For societies and economies around the world to meet their full potential, more people need better jobs. By more people, I mean populations that face roadblocks like degree inflation to accessing gainful employment, particularly the more than 60 percent in the United States and many other developed countries who don't have four-year college degrees. It includes young people who need a first job, and mid-career workers lacking skills for the future. By better jobs, I mean those that pay well enough to sustain a family, and are upwardly mobile, meaning they have the potential for rising pay over time.

Not hourly-wage jobs typically associated with blue collar work, and not *only* the higher-salaried professional roles associated with white collar workers on one end of Autor's barbell. Better jobs are occupations that have historically been called middle-skills jobs—supervisory, administrative, sales—as well as the category of tech jobs that arose in the digital era, which I'd coined as new collar jobs. Most of today's middle-skill jobs require some expertise, and thus hard- and soft-skills training beyond a traditional high school education, but not a four-year college degree to be successful.

Examples across industries include data scientists, cyber analysts, operating room technicians, medical assistants, call center representatives, sales representatives, machinists, mechanics, construction, and other trades.

As David Autor told me, "The message should not be 'college for all.'"

Alternate career paths like P-TECH, apprenticeships, and returnships are meaningful pathways to good jobs. They're already making a difference in many lives. But even with P-TECH's pipeline of 150,000, a step change in scale is needed to improve millions of people's financial circumstances around the world. The more I learned, the more I came to see that there was something those pathways had in common that could be the seeds of a systemic solution: none of these pathways require a four-year degree to launch someone into a good job.

Having a global impact on millions and millions of people demanded more than one-off programs. Embracing talent without traditional degrees had to become a widespread mindset and a massive cultural shift. I felt strongly that IBM, as one of the world's largest technology corporations, had a global responsibility to adopt this mindset because, as I've written, preparing people for the digital jobs being created is to steward good tech. The breadth of doing so was becoming clearer. We were not just creating more jobs. We were addressing a complex societal challenge—lack of access to good jobs—which required assessing, challenging, and changing many interconnected and interrelated participants and processes. This is systems thinking at its finest. I remember thinking, *This is what I've been trained to do my whole life.*

12

Thinking Systemically

"The four-year college degree is increasingly dividing America."

This is among the conclusions of a book I was introduced to by Bob Bradway, the CEO of Amgen. The book, *Deaths of Despair and the Future of Capitalism*, doesn't dismiss higher education as a valuable pathway for many people, but it recognizes that it shouldn't be the only alternative.

The book's authors, Princeton University professors Anne Case and Angus Deaton, explore the rising death rate for middle-aged white people in America. They label the three main causes—suicides, drug overdoses, and alcoholic liver disease—as "deaths of despair."

That so many people in America are dying from causes related to the opioid epidemic is, tragically, no longer a shock. What surprised me is the connection of these deaths to education levels. The authors found that almost all who die from deaths of despair do not have a four-year degree. Mortality rates have long been higher for people with less education, as the authors write. What's notable is that the death rate among white Americans without a college degree is rising, as are other ills.

The authors write that the four-year degree divides us not only in death but also in quality of life. "Those without a degree are seeing increases in their levels of pain, ill health, and serious mental distress, and declines in their ability to work and to socialize. The gap is also widening in earnings, in family stability, and in community."

Data can reveal realities we can't see. But when we do see them, they're hard to ignore.

Embracing an Alternate Reality

Back in the mid-2010s, I was reviewing one of our business units, and one of the team's challenges was the low supply of cybersecurity and tech talent. It still took far too long to fill job openings, and managers weren't always thrilled with all the candidates.

Coincidentally, my next meeting was a review of our P-TECH program. Progress on the number of new schools and student graduation rates looked good. "How many P-TECH students have we hired in the business unit I just reviewed?" I asked my colleagues. The room got quiet before I got the answer.

"Three." How could that be? With a little digging I found out why. Many of the roles the business unit couldn't fill required four-year degrees, which automatically eliminated P-TECH students with associate degrees from even getting an interview.

Dots connected. Requiring a four-year degree was inhibiting our ability to access new pools of talent at scale, and in turn it was inhibiting that talent from accessing us. If we continued to hire non-degreed employees in such small numbers, they'd be viewed as the exception, or an experiment, versus a population we valued and employed as the normal course of business.

The hard work began as we started reviewing job postings and asking ourselves if we described positions in a way that reached the widest group of qualified applicants, or if our job descriptions filtered out potential candidates. Why did we insist on a minimum number of years of experience? Did we always require a bachelor's degree because it was necessary, or did we do so out of habit? Our recruiters scrutinized job requisitions and rewrote many to articulate specific skills the job required. The process was unexpectedly tedious. It was so much easier to just ask for academic qualifications and assume the skills were part of the package!

The skills-based revision exercise was effective, so we expanded it to other roles. Soon we were interviewing and recruiting more people who'd never gone to or finished a traditional college.

Our head of HR became such a fan of skills-based hiring that she called for bachelor's degrees to be removed from all company job postings unless there was a compelling reason for it to stay. We convened a special team to pick which entry-level roles could be modified, and we revised more job requisitions to emphasize critical knowledge, expertise, and abilities. The teams also identified soft skills we wanted new hires to have, like a growth mindset and creativity. We also removed unconsciously biased language that might inhibit people from applying.

Some colleagues were skeptical as we scaled this approach. IBM had always hired employees with college and university degrees, not to mention a lot of PhDs. They worried that de-emphasizing degrees might lower performance standards and work quality.

To address this concern and confirm that hiring for skills first was indeed paying off, we measured the performance of non-four-year-degreed hires in five areas, including innovation, client service, and business results. Compared to degreed colleagues, the non-degreed cohort took a bit more time to come up to speed in some areas during their first year, but their ability to produce defined business results was soon equal to or better than those with degrees. We also found our non-degreed hires exceptionally curious; they invested more time than their degreed peers in their own learning and continuing education, sometimes almost double. And they tended to stay longer, perhaps because they felt a sense of loyalty to IBM for giving them a chance and ongoing options to learn more and progress. Our time and attention were indeed paying off in many ways. About three million people apply for jobs at IBM each year. We saw a 63 percent increase in underrepresented candidates by 2019, and many open positions were staffed faster than usual. That year, approximately 15 percent of new hires in the United States did not have a four-year degree. In 2021, less than half of IBM's open jobs in the United States no longer required bachelor's degrees. Comparatively, in 2016 more than 90 percent did require a degree.

But focusing on skills was about more than hiring. It was a mindset that seeped into our culture and changed everything about talent, from how we sourced, interviewed, promoted people, and developed careers. On the sourcing front it widened our scope, which connected us to other overlooked groups, like mid-career tech professionals that had temporarily left the workforce; people with college degrees but no tech experience; and, neurodiverse talent, whose unique ways of thinking, learning, processing, and behaving make work uniquely challenging.

We also made our hiring teams more diverse and trained interviewers to avoid unconscious bias. We asked interviewees a mix of situational and outcome-oriented questions—"What would you do if . . ." versus just "When did you . . ."—to accommodate the wider range of applicants that skills-based hiring attracted. We became very transparent with our existing employees about the status of their own skills, letting them know just how in-demand those skills were, or would be in the future; what new skills they needed to succeed in the marketplace (not just at IBM); and, how we could help them acquire knowledge they didn't yet have. The company created an entire talent system around skills, which included AI-generated career-path models so people could envision a future unique to them.

Our journey was documented in a Harvard Business School case study by professor Boris Groysberg and senior case researcher Sarah Mehta, who provided the first in-depth look at the lengths we went to transform talent selection and advancement.

I began to see a different future—not just for IBM. I envisioned cities, towns, and rural communities where more people had good jobs, and more companies had the employees they needed.

I called it a SkillsFirst world.

Choosing SkillsFirst

SkillsFirst is a catch-all term that refers to valuing the skills a person has rather than just the degrees they have. More specifically, a SkillsFirst approach to learning, hiring, and advancement means that employers source and select employees based on what people know, their expertise, not just based on their degree or higher education credentials. A SkillsFirst approach can apply to many different jobs and at all stages of a career lifecycle.

In a SkillsFirst world, we're in service of many. For individuals at the start of their working lives, SkillsFirst hiring opens the door to more upwardly mobile middle-class jobs and careers. For people mid-career, SkillsFirst makes new paths possible. For employers, SkillsFirst provides access to larger and more inclusive talent pools, without sacrificing performance, and invites more diverse workforces. It puts in place career paths, promotions, and pay based on skills, and moves the organization to value lifelong learning. For society, SkillsFirst creates more employment opportunities for more people so more citizens can be self-sufficient and realize their potential and experience the dignity of work, which in turn helps bridge inequities and strengthen economies.

In a SkillsFirst world, workers no longer see education and training as one-and-done propositions, even for those who graduate college. Instead, we embrace a lifetime of continuous learning, which is so important in an era where many tech skills become obsolete or less relevant in three to five years.

In a SkillsFirst world, learning agility and growth mindsets are highly prized assets, and the greatest predictors of individual achievement are curiosity and a propensity to keep learning. Workers seek out educational opportunities for themselves and take advantage of those available.

In a SkillsFirst world, employers become "builders" versus just "buyers" of talent. They invent or partner for their own educational programs, adapt courses from other companies, and guide their people through learning journeys, giving employees time for formal classes, experiential learning, and informal exposure to fresh ideas and ways of thinking. In a SkillsFirst world, skills, not just degrees, equate to professional accomplishment and are a prerequisite for advancement. Companies with true learning cultures attract and retain more talent, increase engagement, spark innovation, and are more competitive.

In a SkillsFirst world, governments, educators, and talent developers partner and align with business to make possible alternate pathways into the workforce.

The right language can be a catalyst for the change we seek, and the "SkillsFirst" nomenclature provides a descriptive, pithy entry point to the new world I imagined. It describes a universal mindset, not just a program from one company. The accessible term helped me build belief as I actively championed it inside and outside IBM.

Advocating Broadly

"For years we've heard about the skills gap. The idea that we don't have enough workers with the right skills to get the kinds of jobs that are being created," Jim Cramer told his CNBC audience one day in 2019. "But you rarely hear about solutions to the skills gap."

Jim, the notoriously forthright, ultraprepared host of CNBC's *Mad Money*, had me on his show many times to talk about IBM through its ups and downs, as well as broader topics. In 2019, he had me on to discuss the success of P-TECH. Jim was a big fan of the P-TECH model. He'd met students and even graciously hosted graduates at his Brooklyn restaurant, Bar San Miguel. Jim went to Harvard University and had a successful career as a hedge fund manager, and yet he saw beyond his own experience and recognized the value of alternate pathways into the workforce. That June day in 2019 he interviewed me in the library of the first P-TECH school in Brooklyn as we sat on stools surrounded by shelves of books.

"If you come here, you're going to be on the fast track versus no track, right?" he said, referring to the access that P-TECH provided underserved communities and students.

"Right," I said, "It's a curriculum that's aligned to what industry needs." I shared some of P-TECH's success stats.

We spoke for about ten minutes, and at the end of the interview Jim asked, "What do you say to people who say, you know what, this is a waste of time . . . it's not what IBM shareholders want." I told Jim I wholeheartedly disagreed. Supporting a program like P-TECH and addressing the skills gap went beyond corporate responsibility. It was about economic responsibility.

"I need that workforce for my company. It's good for business," I said. "These are great employees, some of the most loyal and dedicated you'll ever have."

This need to build belief among skeptical or unaware members of the business community—from IBM shareholders, to employees, to other CEOs—was why I spoke so often about P-TECH, the new collar economy, and SkillsFirst.

Every time I sat on a panel or keynoted big events—the World Economic Forum in Davos, the Consumer Electronics Show in Las Vegas, VivaTech in Europe—I capped my main topic with a discussion about stewarding good tech, which included advocating for a SkillsFirst world.

Often I brought IBM's own new collar and P-TECH employees on stage with me to share their stories and showcase their talent. I made them feel as comfortable as possible (think, prepare, rehearse!), but can you imagine the courage it takes for someone not used to public speaking to tell their story in front of twenty people, let alone thirty thousand? I think they summoned the confidence because they believed they were speaking on behalf of a larger part of society, in many cases the communities where they grew up. And they were rightly proud of their own accomplishments. After, I'd talk with them backstage, and their wide smiles and enthusiasm told me they'd do it again. And so I continued to ask. Speaking on such a big stage was a stretch, and they grew from it. So did everyone listening in the audience; hearing people's experiences firsthand personalized the issue, helping to build belief in a SkillsFirst world, one audience at a time.

One year, I got on the agenda of the National Governors Association annual meeting to tell the P-TECH story in a speech broadcast over C-SPAN, which triggered calls from more interested states. Another year, I was preparing for IBM's annual Big Bets conference, where we brought one hundred of our largest clients' CEOs together. The planning team walked into my office and someone suggested that will.i.am join me on a panel. Some thought it was a crazy idea. I loved it. The singer, songwriter, and leader of the Black Eyed Peas formed the i.am Angel Foundation to help transform his hometown, a low-income immigrant community, with scholarships in STEM education. I'd yet to meet will.i.am. When we were introduced, I could see his genius as his creativity, passion, and dedication worked in unison. For as different as we were, we shared a vision about how improving access to education could help transform communities rich in potential. Like-minded thinking brought us together many times, and the collaborative efforts of will.i.am and others outside the business community brought SkillsFirst to audiences I never would have reached, allowing for a more cocreative allyship.

Just as my good tech advocacy wasn't limited to the United States, neither were my attempts to activate a SkillsFirst mindset. In France, I joined President Emmanuel Macron's Tech for Good Summit and cochaired its workforce and education workstream with Jean-Laurent Bonnafé, director and CEO of BNP Paribas. In India, we ran the STEM for Girls program to help educate more than two hundred thousand in the science and technology fields and support Prime Minister Narendra Modi's goals for the education of young women. Another year I brought my leadership team to Africa so they could see for themselves the need and potential of building skills in developing countries. IBM launched Digital Nation Africa, a free, open platform to provide digital skills development for young people.

Change at scale, especially across borders, required keeping the message clear, but more so broad.

A big "ah-ha" moment arrived when I chaired the Business Round-table's workforce commission. BRT member companies, more than two hundred, provide a total of about twenty million jobs, and my BRT colleagues had a sincere commitment to improve recruitment and promotion practices to bring more underrepresented populations into their workforces. Every company had its own process for doing this, so we surveyed BRT members to identify the most effective programs with real outcomes, thinking other BRT companies would then adopt the best. We made some progress, but I found some organizations didn't want to give up their own programs, especially after investing years and money creating them for their communities.

I understood. I felt the same way about P-TECH. The problem was, even the best programs weren't broad enough to address the magnitude of national job inequality.

The way forward was not to insist organizations replace one program with another, but to change mindsets. More people needed to embrace SkillsFirst as an approach, then have the freedom to write their own play-book for implementation. Once I understood this, I realized the real way forward was to build belief in SkillsFirst tenets and benefits and provide broad strokes of how to coconstruct this new reality. If companies came together and aligned and federated their efforts, SkillsFirst could scale faster. My lesson: always choose progress over perfection.

In addition to leading the BRT's workforce commission, I also served on the Trump administration's American Workforce Policy Advisory Board to promote good jobs for more people across the nation. We made real progress, and in 2020 the president issued an executive order that all federal government agencies should hire with the SkillsFirst paradigm.

Also, in New York City, Jamie Dimon and JPMorgan Chase helped to create the New York Jobs CEO Council. I joined their coalition of some thirty companies and community colleges to hire one hundred thousand low-income New Yorkers into family-sustaining jobs. Instead of working independently, the businesses are working together to help education providers and community colleges align their teaching with skills that are in demand. Already, by working together, they've had an impact.

Throughout my advocacy, I was keenly aware that my voice and the voices of workers and businesses were necessary but hardly sufficient to induce long-term, systemic change to a SkillsFirst world. There was another piece of the puzzle. To create new collar jobs we also needed collaboration across traditional lines of federal and state governments, public school systems, community colleges, and private businesses, across multiple industries. "We will not always agree, but progress in job creation will come from open discussion and engagement," I wrote in my 2016 USA Today op-ed. "Together, we must work to reform education, policy, and strategic approaches—in the US and around the world."

I was referring to the laborious, unavoidable work of policy reform, which is necessary to achieve any kind of systems change.

Reforming Policies

There was some tension in the dining room as many around the table were political adversaries. Still, they'd showed up to dinner, which was a big win after a tedious seven-year effort by IBM and others to update a law called the Perkins Act. Soon Congress would vote on the revised law, and in a final push Ivanka Trump invited lawmakers from both sides of the aisle to her home in Washington, DC, for an informal dinner. Ivanka was a staunch supporter of SkillsFirst, and she asked me and a fellow CEO to join the bipartisan gathering to represent the business community. Putting policy over politics, we of course accepted.

The original Carl D. Perkins Act—passed in 1963, under another name— provided states with money to fund community colleges and trade schools for students not attending four-year institutions. The law enabled millions of people, mainly from low-income households, to access vocational jobs. The Perkins Act was reauthorized several times but not thoughtfully updated, and its purpose was floundering in the digital era. IBM was on a mission to update the outdated law to help better align the nation's talent supply with talent demand.

Our collaborative effort aimed to fix the law's main flaw: community colleges and other educational institutions funded through the Perkins Act were not being held accountable for teaching students skills aligned with modern industry needs. In short, community colleges had a lot of power and potential to produce graduates that companies needed, but incentives to meet market demands didn't exist.

For years revisions were discussed, but partisanship prevented progress.

We finally succeeded by taking a big-tent, cocreation approach, and spent years building belief among a diverse coalition—businesses, chambers of commerce, labor organizations, civil rights groups—that participated in drafting the new law. We asked members of those groups to speak to members of the legislature on their own behalf; clearly communicating why the change was needed from all constituents' viewpoints helped build support among lawmakers on both the right and the left. Still, there was hesitancy. Hence the dinner.

We ate and talked about the presumed intentions behind changes to the act and potential unintended consequences. It was a lively debate. When I got the opportunity to make the case, I emphasized the one thing I knew we'd all agree on: jobs. An updated Perkins Act would prepare millions more people for good jobs, in every state, red and blue.

Those seven years and that dinner were not in vain. On July 31, 2018, President Trump signed the Strengthening Career and Technical Education for the 21st Century Act, or Perkins V, into law. It increases funding for more types of learning and education so more students can participate in skills training. It gives states more authority to set their own learning goals, which means more schools now teach skills that regional employers want. Most notably, it holds statewide educators accountable for progress through data like graduation rates, as well as the number of students earning credentials. The federal government can now withhold funding to states that fail to meet performance targets. That's right: if you don't supply what the market demands, you don't get funding. It's a powerful incentive and an example of how accountability can increase access to opportunity.

The passage of the Perkins V Act was more proof that public-private coalitions can solve problems that either entity can't do alone. Did we get everything we wanted? No, but once again perfection didn't stand in the way of progress. It's also a reminder why resilience is so vital when pursuing systemic change!

Putting policy over politics will go a long way toward updating other laws and regulations. Driving any systemic change requires examining legislation and regulations from the perspective of what helps and what inhibits in today's reality. When it comes to creating more economic equity, there are conflicting opinions about what needs to change, from labor laws that set minimum wages, to more unions, to more expansive eligibility for financial aid. There also are widely agreed upon levers that governments can pull, often in tandem with the private sector. The sheer variety proves how many different levers must be pulled to transform broken systems.

Here's my legislative to-do list for a SkillsFirst world:

For one, universal access to affordable, reliable internet connection must be a human right, just like access to water and electricity. Lack of internet access prevents online learning and makes it harder if not impossible to apply for jobs online and work remotely. As with apprenticeships, the United States is woefully behind other countries in providing universal access. It came closer to fruition in 2022 when twenty internet providers agreed to improve and expand subsidized, high-speed internet for millions of low-income households. We just can't let this initiative stall.

Second, we also need more and higher quality wraparound services. Access to training and jobs doesn't matter unless learners and employees can access affordable transportation and childcare so they can get to class or to work and focus their minds because their children or aging parents are well cared for.

Third, I also advocate for more public transparency into educational and employment opportunities. Students and mid-career professionals must have easy insight into market trends and the many and new learning pathways available so they can invest in ones that are right for them. A growing landscape of startups are being funded to address this issue. Some make information consumable to the populations they serve, like providing TikTok-like advice to parents and high school students. Many companies are using artificial intelligence to match jobs and job seekers, and for career path counseling. Others are building markets around talent financing.

Finally, there's also a huge need for the portability and transparency of all types of credentials across schools and employers. There's no uniform way for job seekers to prove their skills other than a résumé or a degree. A national credentialing system will provide a standard way for job seekers and employers to share, recognize, and verify skills attained through classes, certificates, and degrees, as well as experiential learning like apprenticeships. Technologies like blockchain make this possible with immutable ledgers to document an unchangeable record of an individual's history.

This is a lot of change. But innovating to create an alternate reality like a SkillsFirst world doesn't mean we discard everything. We must also ask what must endure.

Knowing What Must Endure

Bachelor's, master's, and doctorate degrees remain essential to the health and growth of economies. So yes, higher education must endure as an accessible option to many. We can increase access by making four-year degrees easier and less financially debilitating to obtain, and more relevant in the marketplace. For example, colleges can count credits from untraditional but credentialed talent developers toward graduation qualification. Holding more colleges accountable for real outcomes, like job placements, would help ensure that the value students receive for their investment in an institution is not just a degree.

The "college or bust" message is embedded in the American Dream narrative—and not just in the United States. It's a myth reinforced by how federal loans and grants are managed. Since 1965, for example, the Higher Education Act's financial aid programs have opened doors for millions of Americans. Now we need to expand eligibility for student loans, as well as Pell Grants, the popular subsidy that helps low-income undergraduates pay for college. Most financial aid is limited to students enrolled at two- or four-year colleges and universities, or at vocational schools meeting strict requirements. The rules need to be loosened to include more talent developers, like tech boot camps and nonprofits that teach skills. Under current law, Pell Grants only apply to programs with fifteen weeks and 600 hours of instruction. And yet, a California emergency medical technician can meet licensing requirements after completing just 170 hours of training. In North Carolina, a Nurse Aide I certification can be completed in 75 hours. Federal law must allow part-time students and mid-career professionals to get Pell Grants and student loans for short-term learning programs as well as apprenticeships, internships, quality certificate courses, and community college classes.

When we take time to look, we'll see the many underpinnings that reinforce the status quo. Imagine if even small things like the Federal Work-Study Program are updated. It has long paid up to 75 percent of wages to college and graduate students working part-time to help them pay for school. The current program provides about $1 billion, but the majority of funds only pay for on-campus jobs, like sorting books in libraries and serving food in cafeterias. Only 25 percent of funds can go toward off-campus jobs at for-profit businesses. By lifting the 25 percent cap, so many more students can work for small, local businesses and gain real world experience, better preparing them for the job market, all while giving small businesses access to more talent.

Changing long-standing positions and institutions is difficult work. Progress happens like molasses. The pace can be infuriating for someone like me with a bias for speed. Talk about the need for resilience! But encouraging our educational institutions to address pressing social issues and letting go of laws that no longer serve us and building on them are other arrows in the quiver to hit a SkillsFirst bull's-eye. Thinking systemically, and through the lens of good power, can unlock meaningful change at scale.

Scaling Principles

At the end of 2020 I retired from IBM after forty years. During my final few weeks, I bid goodbye to colleagues and clients from around the world through countless video gatherings because the raging pandemic kept us from coming together in person. Many of the meetings were region or country specific, and on each I shared my top three memories about how local IBMers had impacted our global transformation and business results, clients, and their country. On countless client video calls, I toasted each person and told them what I personally most admired about their leadership, what I'd learned from them, and why I had such great confidence in my successor, Arvind Krishna. In my last letter to IBMers I wrote, "We shape the companies we work for, and they shape us." It was all bittersweet.

I'd spent my life in service of one company, and I was going to miss it terribly. But I wasn't retiring from work, just from IBM. I'd found another mission that I was passionate about and ready to dedicate my time and attention to.

I have long believed economic opportunity is the best equalizer, and because I equate economic opportunity with gainful employment, it's clear to me that helping a broader swath of people access better jobs is critical and urgent. For me, amplifying my efforts to create a SkillsFirst world is the ultimate translation of good power's progression from me to we to us.

Preparing society for the digital era by helping more people access better jobs is to be in service of the millions of individuals who might otherwise be locked out of the digital economy. It's also in service of businesses that can't thrive unless they can develop or find employees with skills they need, as well as societies that will face instability unless their citizens believe they can have a better financial future.

Scaling SkillsFirst asks that we build belief in new paradigms and accept the crux of the employment divide. So many people are being left out of the workforce not because they lack aptitude or drive, but because they lack access to educational as well as employment opportunities. We'll solve this problem because real solutions already exist and can be scaled.

Scaling requires systems thinking, looking at all parts, and figuring out what must change, and what must endure. Let's be honest about what's no longer working in today's educational institutions and corporate practices. Let's summon wisdom and fortitude to adopt new paradigms and innovate with new models underpinned by revamped government policies and collaborations between the public and private sectors.

Building more diverse and inclusive workforces that embrace people from underserved groups and communities—doing what's right for people, for society, and for businesses—is stewarding good tech.

Finally, the barriers that must be addressed are entrenched, and I'd come to know the major inhibitors to tackle: the overcredentialing of family-sustaining jobs. The mismatch between education supply and employer demand. The lack of multiple pathways to better jobs. Outdated policies and laws. And a one-and-done learning mindset. Addressing these barriers would open the doors to good jobs for all underrepresented and underserved groups. We had a chance to create a rising tide to lift all boats. I'd need a lot of resilience, but I was ready to muster it because the mission was so important.

That mission took on more urgency in the summer of 2020, when tragic events captured the world's attention.

13

Creating a Movement

We don't always recognize pivotal moments while they're happening.

In late May 2020, a little more than six months before I retired, Mark and I were home, like everyone else, quarantining during the Covid-19 pandemic. I was now Executive Chairman at IBM, and Arvind Krishna had begun his tenure as my successor. Our time overlapped to ensure a smooth transition, especially given the large divestiture we'd announced.

Most of my days were spent on videoconference calls with colleagues and clients as we all got used to this new remote way of working. I'd never spent so many consecutive days—almost three months by that time—at my own home in, well . . . ever. I missed meeting with people in person, but I have to say it sure was a reprieve not to be traveling all the time, and especially nice to begin and end my days with Mark. Although having me around so much was novel for him, too. Our home office had become his office since I was always on the road, so I set up my own workspace in our kitchen, with cabinets as my backdrop.

Like most people during this unprecedented period, our TV was often on in the background as we tuned in to daily news. At the end of May, the pandemic news receded when a forty-six-year-old Black man named George Floyd was murdered in Minneapolis, Minnesota. He had been arrested for suspicion of using a counterfeit $20 bill, and one of the white police officers who arrested him, Derek Chauvin, knelt on his neck for nine minutes while Floyd was handcuffed and lying facedown on the street. Floyd became more and more distressed and eventually stopped breathing. Then he died. His autopsy determined his death a homicide. A video of the horrific incident went viral.

For people like me who don't face the hostilities and obstacles of racism, the death of George Floyd and the outrage that followed were another wake-up call to the vast divides between white and Black America. I didn't take to the streets in protest, but I talked to my family and listened closely to what my Black friends and colleagues had to say to better understand what the Black community was experiencing. Ken Frazier, whose decade as the CEO of Merck paralleled my years leading IBM, shared that Floyd's killing was a pivotal event for so many people, white as well as Black, because of how our country collectively experienced it. Everyone was home watching TV, and everyone could see with their own eyes a white police officer kneeling on the neck of a defenseless Black man, ignoring his pleas for help. In the days that followed, the nation also watched as millions of people emerged from their homes to express anger, frustration, and depths of sadness. The outpouring, said Ken, was about more than anger at police brutality. It was about the totality of racism in America, and the widespread belief that Black Americans have never been fully able to participate in society.

Ken and I were among many business leaders looking inward, asking ourselves bigger questions, like how we were dealing with racial inequities and barriers in our own lives, and in our companies. Were we wielding our power in the best of ways? One thing was becoming obvious. We had to do more because what we were doing wasn't having a positive enough impact on the very societies that gave us license to operate.

Gaining Traction

How do we create positive change at the scale of an entire society? To me, this is the ultimate use of good power—the power of us.

Real, widespread change must be systemic, meaning the ways people think and do things every day have to be different than the ways we do them now. Systemic change can begin when unexpected events trigger a shift in collective consciousness, moving millions of people to coalesce around an idea or truth that's been waiting in the wings for just the right cue to burst onto a national or global stage and capture attention. George Floyd's death, and the mass outrage that followed, was just such a moment because it unleashed more widespread reckoning and awareness of racism and inequality—mainly among those of us who aren't Black. When George Floyd died in front of the world, racism had another face we could not unsee.

I admit that I thought I understood the state of racial and economic disparity in our nation, but the data tells a much worse story than even I realized. In the United States, Black individuals are more than twice as likely to live in poverty as white people, according to the US Census Bureau's American Community Survey in 2019. The average national net worth for a Black family is $17,000, compared to $171,000 for a typical white family. The magnitude of this and other income gaps is unconscionable, and the pandemic has made them worse, especially for Black women.

Before the events in the summer of 2020 prompted a wave of reflection among business leaders, some were already committed to addressing today's prejudice and racial equity in a variety of ways, in part by being more open and honest about it in the workplace. An issue that was once a third rail in professional settings had become the topic of conversation and town halls, where employees voiced opinions and shared experiences. IBM had such a gathering about six months before the murder of George Floyd, as part of our normal senior leadership training. I'd invited Shirley Jackson, the renowned physicist and longtime president of Rensselaer Polytechnic Institute, to speak. Shirley was the first Black woman to earn a doctorate from the Massachusetts Institute of Technology (MIT), and one of my favorite role models. In the most positive of ways I consider her a force of nature. Along with Shirley, several of our own Black leaders talked about their own experiences with prejudice. One individual spoke about feeling the weight of the world on his shoulders to succeed, because failure meant not just letting himself down, but the entire Black community and his home country. I remember being struck by how racism manifests in so many subtle but equally demeaning forms. If some of the brightest and most accomplished Black achievers feel its pain, weight, and limitations, I couldn't even begin to imagine the emotions a young person might be carrying.

Conversations like these are beneficial, and it's important that they're happening. But for society to progress, they need to be accompanied by big actions.

It was Ken Frazier who delivered a call to action in the wake of the national protests: "We should do what business does best, provide jobs." Ken knows the value of good jobs for Black families, particularly for younger generations. His father never had more than a third-grade education and worked as a janitor. One of Ken's most vivid childhood memories is getting ready for school, brushing his teeth in the bathroom after his dad had left for work.

"He'd already be gone, but I could still smell his shaving cream," Ken told me once. He grew up sensing the pride and dignity his father took in his job, and it made an impression. Ken went on to attend Pennsylvania State University and Harvard Law School. He joined Merck in 1991, and became CEO in 2011, one of just five Black CEOs in the *Fortune* 500. Ken believes that parental role models can elevate a young person's sense of self, as his father did for him. If every child, and not just Black children, can see family members working hard, it instills in them dignity, confidence, even drive. Such a mind shift at scale can change the country. I agree, given my own upbringing. We can't be what we can't see!

Ken joined with two other senior Black business leaders—Ken Chenault, the former CEO of American Express; and Charles Phillips, the former CEO of Infor; as well as Kevin Sharer, the former CEO of Amgen—to begin formulating a new way to provide employment to disenfranchised Black communities. I understood well their goals—more good jobs for Black individuals. As a white woman, I of course can't speak to the Black experience, but I continued to listen to my colleagues and learn from them. Then it struck me that perhaps I could bring something very valuable to the table: my operational experience with SkillsFirst hiring and advancement. SkillsFirst could help make their vision a reality. I joined their effort.

We all knew that Black talent was plentiful but not always easy to find, even when our companies proactively recruited for it. It's no surprise when you see the data. Over 75 percent of Black people in America between eighteen and thirty-five do not have a college degree, and yet almost 75 percent of "good" family-sustaining jobs require a four-year degree, with many jobs being overcredentialed. There is no question that Black individuals in the United States—and all of America—will benefit from the mass move to a SkillsFirst approach. But to spark a real sea change, thousands of companies large and small need to rethink the way they recruit, manage, and develop talent. Getting multiple corporations to band together and embark on such systemic change is hard, especially if they've got competing businesses. But that year, the catalytic shift in awareness had people hungry to do something different to address inequity in the United States. Plus, corporations were still having trouble finding enough skilled workers, so they had a business incentive, too. Hiring more underemployed Americans was a win-win. If ever there was a time to get businesses to embrace SkillsFirst hiring and advancement, this was it.

More personally, I'd been thinking deeply about how to spend my time after leaving IBM. I was already committed to several boards, including JPMorgan Chase, Northwestern University, and the Memorial Sloan Kettering Cancer Center. Pouring my passion and experiences into championing a SkillsFirst movement was one thing I could do to create meaningful change in the wider world.

Beginning a Movement

In the summer of 2020, Ken Frazier and I did a video call with members of the Business Council, another group of two hundred CEOs, to propose an idea our small working group had conceptualized. We were forming an organization called Coalition of Employers for Economic and Racial Justice (CEERJ). Admittedly, a bit of a mouthful. The coalition would make long-term commitments to hire Black individuals without four-year degrees into upwardly mobile middle-class jobs.

The coalition was in service of three groups: one, people without four-year degrees who need access to employment, starting with Black individuals then expanding to all underserved populations; two, businesses small and large who need to fill open jobs, and want their workforces to be more inclusive and diverse, starting with large corporations; and three, educators and skills developers who need to prepare more people for the jobs of today and tomorrow.

Our approach was also ambitious: systemic change. What did that look like? At the most basic levels, people locked out of good jobs had to shift their perspective and be willing to acquire new skills. Employers had to reinvent who and how they hired, trained, and promoted. And skills developers had to change how and what they taught students, and in some cases how they operated.

Ken, I, and the others spent months trying to convince CEOs and their companies to join us; we all needed employees and yet we weren't tapping into a large talent pool that needed employment. Again and again I stated a truth based on IBM's experience with SkillsFirst hiring: "The problem isn't a lack of talent; it's a lack of access." By December 2020, almost forty major companies had committed to help us achieve our goal: hiring, promoting, and advancing one million Black individuals in the United States without four-year degrees into family-sustaining jobs in ten years. Admittedly, this was a very big bet, and we changed our clunky name to reflect it, and to be more memorable: OneTen. Ken and I agreed to cochair the new organization.

On December 10, 2020, the two of us sat in our home offices and Zoomed our heads into *CBS This Morning* for an interview with Gayle King to announce the launch of OneTen. Gayle began, "I think many people were fascinated that you don't necessarily have to have a college degree here . . . It's been my experience, to be honest with you, that book smarts don't often translate to skills or even your intelligence." Bingo! Gayle, speaking to millions of viewers in her warm, authoritative voice from behind tortoise-framed glasses, was helping us tackle the inhibitor of degree bias. Ken and I went on to describe OneTen's mission, and Gayle's last question to me was pointed. "Are you worried about being accused of excluding people?" I told her OneTen was a startup and while we're focusing on Black talent first, the barriers we address apply to all underserved groups. There was pain throughout the country, white and Black alike. "But like any startup, you have to start somewhere."

Ken and I did more media interviews to build traction. Once the hype died down, we had to go back to the heavy work of delivering on our intentions.

Soon more than sixty of the country's largest companies were on board, including ADP, Allstate, American Express, Amgen, Aon, AT&T, Bain & Company, Bank of America, Cargill, Caterpillar, Cisco, Cleveland Clinic, Deloitte, Delta, Lilly, Gilead, GM, HP, Humana, IBM, Intermountain Healthcare, ITW, Johnson & Johnson, Lowe's, Medtronic, Memorial Sloan Kettering Cancer Center, Merck, Nike, Nordstrom, Northrup Grumman, PepsiCo, Roper, Stryker, Synchrony, Target, Trane Technologies, Verizon, Walmart, and Whirlpool.

As more businesses signed up, each identified anywhere from fifty to five hundred positions that qualified as a potential OneTen job to fill, which meant that it paid a family-sustaining living wage; didn't require a four-year degree, or more than five years of experience; and was not at risk of being automated out of existence. As a cohort, OneTen was amassing a higher and higher SkillsFirst demand, which was a forcing function to tackle another big inhibitor to achieving our goals: the lack of SkillsFirst supply.

Tackling an Inhibitor

Cleveland Clinic, the premier medical facility based in Ohio, joined OneTen because its traditional sources of job candidates weren't providing enough applicants to fill hundreds of open spots.

Dr. Melissa Burrows leads the clinic's talent search, and after spending time with OneTen, she was intrigued by the SkillsFirst approach to hiring. But first they had to find potential candidates. So her recruitment team fanned out in some of the poorest nearby neighborhoods and went door-to-door, visiting about four hundred homes to introduce themselves and tell residents about job opportunities at the clinic. Most of the people they met were shocked to learn that they could qualify for many jobs with good wages, benefits, and career opportunities, which they assumed were out of reach because they didn't have the educational degree or work experience. But in some cases they could learn on the job or take a few classes and get up to speed. For Dr. Burrows and her team, it became clear how many people had no idea about the range of employment options.

Dr. Burrows decided to go back into the community rather than wait for people to come to them. In March 2022, the clinic hosted its first-ever fair, bringing hiring managers and recruiters right into the neighborhoods of Cleveland. In one day, 123 people showed up, and 82 people got job offers that same day.

Cleveland Clinic's CEO, Dr. Tom Mihaljevic, told me that exposure to skills-based hiring has been transformational, not just in finding more qualified employees but also in giving its leaders clarity into the unique issues surrounding Black talent. It's also taken the Cleveland Clinic down new paths to find diverse talent. They're rewriting twenty-seven hundred job descriptions, and they've launched apprenticeship programs for pharmacy technicians and IT professionals and trained three thousand existing employees to become more inclusive managers. In 2021, the clinic exceeded its goal of hiring five hundred Black caregivers by almost double. By midyear 2022, they'd almost achieved their full-year target.

As I have written, the supply-demand mismatch isn't a problem limited to Cleveland. In most cities it is the big inhibitor to connecting more people to better jobs.

I'd come to believe, along with Ken, that increasing the supply of skilled, non-degreed talent would only happen if demand increased. Once again, jobs are the currency to incentivize training and education organizations to rethink and adapt what and how they teach to the needs of the job market. If a community college knows the IBM office in its city has hundreds of annual openings for cyber talent and wants to recruit at the school, the college is likely to bring on more cyber instructors and create cyber curriculum. We saw this with P-TECH.

"Talent programs are driven by critical mass job opportunities, not the other way around," is how Brian Moynihan, the CEO of Bank of America, puts it. The financial services company has become a huge proponent of skills-based hiring for many jobs, including hard-to-fill tech roles.

Moving to a SkillsFirst world is a bit of a chicken-and-egg conundrum: only if SkillsFirst hiring scales can supply scale; but if there aren't enough candidates to fill skills-based job opportunities, then SkillsFirst hiring won't continue to grow. OneTen's philosophy is that if we can get enough companies to align and pool their hiring needs under our big tent and commit to hiring significant numbers of people, those jobs will incent many skills developers to do things differently.

So, just who are the talent developers and skills providers so vital to the success of every economy, and whose effectiveness we need to cultivate? What do they do well and what can many do differently? Starting OneTen taught me a lot about them.

The terms "talent developer" and "skills provider" span a broad landscape of public and private education and training organizations that vary by country. In the United States they vary by state and city, and include the nation's twenty-six hundred four-year colleges, including historically Black colleges and universities (HBCUs). Overall, not enough colleges and universities treat the skills divide as their problem. They consider skills training as the domain of high schools and community colleges. Meanwhile, so many of their degreed graduates leave school with burdensome debt, about $38,000 on average for some 43 million Americans, according to the Education Data Initiative.

The less expensive twelve-hundred-plus community colleges in the United States are a vital path to economic mobility. Close to seven million students enroll in community colleges for credit each year, and they are disproportionately minority, low-income, and first-generation college students. Associate degrees and learning certificates can lead to higher employment and earnings, and a lot of community colleges do exceptional work producing work-ready students for multiple industries in just a few years. The best community colleges collaborate with industry to inform curriculum. They extend their reach into high schools and the mid-career workforce. They embed transferable skills certificates into their programs so students can land higher-paying jobs more quickly. Some provide wraparound services, from tutoring to childcare, and boast strong career placement services. The community colleges that aren't yet meeting the country's needs are a deep reservoir of untapped potential.

Beyond colleges, talent developers also include a bevy of for-profit and nonprofit models: vocational schools, online platforms, virtual courses, labor union education, public-private programs (like P-TECH), employer-led education, military transition programs, and industry-specific credentialing organizations. There are online boot camps that provide immersive, project-based learning, and hybrid programs that pair hands-on job experience with classes. The list goes on, and the quality varies. Some providers have their finger on the pulse of skills demand. Some teach soft skills, too. Some are tech only, while others prep people for jobs in sales, logistics, manufacturing, health care, and other fields.

This is a group ripe for innovation, and a lot of new players are doing fantastic work worth building on. Per Scholas, for one, serves about three thousand people a year with no-cost classroom training. Generation USA serves about five thousand people a year via multimonth training programs taught inside companies, at nonprofits, and at existing educational institutions. Merit America's tech boot camps target working adults who need to earn while they learn, deferring tuition for participants until they're employed. These organizations are impressive, and many have incredible potential to grow at an even faster pace to be in service of millions of people who need work and countless companies that need workers.

Two issues many talent providers can urgently address are alignment and fragmentation. Alignment means more suppliers need to produce workers with the skills employers need, aligning supply and demand. Fragmentation refers to the sheer number of providers that exists; it's just impossible for any hiring organization, even the largest corporations, to deal with so many different and small-scale sources of talent.

OneTen aims to be in service of skills providers' efforts to address these issues, as well as help member companies address their own issues. By the fall of 2022, more than one hundred skills providers had joined our efforts. We're supporting them individually and as a cohort on several fronts. First, helping them to align and teach the hard and soft skills businesses need. Second, helping them connect with more employers to ensure students get placed in good jobs; this will build even more trust and attract more students. Third, helping them implement viable, sustainable business models that hold their organizations more accountable for outcomes and allow them to grow, scale, and produce skilled talent in larger numbers.

OneTen's belief is that if enough of our member companies align and combine their hiring needs, we'll have that critical mass to induce skills providers to evolve what they teach and how they work. In turn, when employers see other companies improving how they hire talent, they too will change. Once again, jobs are the currency that incents change.

Our founding CEO, Maurice Jones, spent his career working in the private and public sectors, and he understands the power of public-private partnerships to achieve large-scale societal change. "It's hard to solve a problem in America without business being part of the solution," he says. "Government and the social sector often try to create something, and then go to business. The real power with OneTen is that we are cocreating."

Executing on our intentions is the biggest challenge, and part of our approach is to establish local ecosystems. First, we picked twenty-five cities and regions where a lot of talent and potential jobs exist; we call these markets. In each market, we're creating employer coalitions to help aggregate skills demands, creating so many similar job opportunities that local skills developers will align curricula to businesses' needs so graduates will get jobs. We're also working with organizations that offer wraparound support services like transportation and childcare. Ultimately, the connective tissue of each regional ecosystem could be a game changer.

Two years in we're still learning a lot, including some "ah-has" about how to scale change when engaging so many different players. For example, OneTen doesn't insist on exact ways our member companies should achieve outcomes. Every corporation is complex in its own way, and getting companies to adopt programs that someone else developed is almost impossible. I'd seen this with apprenticeships: everyone wants to invent their own. This is inefficient, but it's a reality. OneTen's role is to provide the big tent where members can come together to learn from each other, then customize ideas that fit their organizations. Adapt versus adopt.

Our big learning: aggregate, align, and federate, but don't dictate.

Sharing Solutions

The recredentialing of jobs company-by-company is a first step to creating a SkillsFirst world. As I write, OneTen is steeped in helping our members change their HR systems and cultures to embrace skills-based hiring and advancement. That means we're asking everyone to review their job requisitions to prevent overcredentialing, then figure out how to hire and promote hundreds of candidates without college degrees.

The transfer of knowledge among our members happens when our OneTen companies come together in what we call our communities of practice. We have a community for the CEOs, HR leaders, and more. I attend these video calls so I can keep learning and help motivate. I'm always impressed by the level of passion and candor. So many of our members deeply want to contribute to positive change in their organizations and in the world. They come to each call with questions, triumphs, and tactical examples of what they're doing to change how their companies think about talent.

Building belief in SkillsFirst inside companies is a challenge for many. That's why quarterly meetings for all OneTen company CEOs are essential; these leaders need to reinforce that SkillsFirst isn't about compliance or a diversity strategy, but a talent strategy.

Ed Bastian, the CEO of Delta, told OneTen members that the airline removed the four-year requirement from almost all their job roles, including job descriptions for pilots, because there are many ways to receive the prerequisite training. Rewriting pilot job specifications emphasizing skills versus just a degree opened doors to a great number of diverse candidates. Ed said it was equally critical to build SkillsFirst career pathways for both retention and advancement. Many companies like Delta already have very diverse workforces, and with SkillsFirst career pathways their frontline workers can see the path to advancing into better roles throughout the company.

Sharing data and research also help build belief. An analysis of thirty-three million job postings between 2017 and 2019 found that when employers remove degree requirements, they often add to the hard, technical, and soft skills they prefer for a given job. "The degree reset does not seem to reflect any diminution in the complexity of work; quite the contrary, jobs that undergo a degree reset are more likely to specify high-level skills," according to the report from the Burning Glass Institute. In other words, the very process of recredentialing jobs to articulate specific skills can bring in higher-quality candidates. Doing so has economic benefits. Notes the report, "Widening the aperture of the recruiting process to include more non-degree holders can generate real economic returns for employers by reducing the mean time to fill positions and turnover with no major associated reduction in productivity."

A 2017 report by Harvard Business School, Accenture, and Grads of Life on the consequences of degree inflation found that employees with college degrees in middle-skill jobs command higher salaries than non-degreed employees for the same work, and have lower employee engagement and higher rates of voluntary turnover, in part because their job expectations are often higher than non-degreed workers. Degreed hires also required about the same amount of onboarding.

Sharing people's stories is another way to build belief in SkillsFirst because it puts human faces on the paradigm. Your CEO can tell you to adopt a SkillsFirst approach and data can reinforce it, but it's especially powerful when a young woman named Rufaro Zengeni tells you that she emigrated from Zimbabwe to the United States at age seven and didn't complete her four-year degree because she didn't have the funds to pay tuition, and because she had to work to help support her family. It's more moving when she explains how a nonprofit boot camp taught her how to code in JavaScript for free, which led her to a job at JPMorgan Chase and a career as a software engineer. When Rufaro says—as she did to our OneTen group on a call in 2022—that she used to think no one would believe in her because she didn't have a four-year degree, and then asks you to have an open mind and give opportunities to people from untraditional backgrounds who have the abilities and drive to better themselves, you are even more likely to change how you think about talent, and change your approach.

Bridget Gainer, global head of policy and public affairs at Aon, reminded us that it's not as hard as we think to convince companies that there are smart, driven people worth hiring who just don't have a college degree. "Most people in corporate life are only one generation away from someone who didn't go to college. Maybe it's their parents or siblings, so there is a connection and a confidence in investing in someone who did not go to a traditional four-year college."

Still, letting go of degree bias is hard. "A four-year degree is like an insurance policy for hiring, and it's human nature to mitigate risk," says Bridget. "A company needs to give recruiters room to do things differently and take those risks."

I've long said that diversity is a fact, but inclusion is a choice. OneTen companies and organizations are making that choice, and I can tell you that what they're trying to do is a heavy, heavy lift. One decision, one action, one day at a time. Ken and I encourage everyone to stay focused on outcomes, and to treat the hiring of SkillsFirst Black talent with the same level of rigor and care that they give to other business initiatives. We set goals and measure progress. And while it's easy for all of us to get caught up in numbers like one million hires, I try to remind myself that behind the data are real people who have stories and dreams and families.

On a OneTen group call last summer, Aleta Howell, the global lead of DEI recruiting and business strategy for Cisco Systems, made a great point. Even people who graduate four-year colleges don't have 100 percent of the skills they need to get promoted to a new job, entry-level and beyond. We all take on roles we have to grow into, so why should it be any different for people without traditional degrees? We all learn as we go.

So much of systemic change is about shifting our own perspectives, right?

Before our group call ended, Aleta said something else that made me smile. "I love my job, and I truly believe in my heart that this is a movement."

A movement. Isn't that what we're after? Yes, it is.

I've asked myself, *How will we know when we've arrived?* Here's the thing I've learned about trying to create positive change at scale. Any quest to achieve large, meaningful, measurable results is often at odds with the sheer size of the problems it's trying to solve. Sometimes change is so ambitious, the breadth so grand, that it takes time, so we may never get to see our visions become full-scale reality. But that's the nature of stewardship, and it doesn't mean we don't do everything in our good power to try.

Final Reflections

Sometimes we have to look back to look forward, and I see now that championing SkillsFirst today is a natural culmination of my life experiences and learnings, stemming all the way back from my childhood.

Our youth and early career often seed our core beliefs and character traits. For me, these were the years I discovered "the power of me" to create positive change in my life. I also observed how access to education and employment can unleash potential. Most of all, I learned the value of curiosity and staying curious. Lifelong learning gives us the confidence we need to engage more people, bridge divides, and find new solutions, which are so very essential to achieving progress toward a better end for all.

As my career progressed, my perspective broadened and I began to grow into the kind of leader I admired and strived to be—one that leads with values and respect for others as well as rigor and accountability. I began to apply "the power of we," discovering the good power principles that can drive all kinds of change.

I saw how being in service of others, and considering the needs of multiple stakeholders, shapes our behavior and outcomes. When we aspire to meet the needs of many, not just a few, we can do the most good for the most people, and meet our own needs too.

I experienced how building belief in a mission unleashes the discretionary effort and talents necessary to achieve real and difficult change. When we exercise our influence versus exerting authority, we bring people together to embrace a new reality, bridging difference through common purpose and cocreation.

I realized that knowing what must change and what must endure is key to making the tough choices that lasting change demands, and in parallel makes us pay equal attention to how work gets done, not just what work gets done.

I tried to steward good tech in a world where every organization is infused with technology, and determined that if values underpin all we do and inform our decision-making, then change won't happen in a vacuum or at the expense of other people.

And I mustered resilience many times, which allowed me to take risks and keep the momentum of change going, even when the journey got tough and I felt uncomfortable.

I hope I've shown how these principles ladder up over time, as we acquire them through experience, high-stakes assignments, and practice. Not all of them are relevant at every stage of our work, but individually and in sum

I have come to believe that the principles of good power can help us navigate the tensions inherent in leadership, in problem-solving, and in trying to bring big ideas to life. I encourage you to do just that, and harness "the power of us" to create change at scale, in whatever way matters to you.

While I hope you'll join the SkillsFirst movement, my guess is that you have a passion or mission of your own that's the culmination of your life experiences and learnings. I urge you to pursue it. Don't be intimidated by the scope of your aspiration or the magnitude of its challenge, and don't be led to think that you can't make a difference. Trust your heart, and consider how the principles can be used, over and over, to bring your vision to fruition. After all, good power is simply a way to do hard, meaningful things in positive ways, right?

Whatever change you seek—for your life, your work, or our world—you're going to be uncomfortable at times, but don't let that stop you. Go for it now! Our world needs you to "be the storm."

Dear Reader,

Thank you for giving me your most valuable asset - your time. Before we part ways, one final thought from me to you.

Whatever your ambitions, you'll not only be remembered for "what" you achieve; your greatest legacy just might be "how" you achieve it. Keep that in mind every day, and I promise that you will be proud of the life you live.

With gratitude,

Ginni

INDEX

ACKNOWLEDGMENTS

Writing this book has been one of the hardest things I've ever done. In fact, I never intended to write a book, but after I retired from IBM in 2020, people urged me to share what I'd experienced. Personally, I was most passionate about an issue bigger than myself: the urgent need to prepare society to thrive in our digital era by creating more jobs for more people, and how the SkillsFirst movement can create economic opportunity for so many and heal divides. I thought a book helping to drive this type of societal change, filled with facts, studies, stories, descriptions of barriers, and implementation details, would find an audience.

Robert Barnett, the acclaimed lawyer and renowned book publishing expert, guided me down a different path. He persuaded me to go outside my comfort zone to tell my personal and professional story, recount events that shaped my beliefs about how I lead, as well as share experiences that led me to my SkillsFirst journey. For that and more wisdom, I thank you, Bob.

This book was conceived and written in collaboration with Joanne Gordon, an unbelievably experienced and gifted writer, who is both thorough and patient. Joanne pushed me to look deep within myself, to talk more about how I felt versus what I saw, all things my analytical, engineering mind did not do naturally. She pored through my archived documents and articles and made sure everything written was accurate and fact-checked. She helped me take a lifetime of facts and stories, plus my ideas about the future, and weave them into a narrative with the intent to inspire and benefit anyone. With that intent, the book became a sort of memoir with purpose. Joanne settles for nothing less than excellence, and I am beyond grateful that I found her.

To my insightful editor, Melinda Merino, and the editorial department at Harvard Business Review Press: thank you for your passion and respect for my story and my work. From the beginning, you believed that I had a history and important ideas worth sharing with the world, and you provided encouragement and direction along the way. The entire HBR Press team—including Jennifer Waring, Stephani Finks, Sally Ashworth, Akila Balasubramaniyan, Jordan Concannon, Julie Devoll, Lindsey Dietrich, Ed Domina, Brian Galvin, Erika Heilman, Alexandra Kephart, Jon Shipley, and Felicia Sinusas—helped steer and shape the book through production, design, and marketing.

Preeti Wali has been a constant, enthusiastic, and trusted adviser since before the book was even a vision, and she gracefully orchestrated the book's journey from draft to publication, no small feat.

I am also grateful to my trusted PR and digital partners, including Bully Pulpit Interactive (BPI) and Mark Fortier and his dedicated team.

A deep thanks to the more than fifty people who shared memories and perspectives to help me reconstruct the past and address complex issues, as well as to the IBM team for validating many of the facts, figures, and experiences I share in these pages.

I am also grateful to those who graciously gave their time and attention to read drafts and provide honest feedback. Keith Yamashita's thoughtful input was especially perfect at exactly the right time. Thanks also to Jonathan Adashek, Michelle Browdy, Rob DelBene, Nina Easton, Diane Gherson, Maria Reeves Hayes, John Kelly, Ken Keverian, Bridget van Kralingen, Arvind Krishna, Tina Lundgren, Kathleen MacLennan, Jesus Mantas, Maureen Nally, Pattie Sellers, and Bob Weber.

Sarah Greenberg and Julie Tate's skills and diligence were also instrumental to the book's reporting and research process.

I have been lucky to work with and for so many incredible people. Some are mentioned in the book, although many others are not. I learned so much from all of them, including Janice Cafmeyer, Pat O'Brien, Bob Howe,

Fred Amoroso, Doug Elix, and of course Lou Gerstner. I am who I am in part because of each of you.

To all the members of the IBM Board of Directors between 2011 and 2020: Your steadfast guidance and support enabled IBM to take the actions needed to reinvent itself for the eras of hybrid cloud and AI. I learned a great deal from each and every one of you, and I am full of gratitude for your service and wisdom.

To all my direct reports at IBM over four decades, words cannot express the depth of my appreciation for your hard work and talents. Many of you led IBM through its most difficult transformation with endless commitment, energy, and expertise. Your dedication to a company and its purpose was and is boundless. I am also forever thankful to your friends and family for the support they provided you, and the sacrifices they made so you could focus on IBM.

To all the IBMers that I've had the opportunity to work with shoulder to shoulder: You lived IBM's values in good times and bad, and I could not be more proud that you were and remain "in service of" our clients. It was my honor to be your colleague.

To my clients through the years and from around the world: Being in service of you and your companies has been my greatest privilege. I've learned a tremendous amount about leadership, followership, and stewardship from each of you, and I thank you for allowing me and IBM to be part of your journey. I feel extremely fortunate that so many of you have also become my lifelong friends.

To all the people committing their hearts, minds, and their companies' efforts to drive the success of OneTen, thank you. There are so many other things you could spend your time on, yet you have elected to dedicate yourself to this most important effort. Ken Frazier, Ken Chenault, Charles Phillips, and Kevin Sharer—I am honored to be on this mission with you. To OneTen member companies and their CEOs, thank you for being willing to embrace a SkillsFirst culture and for your long-term commitment to OneTen's mission: Accenture, The Adecco Group, ADP, Airbnb, Allstate, American Express, Amgen, Aon, AT&T, Bain & Company, Bank of America, Berkshire Hathaway, Berkshire Hathaway Energy, BNSF Railway, Bright Horizons, Care.com, Cargill, Catalyte, Caterpillar, Chubb, Cisco, Clario, Clayton Homes, Cleveland Clinic, ConSol USA, Deloitte, Delta, Dow, Elanco Animal Health, Emerald, Federal Reserve Bank of San Francisco, General Motors, Genpact, Gilead, Goldman Sachs, Hikma, HP, Humana, IBM, Illinois Tool Works, Intermountain Healthcare, ITW, JetBlue, Johnson & Johnson, JPMorgan Chase, Lilly, Lowe's, Medtronic, Memorial Sloan Kettering Cancer Center, Merck, Nagarro, NBA, Nike, Nordstrom, Northrop Grumman, NYU School of Professional Studies, PepsiCo, Randstad, Roper, RWJBarnabas Health, Samsung Electronics America, StoneEagle, Stryker, Supplemental Health Care, Synchrony, Target, Trane Technologies, United Airlines, Verizon, Walmart, Weill Cornell Medicine, Wells Fargo, Whirlpool, and Yum! Brands. An additional thank you to all OneTen members who joined us after this book went to press.

Mark and I want to thank our closest friends, including John and Glenda, Barb and Bill, Ron and Mary Jane, Rick and Claudia, Gerry and Diane, and Alex and Pat. For decades you've listened, supported, and encouraged us, shed tears for us, and celebrated so many milestones with us. We are better people because of you, and lucky to have you in our lives.

To my entire family: I'm blessed to have a lifetime of unconditional love and support from each of you. You've always been great pillars of strength, and it's no surprise that I received the same support as I embarked on telling our family's story in this book. In many ways, my story is your story, too. Thank you for allowing me to share it.

And finally, to the love of my life, Mark. None of this would have been possible without you. And, without you, none of this would have real meaning. In the storied words of Led Zeppelin that you always quote, "If the sun refused to shine, I would still be loving you. When mountains crumble to the sea, there will still be you and me."

ABOUT THE AUTHOR

GINNI ROMETTY is a leader, innovator, and convener who believes that how we work and lead is as important as what we achieve. As the ninth Chairman, President, and CEO of IBM, Rometty transformed the one-hundred-year-old company, reinventing 50 percent of its portfolio, building a $25 billion hybrid cloud business, and establishing IBM's leadership in AI and quantum computing. She drove record results in diversity and inclusion and supported the explosive growth of an innovative high school program, P-TECH, to prepare the workforce of the future in more than twenty-eight countries. Through her work with the Business Roundtable, she helped redefine the purpose of the corporation. Today she is a champion of SkillsFirst learning, hiring, and advancement—a movement to connect people without a four-year college degree with good jobs. In 2020 she cofounded OneTen, a coalition of companies and educators committed to upskilling, hiring, and promoting one million Black Americans by 2030 into family-sustaining jobs and careers. Rometty serves on multiple boards, including JPMorgan Chase and Memorial Sloan Kettering Cancer Center, and was named *Fortune*'s number-one Most Powerful Woman three years in a row. She was honored with the designation of Officier in the French Légion d'Honneur and is a member of the National Academy of Engineering.